Politics, Discourse, and American Society

Politics, Discourse, and American Society

New Agendas

Edited by
Roderick P. Hart and
Bartholomew H. Sparrow

ROWMAN & LITTLEFIELD PUBLISHERS, INC.
Lanham • Boulder • New York • Oxford

ROWMAN & LITTLEFIELD PUBLISHERS, INC.

Published in the United States of America
by Rowman & Littlefield Publishers, Inc.
4720 Boston Way, Lanham, Maryland 20706
www.rowmanlittlefield.com

12 Hid's Copse Road
Cumnor Hill, Oxford OX2 9JJ, England

Copyright © 2001 by Rowman & Littlefield Publishers, Inc.

British Library Cataloguing in Publication Information Available

Library of Congress Cataloging-in-Publication Data

Politics, discourse, and American society : new agendas / edited by Roderick P. Hart and
Bartholomew H. Sparrow
    p. cm.
   Includes bibliographical references and index.
   ISBN 0-7425-0070-5 (alk. paper) — ISBN 0-7425-0071-3 (pbk. : alk. paper)
    1. Communication in politics—United States.   2. Communication—Political
aspects—United States.   3. Political participation—United States.   I. Hart, Roderick P.   II.
Sparrow, Bartholomew H., 1959-

JA85.2.U6P65   2001
320'.01'4—dc21

                  00-068848

Printed in the United States of America

∞™ The paper used in this publication meets the minimum requirements of
American National Standard for Information Sciences—Permanence of Paper
for Printed Library Materials, ANSI/NISO Z39.48-1992.

For
Theodore H. Strauss
Devoted spouse, loving father, loyal friend

Contents

Preface

This volume is one of two books (the other is *Communication in U.S. Elections*) emerging from a unique scholarly conference held at the University of Texas at Austin in the spring of 2000. The conference was special in several ways. For one thing, it was the first major event sponsored by the Annette Strauss Institute for Civic Participation, a research and outreach center on campus devoted to understanding, and improving, civic engagement in the United States. The institute is named after the former mayor of Dallas, who had an extraordinary ability to get different people to work together for the benefit of the community. The legend of Annette Strauss went well beyond the confines of Dallas, Texas. By the time of her death in December of 1998, Strauss had received virtually every civic award given in that city as well as many of those bestowed at the state and national levels.

In a real sense, the story of Annette Strauss is the story of the institute itself. In an era in which voter turnout rates are dropping, and dropping persistently, we as a society must find creative ways of reversing that trend. In an era burgeoning with exciting new modes of communication—cable television and the Internet, for example—we must find ways of using those technologies to bring people together and make civic dialogue once more a reality. The challenge of the institute is thus to blend one of the oldest human instincts—the need for community—with new ways of helping people help one another. Rarely have science and society had as much in common.

It was in this spirit that twenty-two young scholars were brought to campus for a conference called "New Agendas in Political Communication." The idea of the conference was to assemble a diverse group of scholars broadly interested in political communication, persons who were at the early stages of their careers but who had already demonstrated considerable scholarly potential. The plan was to capture the energy and imagination of some of tomorrow's best scholars in two disciplines—communication and political science—and to listen to them as they set out new research agendas. In addition, an effort was made to ensure that roughly half of these scholars were [students of culture (such as those in the current volume), while the other half took a more social scientific approach.] In short, we wanted to produce as much cross-pollination as possible so that no new idea would go unheard or untested.

This book is the result of our labors. In each case, the authors have done exactly what was asked of them: (1) stake out a broad area of investigation demanding new (or renewed) scholarly attention; (2) present original research findings showing how their work furthers that agenda; and (3) suggest the most important questions the sub-area should address in the future. This volume examines the complex intertwinements between U.S. politics and the culture surrounding it. It is often not easy to tell where politics begins and where culture ends, and that has been especially true in the United States, a nation pockmarked with diverse cultural elements from its beginnings. The authors represented here consider such powerful factors as ethnic identity, legal interpretation, media institutions and journalistic routines, the polling industry, the lessons of history, and the revolutionary effects television has had on the nation that invented it. It is far too early to tell where these forces are taking us but the authors in this volume help us begin the journey.

Naturally, these authors are not the only young scholars working on such matters. Indeed, research in political communication has never been a more active or productive endeavor. But because financial resources for the New Agendas conference were limited, we were unable to invite a suitably international group of scholars. We have tried to turn that liability into an asset here by focusing [exclusively on American society, teasing out the subtle cultural factors that make the nation distinctive. Or so we assume. Future research will no doubt put these cultural assumptions to the test and track the phenomena identified here] in cross-national contexts.

This book, and the New Agendas conference itself, could not have been produced without the contributions of several exceptional individuals. I begin by thanking Annette Strauss's family, whose vision, concern, and generosity of spirit have been a personal inspiration to me, as well as a reflection of those same qualities embodied in Mrs. Strauss herself. I hasten to thank my co-editors—Bat Sparrow for this volume and Daron Shaw for *Communication in U.S. Elections*—for their vision and hard work throughout this project. It is gratifying to have colleagues and friends of such depth and character.

The New Agendas conference would not have gone as smoothly without the personal ministrations of Bill Jennings, a smart and resourceful doctoral student for whom no task is too large and for whom my expressions of gratitude are eternally insufficient. The editors are also grateful to Rowman & Littlefield Publishers, especially to Jennifer Knerr and Brenda Hadenfeldt, who immediately saw the wisdom of bringing together twenty-two bright young scholars and who went out of their way to help make that happen.

Thanks are also due to Professor Jim Fishkin, chair of the University of Texas Department of Government, who spoke at the conference banquet, and to his departmental colleagues—Melissa Collie, Bob Luskin, Brian Roberts, and Jeff Tulis—who read papers in their areas of expertise and who served as discussants. We also appreciate those in the College of Communication who performed similar functions—Max McCombs, America Rodriguez, and Chuck Whitney. We appreciate, too, the graduate students who chaired the sessions and helped in other important ways: Courtney Dillard, Nancy Jennings, Spiro Kiousis, Kevin Kuswa, Anna Law, Zizi Papacharissi, Kanan Sawyer, and Scott Truelove. As always, the staff assistance provided by Deanna Matthews and Margaret Surratt was extraordinary.

Finally, we want to thank three individuals who have become unparalleled friends of the Strauss Institute. Dr. Sheldon Ekland-Olson, provost of the University, Dr. Richard Lariviere, dean of the College of Liberal Arts, and Dr. Ellen Wartella, dean of the College of Communication, have supported us from the beginning, providing financial support to get us started, and believing all the while in our work. These three individuals give new meaning to the phrase enlightened leadership.

Politics, Discourse, and American Society is neither the first word nor the last on its subject, but it is an earnest attempt to identify what we seem to know about the cultural forces shaping American politics and to report on some promising research programs designed to probe these phenomena in depth. The scholars whose work is presented here are just beginning to ask their questions and get their answers. They have more to learn and, happily, they have the energy and intelligence to learn it. For all of these reasons, it has been a personal pleasure to learn from their New Agendas.

Roderick P. Hart

1

Tocqueville and Political Communication in America

Bartholomew H. Sparrow

In *Democracy in America* Alexis de Tocqueville identified the causes and impact of democracy in the United States (and, by implication, in France). Tocqueville also described and analyzed the political culture and sociology of the young United States. Intriguingly, he even wrote about political communication—specifically, the press. Curiously, however, little has been written on Tocqueville and his views of the American press or, for that matter, on the related subjects of popular culture and commerce (but see Adhikari 2000; Karl 2000). His views on the press and popular culture remain under-studied, in contrast to the attention paid to his writings on liberalism, democracy, equality, social mores, the legal system and the Constitution, federalism, and race (see, for example, Boesche 1987; Commager 1993; Smith 1997; Zetterbaum 1981).

Nevertheless, the press is central to Tocqueville's view of democracy and government. Newspapers are indispensable to the existence of "associations," Tocqueville observed, and it is these associations that preserve democratic government. Tocqueville recognized their power early in the second volume of *Democracy in America*:

> Only a newspaper can put the same thought at the same time before a thousand readers.
>
> A newspaper is an adviser that need not be sought out, but comes of its own accord and talks to you briefly every day about the commonweal without distracting you from your private affairs.
>
> So the more equal men become and more individualism becomes a menace, the more necessary are newspapers. We should not underrate their importance if we thought they just guaranteed liberty; *they maintain civilization . . . without newspapers there would be hardly any common action at all.*

> A newspaper is not only able to suggest a common plan to many men; it pro-
> vides them with the means of carrying out in common the plans that they have
> thought of for themselves. (Tocqueville 1969, 517–18; emphasis added)

For Tocqueville, the press at once engenders collective identity and makes
collective action possible.

By connecting persons and associations, newspapers foster democratic
government and discourage tyranny (Tocqueville 1969, 520). "The enormous number of American newspapers" produces "a great number of small
local powers," and thereby promotes both local and national liberty (Tocqueville 1969, 519). Tocqueville also pointed out that:

> in democratic countries it often happens that a great many men both want and
> need to get together cannot do so, for all being very small and lost in the crowd,
> they do not see one another at all and do not know how to find one another.
> Then a newspaper gives publicity to the feeling or idea that occurred to them
> all simultaneously but separately. They all at once aim toward that light, and
> these wandering spirits, long seeking each other in the dark, at last meet and
> unite.
>   The newspaper brought them together and continues to be necessary to hold
> them together.
>   In a democracy an association cannot be powerful unless it is numerous.
> Those composing it must therefore be spread over a wide area, and each of
> them is anchored to the place in which he lives by the modesty of his fortune
> and a crowd of small necessary cares. They need some means of talking every
> day without seeing one another and of acting together without meeting. So
> hardly any democratic association can carry on without a newspaper.
>   There is therefore a necessary connection between associations and newspa-
> pers. Newspapers make associations, and associations make newspapers. . . .
> Thus, of all countries on earth, it is in America that one finds both the most as-
> sociations and the most newspapers. (Tocqueville 1969, 518)

Newspapers facilitate association even as their readership itself constitutes
an association.

Even with the numbers of associations and newspapers—and therefore
the many expressions of political sentiment and the necessary dispersal of
political power—"the power of the American press is still immense. It makes
political life circulate in every corner of that vast land. . . . When many or-
gans of the press do come to take the same line, their influence in the long
run is almost irresistible, and public opinion, continually stuck in the same
spot, ends by giving way under the blows." After public opinion, the press
was the "first of powers" in the United States (Tocqueville 1969, 186).

But when viewed through today's eyes, much of Tocqueville's analysis of
the press seems inaccurate—not surprisingly, perhaps, since he was writing
in the 1830s. For example, comparatively more newspapers were published

then, with the result that there was a much greater fragmentation of political power. As Tocqueville found:

> There is hardly a hamlet in America without its newspaper. Of course, with so many combatants, neither discipline nor unity in action is possible, and so each fights under his own flag. It is not the case that all the political newspapers in the Union are lined up to support or oppose the administration, but they use a hundred different means to attack or defend it. Therefore, American papers cannot raise those powerful currents of opinion which sweep away or sweep over the most powerful dikes. (Tocqueville 1969, 185)

With the rise of the norm of objective journalism dating from the Progressive Era, the establishment of large newspaper groups, and the end of almost all two- and multinewspaper towns, however, the political diversity among newspapers described above by Tocqueville has narrowed considerably.

A second and perhaps more important difference is the great increase in the profitability of newspaper publishing and media enterprises and, pari passu, the change in journalists' status. For Tocqueville,

> competition prevents any newspaper from hoping for large profits, and that [fact] discourages anybody with great business ability from bothering with such undertakings. Even if the papers were a source of wealth, as there is such an excessive number of them, there would not be enough talented journalists to edit them all. So generally American journalists have a low social status, their education is only sketchy, and their thoughts are often vulgarly expressed. (Tocqueville 1969, 185)

This situation contrasts sharply with the current concentration and consolidation of newspapers (and media firms) and the consequential diminution of competition. Revenues derived from newspaper publishing and from broadcast and cable franchises are the source of large profits, and media companies are managed to that end. Too, journalists in Washington, New York, Los Angeles, and other large cities are typically well known, well off, and well educated—often more famous than the presidential candidates they report on.

In addition, it is no longer easy for an individual or group to start a newspaper or magazine (or, for that matter, to obtain a television or radio station, or a network of stations). The print and video markets, which have become increasingly lucrative and consolidated, now constitute oligopolies where a handful of media companies dominates. Newspaper publishing used to have almost no barriers to entry: "printers need no licenses, and newspapers no stamps or registration; moreover, the system of giving securities is unknown." Accordingly, as Tocqueville saw it, "it is a simple and easy matter to start a paper; a few subscribers are enough to cover expenses, so the number of periodical or semiperiodical productions in the United States surpasses all belief" (Tocqueville 1969, 184).

Finally, it cannot be claimed that "the United States has no capital; both en-
lightenment and power are dispersed throughout this vast land; therefore the
rays of human intelligence, instead of radiating from one center, cross each
other in every direction; there is no place in which the Americans have located the general control of thought, any more than that of affairs" (Tocqueville 1969, 184). Washington, D.C., is clearly the political capital of the United
States (and New York the commercial and financial capital), and what holds
for Washington political insiders—politicians, consultants, lobbyists, journalists, political analysts, high-level civil servants—often holds for the country
as a whole (Carpenter 1994; Hertsgaard 1988; Page 1996; Patterson 1994;
Smith 1988).

In short, the present situation of the media in the United States differs significantly from Tocqueville's account of the American press. Ownership is increasingly concentrated; the media have the power to circumscribe and
channel political discourse (that is, to promote "powerful currents of opinion"); journalists are smart and wealthy celebrities; it is very hard to break
into newspaper or magazine publishing or to get into the broadcasting or cable business; and political communication and political power do, by and
large, emanate from the nation's capital.

Despite the difference between the press in the past and the media in the
present, others of Tocqueville's writings on culture, society, and commerce—where he often did not focus directly on the press but wrote of
Americans' character and of broader developments within the United
States—are remarkably prescient. For one, Tocqueville perceived that the
power of newspapers would grow.

> As equality spreads and men individually become less strong, they ever in-
> creasingly let themselves glide with the stream of the crowd and find it hard to
> maintain alone an opinion abandoned by the rest.
>
> The newspaper represents the association; one might say that it speaks to
> each of its readers in the name of all the rest, and the feebler they are individu-
> ally, the easier it is to sweep them along.
>
> The power of newspapers must therefore grow as equality spreads. (Tocque-
> ville 1969, 520)

He also noted the ability of the press (or the media) generally to put the
same thought or image in the heads of thousands or even millions of people
simultaneously (as noted above), an observation highly relevant to a society
where 99 percent of households have televisions and almost 70 percent subscribe to cable television. The media are very much in a position to shape
political discourse. That was true in Tocqueville's day and it is especially true
today.

Tocqueville's comments on the power of newspapers—second only to
public opinion—and on the psychology of Americans (similar, in fact, to

those of Walter Lippmann [1922]) clearly underscore the ability of the press to influence public opinion. This ability is especially worthy of note when the media constitute big business and where there is a capital city to which reporters, editors, producers, publishers, and media executives gravitate.

Tocqueville's discussion of the psychological disposition of Americans suggests that indulgent, materialistic, and oversimple messages will prevail: "A breathless cupidity perpetually distracts the mind of man from the pleasures of the imagination and the labors of the intellect and urges it on to nothing but the pursuit of wealth. Industrial and commercial classes are to be found in all other countries as well as in the United States, but only there is the whole community simultaneously engaged in productive industry and in trade" (Tocqueville 1969, 455). Added Tocqueville, "In America the taste for physical well-being is not always exclusive, but it is general; and though all do not feel it in the same manner, yet it is felt by all. Everyone is preoccupied caring for the slightest needs of the body and the trivial conveniences of life" (Tocqueville 1969, 530). "Love of comfort has become the dominant national taste," he found. "The main current of human passions running in the direction sweeps everything along with it" (Tocqueville 1969, 533).

Since Americans have little appetite for sustained or deep thought, in Tocqueville's view, the danger was that the content of the press (and media) would be superficial and transitory—just like Americans' taste in literature.

> Fine nuances will pass them by. With but short time to spend on books, they want it all to be profitable. They like books which are easily got and quickly read, requiring no learned researches to understand them. They like facile forms of beauty, self-explanatory and immediately enjoyable; above all they like things unexpected and new. Accustomed to the monotonous struggle of practical life, what they want is vivid, lively emotions, sudden revelations, brilliant truths or errors able to rouse them up and plunge them, almost by violence, into the middle of the subject. (Tocqueville 1969, 474)

The texts Tocqueville described resemble much of today's fare on television and in the nation's newspapers and magazines—entertainment that demands little thought or effort on the part of viewers and readers.

Coupled with the Americans' "taste for physical pleasures" (Tocqueville 1969, 536) was the allure of money: "In democracies nothing has brighter luster than commerce; it attracts the attention of the public and fills the imagination of the crowd; all passionate energies are directed that way" (Tocqueville 1969, 553). Although Tocqueville did not make the connection between the dominance of consumerism and the condition of the American media, the linkage is implicit in Tocqueville's own writings if one extends his analyses to the present.

Of course, Tocqueville could not have foreseen the growth of the influence of business in the United States, first in the latter half of the nineteenth century and now at the beginning of the twenty-first. Nevertheless, he observed that "the manufacturing aristocracy which we see rising before our eyes is one of the hardest that have appeared on earth." He then qualified the observation: "But at the same time, it is one of the most restrained and least dangerous." Still, "friends of democracy should keep their eyes anxiously fixed in that direction. For if ever again permanent inequality of conditions and aristocracy make their way into the world, it will have been by that door that they entered" (Tocqueville 1969, 558).

Today's combination of popular culture with the rampant commercialization and the concentration of the media industries conjures an unsettling picture, one resembling the "soft tyranny" that Tocqueville described. In fact, democratic government in the United States is currently at risk if one takes Tocqueville at his word: "Among the causes favoring the maintenance of a democratic republic" was the fact that "America has not yet any great capital, whose direct or indirect influence is felt through the length and breadth of the land." This fact, for Tocqueville, was "one of the primary reasons why republican institutions are maintained in the United States." In addition, "to subject the provinces to the capital is to place the destinies of the whole empire not only into the hands of a section of the people, which is unfair, but also into the hands of the people acting on their own, which is very dangerous" (Tocqueville 1969, 279). Given the centralized political communication of Washington-based journalists working for huge, for-profit media companies, one wonders.

The foregoing interpretation of Tocqueville and political communication in America coincides with recent analyses of the U.S. media that show them to be concerned, first and foremost, with securing advertising dollars, obtaining higher viewer ratings, and garnering higher quarterly earnings. The content in the nation's newspapers, magazines, and television programming is consequently geared to appeal to the least common denominator among readers and the viewing audience: topics like crime, sports, the weather, disasters, sex, and celebrity (see, for example, Alger 1998; Bagdikian 1992; McChesney 1999). Furthermore, the media typically operate closely with the executive branch and the Congress when it comes to core political issues, consistent with Tocqueville's admonition that a narrow sector of people living in the capital may run the government (Carpenter 1994; Hertsgaard 1988; Hess 1986; Sigal 1973; Wicker 1975).

All the same, this dark picture of the media and popular culture does not present a complete perspective on political communication in the United States. Few would make the claim that the destinies of the provinces (the separate states) and the nation as a whole are subject to just one section of the people (Washingtonians), for instance. If political communication emanates from and is centralized in Washington, D.C., it is also true to say that the messages and pictures of politics also circulate *through* the nation's capital, where the origin of a particular idea or image may lie far beyond the Beltway. Even should the media be owned by a relatively few companies, moreover, there still exists significant diversity in the content offered in the print and video media; moneymaking is ultimately an amoral enterprise. In short, the political system is less monolithic than the picture of political communication that Tocqueville drew. Political authority in the United States is not yet exercised as a "soft tyranny."

Tocqueville's work goes only so far in its analysis of political communication, popular culture, and commercial society. It is the virtue of the contributors to *Politics, Discourse, and American Society* that they revisit political communication in its larger context within a vast, commercialized, and complicated democratic polity. Although the several authors do not address Tocqueville specifically, they research previously unexplored aspects of political communication and popular culture, and indicate where further research should be directed. In quite different ways they illuminate, qualify, and amend Tocqueville's interpretation of political communication in America.

Presidential Discourse in a Complex Nation

In the first two chapters, Vanessa Beasley and David Crockett indicate how the U.S. president himself is constrained by society. Although the president may personify American politics and serve as the lightning rod for the media's demand for news, the Beasley and Crockett chapters show that it is not simply the case that political discourse is disseminated top-down, from the president (and his advisers) to the public (see, for example, Kernell 1997; Tulis 1987). Instead, Crockett and Beasley point to presidential communication as being reflective of a much wider political conversation. As participants in this broader discourse, presidents cannot simply speak their own minds or act on a supposed mandate and hope to be effective.

Beasley studies more than a century of presidential communication as contained in State of the Union messages and inaugural addresses, and shows how presidential discourse is grounded in popular rhetoric. Citing examples from presidential addresses, whether of Presidents Herbert Hoover, John F. Kennedy, or Gerald Ford, Beasley shows that presidential statements themselves partake of popular discourse. Presidential speech responds to the attitudes, beliefs, and diversity of the American public. In their very language, the speech of U.S. presidents reveals that they administer a populous, heterogeneous, and democratic nation. Nor is the speech of the American citizen revealed in presidential rhetoric simply that of a passive consumer. On the contrary, presidential speech is pregnant with the hopes, visions, and ideals of the American public—even if at times prejudiced or uninformed. Ultimately, presidential speech is fictitious speech, one that promotes a civil, religious and idealized model of American identity. The president can do no other.

Crockett makes the point that successful presidential communication depends on more than just the talents and efforts of people who shape, direct, and advise presidential communication. Rather, it depends on historical context. Building on the work of Stephen Skowronek, Crockett uses the examples of "opposition presidents"—presidents who find themselves in situations where they face governing majorities of the opposition party (persons whom Skowronek calls "preemptive presidents")—to show how presidents are not all equally able to "go public" (as Samuel Kernell has it: 1997). Crockett studies the presidencies of Dwight Eisenhower and Bill Clinton—presidents whom one might not typically view as being in parallel situations—and shows how the indirect approach taken by Eisenhower, and by Clinton (after the disastrous 1994 midterm election and in his second term) is much more successful than a direct appeal or challenge to Congress.

In short, presidents do not dictate political communication as they might wish. If they are to be successful (at least for those preemptive presidents who wish to be successful in reaching ideological goals), their speech needs to reflect the limits imposed by the Congress and the larger political climate in which they are embedded. Both the party system and popular sovereignty—phenomena illuminated by Tocqueville elsewhere in *Democracy in America*—mitigate the probability of presidential tyranny and serve to equalize their stature vis-à-vis the electorate. Political communication is not centralized simply in Washington, D.C., or, by extension, in the person of the U.S. president.

National Beliefs and Political Identity

The next two scholars point to additional factors that supplement and mitigate the possibility of a commercialized and centralized political communication. Jill Edy and Amy Bunger look at two crucial dimensions of political discourse—renderings of the past and political rights, respectively—and suggest that rather than commerce or politics controlling political discourse, other associations and even individuals exert significant influence on how politics is understood. They find political discourse to be surprisingly indeterminate.

Bunger looks at the legal scholarship on political rights—a central and often assumed part of political life in the United States—as represented over the last one hundred years in the pages of four premier law journals. She discovers that the presentations and understandings of political rights are negotiated, in effect, and that individual scholars, politicians, and jurists may play key roles in the conceptualization of "positive" and "negative" rights. Bunger's research suggests that rights have a genesis and trajectory somewhat independent of political leaders, the mass media, and the public at large, even as rights talk may at the same time have important implications for politics and society.

Edy studies the use of the past in political discourse. In her study of the subsequent journalistic accounts of the 1965 Watts riot and the 1968 Democratic National Convention, Edy too finds that collective memory gets negotiated, that it is not controlled by any one political actor, and that it can be subject to chronic contestation. The past may appear to be settled, only then to be rediscovered and reinterpreted. Collective memory—and the framing of past events and the political appeals that attend its interpretation—thus exerts its own influence on and has its own life within American politics.

Both Bunger and Edy suggest that national beliefs and political identity are to a surprising degree unresolved, and that the resolution as to how rights and history are understood is not reducible to politicians' self-interest, commerce, or the organizational motives of media companies. Instead, they indicate that scholars need to attend to the persons, organizations, and issues involved in the evolution of any one legal concept or remembered event.

The Mass Media and Lay Understanding

Regina Lawrence and J. H. Snider, in the next section of the volume, come closest to examining political culture consistent with Tocqueville's fears. Both contributors look searchingly at the influence of the media on two almost invisible parts of political discourse. Lawrence studies the process by which unexpected events obtain political significance, and Snider explains the logic by which political discourse on national information policy gets suppressed.

Lawrence explores "event-driven problem definition," or how it is that unforeseen events get interpreted and labeled as political issues. She looks at who participates in the struggle over the meaning of an unforeseen event after it occurs, and which problem definitions come to dominate. While there is no formula for predicting which events (such as the bombing of the Oklahoma City federal building or the *Exxon Valdez* oil spill) will produce the most problem-defining activity, Lawrence provides five criteria of problem selection: the scope of harm, the similarity to other events, the probability of dramatic narrative, the interest to key audiences, and the extent of public reaction.

Lawrence studies the news coverage of the Columbine High School shootings on April 20, 1999, in Littleton, Colorado, and shows that the media played a significant part in the complex process of issue definition chiefly through their selection of news sources (that is, which individuals and groups get their views publicized). Lawrence finds that the media gave voice to a wide range of participants in the winnowing process following the event, a period during which the number of explanations and proposed solutions were narrowed to just a few problem definitions. Lawrence suggests that two factors are most relevant in establishing the prominence and longevity of a problem definition: the newness of the problem (not that any problems come out of thin air), and the likelihood that the problem be institutionalized (that is, the degree to which they are picked up by other institutions).

Snider studies the Telecommunications Act of 1996 as an example of situations of asymmetric information between agents and principals. Snider uses a cost–benefit analysis (or rational choice approach) to illustrate how the supposed agents (local TV broadcasters) are able to act opportunistically, hiding their behavior from their supposed principals (the viewers). Content analysis cannot help researchers detect bias in this case (and others like it) because local TV news archives are not accessible to scholars, media owners can exert indirect as well as anticipated bias over elected representatives, and because the scope of the media's bias is constrained to this one issue of information policy.

Snider draws a parallel between the media's behavior in influencing the coverage of information policy to the situation that members of Congress (the agents) have with respect to voters (their principals) in order to explain industrywide behavior of media firms and how they prevailed in the passage of the Telecommunications Act of 1996, despite the absence of direct evidence of their influence on members of Congress. The supposed firewalls between TV owners and reporters, and between special interests and U.S. representatives, were ineffective in preventing the grant of the broadcast spectrum worth an estimated $70 billion to media owners. The upshot, Snider concludes, is that "local TV broadcasters, network TV broadcasters, daily newspapers, cable news networks, and other news outlets have common interests adverse to the public." Nor is it clear, Snider writes, that the political parties or competing special interests are powerful enough to counteract the influence of the media industry.

Both the Lawrence and the Snider chapters point out the degree to which the media act conjointly with political and commercial interests. This is the implication of Lawrence's work, since members of the media interact with government officials, as well as members of organized interests, in the problem-definition period following an unexpected event. It is the direct lesson of Snider's analysis of how broadcasters influence information policy. Both authors hark back to Tocqueville's concerns about centralized political power and the dominance of commerce in the United States.

Enlarging the Public Sphere

Lisbeth Lipari and Paul Waldman address a different agenda: the role of individual members of the public in political discourse. Rather than looking at personal opinions as reflected in public opinion surveys or focus groups, both Lipari and Waldman point to the more complex reality of citizens' views of politics and government. Lipari's work points to how the design and use of public opinion surveys has political implications; Waldman shows how little genuine discussion on politics takes place among Americans (in contrast to Tocqueville's reportage of Americans in the 1830s).

Lipari examines public opinion surveys on social welfare policy to show the influence of polling in political discourse. She finds that polling is at once a symbolic form, a kind of discursive social interaction, and an ideological form. In her study of the Roper Center's POLL database, Lipari discovers that as many questions get asked about welfare as are asked about taxes or defense, even though far more gets spent on defense, or passes through the tax system, than gets channeled to welfare programs. Lipari also finds, not surprisingly, that much depends on the wording and ordering of questions on welfare, that polling questions consistently assume welfare to be a "problem" (rather than a policy solution or contested issue), and that welfare is almost never connected to motherhood or parenting. These and other findings of Lipari all indicate that polling is hardly an objective and representative instrument. Rather, the design and publicizing of survey research is very much a constructed political discourse—constructed by polling firms, media companies, and organized interests. The fact and quality of this construction has significant implications for policy outcomes.

Waldman looks at public opinion at the interpersonal level. He argues that perhaps the most meaningful way that citizens engage in politics is the degree to which they discuss it. If discussion is genuine, he argues, then there is a chance for education and persuasion about the common good: prejudice or privilege cannot carry the day if persons discuss things with one another as equals; when they truly listen to one another, the norm of political equality is reinforced. Furthermore, the interpersonal discussion of politics fosters peoples' beliefs in their political efficacy and encourages additional political participation. Discussion is thus a form of interpersonal political participation, Waldman argues, distinguishable from individually held opinions.

Waldman's research shows that about one-half of the electorate is made up of infrequent political talkers. Importantly, however, those with less education and lower incomes participate in political discussions less than once or twice per week. Nor, he finds, is discussion among spouses or close friends likely to result in political learning, since there is usually little disagreement in such settings. And it is through disagreement, when views are subject to challenge, that people acquire new information and new opinions. Despite the value of certain recent experiments in public deliberation and civic journalism, there appears to be little popular participation as an empirical matter. Accordingly, it becomes very difficult indeed to discover what real people feel about real politics in the United States.

Waldman's and Lipari's work makes it clear that a study of the public sphere needs to include more than the snapshots of individual opinions reflected in polling data. Watching political spectacles and publicized poll results may foster an impression of political information and civic engagement, but Lipari and Waldman show that these do not recover meaningful public opinion for the electorate—consistent with the work of Eliasoph (1998), Gamson (1992), and Hart (1994). This finding is also, of course, consistent with Tocqueville's concerns about a passive and distracted American people who attend to their own pleasures, tamely follow what seems to be majority opinion, and are thus vulnerable to a kind of servitude.

Popular Venues, Popular Politics

The last section of the volume considers the extent to which political discourse is, in fact, part of popular culture. Tocqueville does not write much about popular entertainment, and obviously cannot have predicted the technological and industrial developments that have transformed political communication. David Ryfe, Jeffrey Jones, and Shawn Parry-Giles each look at ways in which political discourse is founded on—indeed, defined by—the mass public.

Ryfe investigates President Jimmy Carter's and President Bill Clinton's uses of the town hall meeting, an innovation of Carter and one resurrected by Clinton. Ryfe sees the town hall meetings as constituting a new cultural form, one harkening back to the Puritan town meetings. Contrary to the strategic view of political communication common among scholars of political speech, Ryfe writes that in town hall meetings presidents are not in control of their speech, but rather follow institutionalized codes.

Town hall meetings occupy peculiar ground. They constitute deliberate attempts to reach out to the public (and to bypass the elite press), and to remove the distance of a formal White House address or the indirectness of a press conference. Yet Ryfe points out that each of Jimmy Carter's meetings had about 1,500 attendees—more a gathering of fans than a genuine grouping of "real people"—and they were inconsistently televised (and by the Public Broadcasting System, not by the TV networks). President Carter used a lectern with the presidential seal, evocative of presidential authority rather than of democratic equality and, despite the rolled-up shirtsleeves, stayed formal and presidential.

President Clinton, in contrast, had meetings with only several hundred attendees, used just a stool, and fielded questions from members of the audience in their seats (questioners used fixed microphones at Carter's meetings). In his regionally and nationally broadcast town meetings, Clinton used much more personal and much less formal language with his audience. Even so, he spoke of policies rather than his own experiences, had scripted and preplanned responses, and used the meetings much as he would a press conference, treating the questions as a springboard for his own messages.

Ryfe concludes that the town hall meetings are not a part of the "going public" strategic logic. (Clinton held no town meetings in his second term in office, and Presidents Ronald Reagan and George H. W. Bush eschewed holding them at all.) Rather, the electronic town meetings occupy an uncertain middle ground that itself manifests profound ambiguities whereby a democratically elected president interacts directly with groups of citizens.

Jones finds another important realm of popular discourse: the politics revealed in the entertainment culture of politicians qua celebrities, late-night comedians talking politics, or political news as soap opera (for example, the Clinton impeachment, the Clarence Thomas hearings). In his chapter, Jones compares ABC's *Politically Incorrect with Bill Maher* and *This Week with Sam Donaldson and Cokie Roberts* in their treatments of the Clinton–Lewinsky scandal. Jones shows how the political discussion of politics and social issues by minor celebrities and nonexperts in an entertainment show differs from the discussion of inside-the-Beltway experts and journalists in a conventional political talk show.

Whereas the conversation on *This Week* focused on Clinton, the fact that he lied, and the repercussions therefrom, the discussion on *Politically Incorrect* centered around what Clinton lied about and why he might have done so. Jones argues that the discussion in *This Week* reflected "political sense," a learned intellectual system with its own rules and understandings of proper behavior, not unlike that used by lawyers or natural scientists. The discussion on *Politically Incorrect,* in contrast, framed the president's behavior differently, depending on whether Clinton was seen as principally a "leader" or as a "human." The panelists on *Politically Incorrect* perceived the president in commonsense terms that made his sexual misconduct nonexceptional—not unlike the reports of actor Hugh Grant's behavior—no matter what their ultimate views might have been about Clinton's behavior.

For all of the resistance of academics and Washington insiders to what they see as the degradation of celebrity politics (epitomized by an "ethos of consumption," as Jones puts it), the case of the Clinton presidency suggests that the universalistic and personalistic content of the entertainment politics in *Politically Incorrect* ultimately made more sense to Americans than the judgmental and moralistic political sense evident in *This Week.*

Shawn Parry-Giles explores "political authenticity," which she identifies as "a symbolic, interactional, and highly contested process" by which political candidates attempt to articulate a political image of genuineness. But the media are the agents for this process of authenticating candidates, where they evaluate politicians' messages through their visual and verbal production processes. Authenticity may be gauged by motive, a candidate's rationale for running for office, consistency, the avoidance of vacillation and hypocrisy, geography, the association of a candidate with a particular place and region, or the presence of oppositional opinions held by the candidate, ones that run contrary to public opinion and conventional wisdom. (Parry-Giles does allow that there may be other markers of authenticity.)

The quest for political authenticity is no stand-alone search for someone's true self, however. Rather, it is a social and political phenomenon that exists both within the journalistic community and as a social movement, in each case the result of the anxiety provoked by the Vietnam War, Watergate, Iran–Contra, and other scandals. In a world of political disaffection, the search for authenticity is a rebellion against image. The recent prominence of Jesse Ventura, Bill Bradley, and John McCain suggests that the search for and presentation of authenticity remain a central part of contemporary political culture.

In order to illustrate the quest for authenticity, Parry-Giles looks at how the media assessed the authenticity of Hillary Rodham Clinton in the early stages of her candidacy for the U.S. Senate from the state of New York. Parry-Giles indicates how the media work to establish their own authenticity of presentation through the insider access of reporters and media personalities (such as Andrea Mitchell, Katie Couric, Christianne Amanpour), the repetition of news stories, the consultation of a few experts (such as David Maraniss, Gail Sheehy), and the editing of visual images. Yet because these sources, reporters, and experts who attempt to authenticate Hillary Clinton cannot know her inner self, and because the video-editing process is compromised for the sake of storytelling, Parry-Giles argues that the media engage in practices that inauthenticate a candidate's image. By decontextualizing and recontextualizing visual images of Hillary Clinton, the media reveal their own inauthenticity.

This last group of chapters illuminates both the direct and indirect presence of popular culture in political communication. Ryfe shows the direct presence of the public in town meetings. Jones describes the direct and indirect influence of popular culture, comparing *Politically Incorrect* to *This Week*. And Parry-Giles uncovers the media's own role in presenting and assessing candidates' authenticity, even as the political culture that encompasses both journalists and the public at large leads the media to search for and evaluate genuineness among politicians.

The facts of televised town meetings, television talk shows, and media quests for authenticity may lie beyond the ken of Tocqueville, but their appearance is testimony to the impact of popular culture on political communication—congruent with Tocqueville's analysis. Institutions such as presidential town meetings (or the now-regular practice of presidential debates, for that matter) have origins in the ideals and history of democracy, equality, and political accountability in America. Similarly, television executives want to produce inexpensive shows that attract the right audiences, but the result may be that the politics of entertainment is more valuable to the electorate (and to media coffers) than political talk shows featuring insiders. The triumph of commercial considerations is, again, consistent with Tocqueville's writing. Last, an exploration of the politics of authenticity suggests the power of the media to frame and even manipulate political communication. Yet the facts that the public hungers for authenticity and that the media attempt to assess the authenticity of political candidates once more reveal the influence of popular culture on persons across the whole of the political system, from politicians, to journalists and their bosses, to the electorate. This, too, accords with Tocqueville's appreciation of public opinion, popular trends, and the power of the press.

"The common interests of civil life seldom naturally induce great numbers to act together," Tocqueville commented. "A great deal of artifice is required to produce such a result" (Tocqueville 1969, 521). Political community has to be fashioned, associations make this construction possible, and the media are preeminent among associations in their ability to connect persons and produce common action. Tocqueville may thus be seen as a precursor to contemporary scholars who write on the construction of politics and the fact that it is the media that largely provide the images, words, pictures, and phrases that circumscribe, delineate, and constitute political reality (Edelman 1971, 1988; Merelman 1984; Hart 1994).

Research in political communication, however, credits three different actors for this construction. The interpretation of politics can happen at the executive level—top-down, as is most obvious in cases of foreign policy—where the media typically serve as conduits for the messages of the president and his aides, other high-level governmental officials, ranking members of Congress, and other experts as commonly recognized by leading Washington- and New York-based journalists (Carpenter 1994; Hertsgaard 1988; Hess 1986; Sigal 1973; Wicker 1975).

Alternatively, the media themselves may do the political construction, as Patterson (1994), Sabato (2000), Graber (1993), and others (Cook 1998) indicate. Unfortunately, the media typically focus attention on the "horserace" of politics, criticize and deconstruct the statements and actions of individual politicians and candidates, and exaggerate political information for the purpose of attracting readers and viewers (Hart 2000; Patterson 1994).

Sometimes, though, individuals may make sense of politics on their own (Neuman, Just, and Crigler 1992; Mutz 1994; Just, Crigler, and Alger 1996). Individuals may resist or be inured to the communication of political elites or the media, and may have their own understanding of politics as a result. Although this third category is often labeled "constructivist," politics clearly gets constructed by all three actors. Political communication, I would argue, has for a long while been thought of in this way—that is, through a linear "media-effects" model whereby the message-initiator, the journalist-transmitter, or the citizen-recipient is the key variable in making sense of political reality.

Each of the contributors to *Politics, Discourse, and American Society* implicitly rejects such a media-effects model. By examining parts of political communication that have typically been unexamined or taken for granted, the authors illuminate the interwoven quality of political communication today. They thereby point to a much more complex, less determinate interaction among politicians, media personnel, and the public.

Beasley and Crockett, for example, reveal that presidential communication is more than "presidential." Beasley shows that it very much reflects popular speech, and Crockett uncovers how the larger political context may both direct and constrain presidential speech and action. Edy and Bunger point to important instances of political communication that take place outside the three-actor model. Edy shows the complex and contested ways in which the past is rendered meaningful (and where all kinds of voices may enter into the interpretation of the past), and Bunger points to the influence of individual legal scholars (or even of plaintiffs, defendants, or judges) in creating a larger political discourse on the evolution of positive and negative rights.

Lawrence and Snider examine the larger political world in which the media operate. Their accounts suggest that both the political/official voice and the people's understanding of politics are subsumed by the media. For Lawrence, newspapers, newsmagazines, and television serve as the mediators of nationwide conversations about how to define important problems. Media personnel thus get to decide who gets access (the sources) and what meaning gets imparted to unexpected events such as the Columbine tragedy. For Snider, legislators infer the power of the media (television broadcasters) from their own principal–agent relationships, where the legislator (or reporter) is pledged to serve the public, but is in fact greatly influenced ("biased") by special interests (broadcast owners).

Lipari's and Waldman's studies of public opinion indicate that the standard measures of public opinion—presumably people's own notions of politics—do not actually measure a genuine "public opinion." Lipari suggests that the media and the designers of public opinion surveys use polling for their own political ends, whether intentionally or inadvertently. Waldman, by describing the paucity of actual political discourse that takes place in the day-to-day world, points to the emptiness of "public opinion." What passes for public opinion often scarcely reflects popular will, and is likely to be vulnerable to manipulation by political elites since, as he points out, the smaller the sphere of political discussion, the lower the probability that political opinions are grounded in reason, and the larger the arena in which policymakers have uncontested latitude.

Finally, the Ryfe, Jones, and Parry-Giles chapters address the reality of popular culture's recent influence on politics, influence which has led to the creation of hybrid institutions of political communication: the town meetings occasionally held by U.S. presidents; the new breed of political comedy talk shows (a subset of politics as entertainment); and the visual/verbal quest for authenticity. Again, Ryfe, Jones, and Parry-Giles take one outside the conventional three part understanding of political communication to view certain new outcroppings of political expression in popular culture.

In sum, the authors in *Politics, Discourse, and American Society* allow for a more sophisticated understanding—if a more entangled and open-ended understanding—of political communication. By exploring what have been largely unexamined phenomena heretofore, the research agendas proposed here echo and extend many of Alexis de Tocqueville's original interests and concerns. The contributors follow Tocqueville in that they see politics as intimately connected to American culture: an amalgam of social psychology, history, and commercialism that makes U.S. democracy distinctive (see, for example, Almond and Powell 1966). Because many of the chapters are critical of present-day practices, the volume is Tocquevillian once again in its willingness to look at democracy with a keen analytical eye. While the work presented here is more exploratory than conclusive, it is united in its quest to use the lens of culture to make better sense of American political experience. It seems reasonable to imagine Alexis de Tocqueville smiling appreciatively at such a quest.

2

Identity, Democracy, and Presidential Rhetoric

Vanessa B. Beasley

Amid the millennial madness of the late 1990s, as the American people worried anxiously about the well-being of their financial and technological institutions, there was one institution whose health seemed better than ever: the U.S. presidency. While it may seem odd to call the Clinton years healthy, I refer here not to the specific predilections or pathologies of the last chief executive of the twentieth century but to the executive office itself, at least as it was portrayed on the nation's television and movie screens. If American popular culture is a reliable indicator of political trends, the U.S. presidency was alive and well at century's end.

The American presidency was a key focal point of at least thirteen major U.S. motion pictures from 1995 through 1999, representing a substantial increase from the four movies that similarly featured that institution during the first half of the decade.[1] During the late 1990s, the presidency also became the setting for a dramatic weekly television series, NBC's *The West Wing*, whose popular appeal quickly surpassed that of standard coverage of the real presidency on outlets such as C-SPAN. Other scholars have noticed similar trends, with some observers arguing that such increased interest provides further evidence of the peculiar but dangerous convergence of entertainment and democratic governance in contemporary times (Nelson 1998). Others have suggested that in an age when Americans are said to hate real politics, tuning in to its virtual counterpart can make them feel sufficiently involved, informed, and clever (Hart 1997). In this chapter, however, I offer an additional explanation. Perhaps the American people watch the presidency closely because they know something that most scholars may not know—that they, the American people, have a unique type of power over their presidents.

Claiming that the American people influence their chief executives may sound unremarkable. Observers of U.S. politics know all too well the myriad ways in which the American people habitually seek to influence politicians through votes, money, and lobbyists. I refer here to a type of popular influence that has gone largely uninvestigated within studies of political communication in the United States: how the American people, through both the circumstances and symbolism of their diversity, affect how their elected officials speak in public.

The statistical and sociological facts of the American people's diversity may at first appear disassociated from increased public interest in the presidency, real or imagined, or to the possibility that this increase has something to do with popular power. Perhaps we should consider one striking similarity between national politics and popular culture in the United States. In order to thrive in the voting booth or at the box office, players in both arenas must carefully construct messages designed to appeal to the tastes, experiences, and dreams of a potential audience of up to 270 million people who share very little in common. Presidents cannot afford to appear more sympathetic to one such group than to another, especially if these groups have known antipathies toward each other, as then-candidate George W. Bush learned after his ill-received visit to Bob Jones University in the 2000 primaries, for example.[2] Similarly, movie directors must think twice before making on-screen villains appear too similar to members of a specific ethnic group in the United States. In order to gain as wide an audience as possible, both types of messages must respond to "the people" as a whole.

How do they respond to such challenges? It is well known that presidential speechwriters and entertainment screenwriters alike have increasingly turned to quantitative indices (such as opinion polls) or qualitative sources (such as focus groups) to get a sense of what "the people" want. While this research alone suggests that "the people" have power over what goes into political and/or popular messages, another approach teaches us even more about such popular influence. Once the speech has been given or the movie has been screened, what image of "the people" has been created? What can we learn by treating such texts as not only written *to* and *for* "the people" but also *by* them?

I suggest that we do not yet know enough about the nature, functions, or consequences of the democratization of U.S. political discourses. What does it mean to say that "the people" reside rhetorically in such texts? How have they been characterized in political discourses, either explicitly or implicitly, and have these characterizations changed across time? If so, how, and if not, why not? How, specifically, does their implied presence affect these texts? What does it allow these messages to say and what does it forbid them? Lastly, and most importantly, what implications, if any, do such rhetorical moves have for "real" U.S. politics and culture?

Although we might easily look to texts from popular culture to learn more about such matters, I limit my discussion here to the phenomenon of presidential rhetoric. Because of its considerable legislative, material, and symbolic import, how presidential rhetoric depicts the American people can have very real consequences for the nation. Similarly, how the American people constrain their elected leaders' rhetorical choices can also have implications for democratic governance. The new agenda advanced here examines both of these questions—how U.S. presidents "write" the people and how the people "write" the U.S. presidency—and, in doing so, urges scholars to learn even more about the possibilities and limitations of discourse and democratization.

In approaching this problem, I first elaborate on why it might be useful to think of presidential rhetoric in democratizing ways. Perhaps most obviously, such a conception helps us better understand the nature and limits of presidential power within a diverse culture. Then I offer empirical examples of what such an approach to presidential discourse can reveal. In concluding, I suggest that these insights may have implications that go beyond the scope of presidential rhetoric. Learning more about the nature and functions of democratization may help us better understand some of the enduring questions and contradictions of the American experience, including why many Americans are more inclined to watch movies about presidents than they are to vote for them. First, however, let us consider how a democratizing view of presidential rhetoric might add to our understanding of political power in the United States.

PRESIDENTIAL POWERS AND CONSTRAINTS

To suggest that the demographic diversity of the American people could affect how presidents speak is also to introduce larger questions of the nature of presidential power. Several generations of scholars have been interested in such questions, probably because they reflect one of the most enduring and intriguing paradoxes of the American presidency, where the individual officeholder is undeniably the most powerful and yet also perhaps the most challenged individual on Earth (see Cronin and Genovese 1998). Within studies of the U.S. presidency, at least, understanding executive power, or appreciating what presidents can do, also means understanding what they cannot do (Neustadt 1990).

Most observers of the presidency have located both its power and its constraints within three basic sources: the institution or office, the individual officeholder, or the citizenry or *demos*. The notion advanced here—that the American people influence their chief executives by forcing a democratization of their discourse—is clearly most compatible with the third source, but it also relates to the first two. Indeed, viewing presidential rhetoric in de-mocratized terms may help us see how all three sets of powers and con-straints interact to maintain a diverse American democracy. Before exploring this possibility, I first review how these three forces have been traditionally assumed to function.

Institutional Power/Constraints

So concerned were the Founding Fathers about the unavoidable truth that (in Alexander Hamilton's succinct words) "men love power" that they sought to incorporate resistance to its charms into the very structure of the Ameri-can political system (Dahl 1998, 73–74). Perhaps the best known of these safeguards is the formal separation of powers. Although there is some dis-agreement on the nature and limitation of this separation (Bessette and Tulis 1981), the "doctrine of the Separation of Powers comprises . . . one of the two great structural principles of the American constitutional system," ac-cording to Edward Corwin's classic work *The President: Office and Powers* (1948, 9). No one branch of the federal government is assumed to have enough power to act independently (and thus perhaps capriciously) from the others on significant matters of state. From a purely institutional stand-point, a president's "getting what he wants is supposed to be hard," as Richard Neustadt noted (1990, xvii). Even presidents as skilled in dealing with Congress as Lyndon Johnson can bristle under these constraints. In-stead of getting to "be as big a man as he [could] be," LBJ is reported to have once lamented that "the only power I have is nuclear, and I can't use that" (Shogan 1992).

Another institutional set of powers and constraints lies within the presi-dency itself, at least according to Stephen Skowronek. Skowronek's notion of the presidency as a "governing institution inherently hostile to inherited governing arrangements" emphasizes the limited options that chief execu-tives have in how they manage this inheritance. Skowronek sees such choices as being driven by three distinct impulses (order-shattering, order-affirming, or order-creating), with all three resting upon the ability of a pres-ident to formulate and articulate his agenda in response to "previously es-tablished governing arrangements" (1993, 20). To the extent that Skowronek is correct that this need is inherent within the office of the presidency, the ghosts in the Oval Office themselves provide another institutional check on presidential power.

Individual Powers/Constraints

The specter of ghosts in the White House evokes another distinct tradition within presidential studies, however. A second type of research locates presidential powers and constraints more squarely on the shoulders of individual officeholders. A well-known example of this line of inquiry comes from James David Barber, whose assessment of individual leaders' personalities enabled him to explain and predict presidential tendencies in *The Presidential Character* (Barber 1972). Within this model, presidential powers and constraints are understood as functions of biography and psychology.

To understand the man is to understand his times, however, and so historical and biographical studies of individual presidents can also be viewed within this line of research. We would know far less about FDR's quintessential exercise of power as a "lion" or a "fox," for example, as well as the unprecedented historical exigencies and political constraints that forced him to make such transformations, without James MacGregor Burns's work (Burns 1956). Similarly, even if we assume that Harry Truman inherited many of Roosevelt's biggest presidential problems à la Skowronek, it still takes the skillful, detailed storytelling of David McCullough to reveal how Truman marshaled his personal talents and overcame past commitments to rise to the occasion (McCullough 1992).

Scholars in the field of communication share many of the same impulses that motivate historians to look for a deeper understanding of individual leaders. The "great man" tradition is often expanded to include the "great speeches" that have been offered both as an exercise in power and as a response to situational exigencies. Sometimes the speeches themselves are the subject of attention (see, for example, Wills 1992; Lucas 1986; Hillbruner 1974), while other analyses place the speech within a greater context of presidential action (see Zarefsky 1986; Vartabedian 1985; Hikins 1975). In either case, the theoretical assumption underlying these investigations is typically that presidential power is located within the president and made manifest through his words, carefully chosen though they may be to fit the occasion at hand.

Popular Power/Constraints

A third set of constraints on presidential action is ostensibly more democratic and yet arguably far less constitutionally based than the first two. Simply put, the American people are themselves thought to both lend power to and take power away from the president. Yet due to theoretical and practical problems with the notion of popular sovereignty, popular power in the United States has traditionally been discussed by scholars in somewhat limited and even negative ways.

Alexis de Tocqueville may have been encouraged by "the principle of the sovereignty of the people in America," but subsequent commentators have been far less optimistic. Indeed, many contemporary scholars have denied or even mocked this source of presidential power. Some doubt its very possibility, wondering whether "the people as a whole ever do engage or ever

have engaged in extensive public deliberation on an egalitarian basis in order to resolve directly any concrete issues of public life" (Smith 1997, 36).
Others have even gone so far as to label this concept a "fiction" (Morgan
1988). Still others choose to, either implicitly or explicitly, challenge the notion by instead advancing pluralism, in which "a rough approximation of the
public interest [will] emerge out of open, competitive struggle in the political
free market" (Huntington 1981, 7). Within these theories, groups of the people, rather than "the people" themselves, are the major players (Baumgartner
and Leech 1998, xv), with presidents presumably appealing to "special interests" according to their own political needs.

As difficult as it may be for contemporary observers to theorize or put into
practice, however, popular sovereignty was apparently included in some of
the founders' original visions of American democracy. Yet even these discussions imply a fear of power truly derived from the *demos*, especially to
the extent that popular sovereignty was assumed to be made manifest solely
through public opinion. As Jeffrey Tulis explained, "identifying and em-
bodying the proper weight to give popular opinion and the appropriate institutional reflections of it" was an important yet deeply problematic issue for
the founders (Tulis 1987, 34). They eventually solved this problem in part by
seeking a means of presidential selection, the electoral college, that could
"elicit the sense of the people" without succumbing to the problems implicit
in "mass politics" and the attendant "shifts in public opinion" (Tulis 1987,
34–35). Thus, the third location of presidential power, the American people
themselves, is presumably exercised at the ballot box or, in the age of a
rhetorical presidency, through opinion polling.

In the preceding paragraphs, I have presented an overview of three loca-
tions of U.S. presidential power and constraints: as found in the office, as
found within the man, and as emanating from popular opinion. Each of these
explanations offers us a piece of the larger puzzle of how the American presidency functions, but one wonders if an important piece is still missing.

The first two models assume a traditional top-down direction of presidential power, while the third, the only one that considers popular sovereignty,
limits the expression of these bottom-up sentiments to voting and polling.
Yet such static, elite-driven models of democratic power seem ill fitted for
American democracy, given its dynamic multiple traditions, which include
laissez-faire individualism, populism, egalitarianism, and liberalism (Smith
1997). What might it mean, then, if we combined all three of these models to
account for a more genuinely democratic sense of American presidential
power and its constraints? What might it mean to conceive of both executive
powers and constraints as operating within some sort of "middle space,"
where political meanings are negotiated in the symbolic interaction between
the office, the leader, and the led? And what might it mean if we could see
evidence of this negotiation within the discourse itself?

The preceding questions seem especially important in the case of the United States, whose status as the only nation thus far able to "make a federal, multi-ethnic state work" suggests that the country has somehow uniquely managed felt needs and suspicions within a multicultural democracy (Schlesinger 1992, 11). To the extent that diversity and democracy have coexisted in relative peace throughout the nation's history, the United States might be an excellent example of a country where both top-down and bottom-up definitions of national identity somehow commingle. From the bottom-up perspective, for example, citizens have been able somehow— one civil war notwithstanding—to juggle the competing needs of different groups within a hyperpluralistic political economy. At the same time, from the top-down viewpoint, chief executives have been able to preside over the resulting wrangling even while articulating a consistent sense of national identity.

But neither the evolution of this idiom nor U.S. presidents' roles in its creation can be sufficiently explained by the previous models of presidential power and constraints. The rhetorical creation and maintenance of "the people" has not been a function solely of one particular institution, nor has it been the sole responsibility of one or more presidents, nor has it been the outcome of a single set of popular feelings. It is, instead, the product of three forces, with governmental structures, democratic leaders, and citizens themselves all actively participating in these mediations. Within such an environment, "the American people" can be thought of not only as a sociological entity or a political necessity but also as a rhetorical construct created by multiple sources. In the words of Benedict Anderson, the American people can be viewed as representing an "imagined community" in which "members . . . will never know most of their fellow members, meet them, or even hear of them, yet in the minds of each lives the image of their communion" (Anderson 1991, 6).

This image of communion must be continually manufactured, articulated, and maintained to be functional. In order to learn more about how this image of shared American identity has been negotiated within this "middle space" of shared meanings, an empirical investigation of presidential rhetoric seems very much in order.

IDEAS AS IDENTITY

It is easy to imagine how presidential rhetoric could serve to mediate democratic tensions. "Aspirants to power require a population to lead that imagines itself to be a 'people,'" Rogers Smith has observed, "and . . . they need a people that imagines itself in ways that make leadership by those aspirants possible" (Smith 1997, 6). Sensible and accurate as Smith's comments may be, he could just as easily have been describing the needs of Adolph Hitler as those of Grover Cleveland. But U.S. presidents face a special set of constraints and these needs relate to the special facts of American democracy. What can presidential discourse tell us about the uniqueness of the United States? How have U.S. presidents encouraged their constituents to imagine themselves in ways that, so far, have worked to allow diversity and democracy to coexist with special force and utility?

To answer these questions, I began by sampling discourses from 1885 in order to include the peak immigration years of the late nineteenth century, when waves of nativism flooded the citizenry, and ended the study in 1992, a year plagued with post–Rodney King fears about racial differences in the United States. In order to maintain a comparable database for Presidents Cleveland through Bush, I analyzed each of their inaugural addresses and State of the Union messages. These particular texts had the benefit of capturing uniformly epideictic moments in which chief executives might be expected to ritualistically "elicit the sense of the people." As I analyzed each of these texts, I paid especially close attention to times when chief executives have had to acknowledge their constituents' many differences and, at the same time, reify a united American people.

"One cannot believe that the Presidency is the embodiment of all the nation's people," rhetorical scholar Walter Fisher has written, "[y]et one can believe it absolutely" because the presidency is a "real-fiction, combining matters of fact and faith" (Fisher 1980, 121). The facts may show that the American people have always had wildly divergent needs, but the fiction that citizens increasingly choose to believe is that the presidency somehow embodies their commonalties. In my study, I found numerous examples of presidents balancing such needs in ways we might expect—by promoting a civil religious and thus ideational model of American identity—but also in some ways that could not be predicted.

In 1944, Gunnar Myrdal wrote that "Americans of all national origins, classes, regions, creeds, and colors, have something in common: a social ethos, a political creed" (1944, 1). Long before the Swedish observer had decided that this "American Creed" of "high and uncompromising ideals" was the source of the nation's democratic unity, U.S. presidents were espousing a strikingly similar set of beliefs as the hallmark of American identity. Yet most presidents have not spoken of these beliefs in terms of their "social ethos" or overtly political nature (as Myrdal and other scholarly observers would). Instead, most presidents have described them by using civil religious themes to signify a higher, if at times somewhat vague, purpose for the United States and its people. By tapping into these themes, presidents have promoted a strikingly ideational model of American identity—based not on biology, heredity, or other characteristics associated with the ancien régime—but one that is instead theoretically open to anyone willing to set aside old beliefs in favor of new ones. In these moments lie our first insights into how the circumstances of American diversity have constrained presidential speech: chief executives have avoided defining national identity in terms that would obviously favor one group of citizens over another, choosing instead to discuss such matters in ways that would make it available to all.

In his 1976 State of the Union message, for example, Gerald Ford explained that although Americans "come from many roots and we have many branches . . . Americans across the eight generations that separate us from the stirring deeds of 1776, those who know no other homeland and those who just found refuge among our shores, [can] say in unison: I am proud of America, and I am proud to be an American. Life will be a little better here for my children than for me."[3] No matter what one's origins or ethnicity, President Ford argues, what makes one an American is the "refuge" one can find "among our shores." Yet what makes this refuge a haven is essentially a *set of feelings*: pride in America and the belief that "life *will be* a little better here for my children than for me."

These sentiments echo ones that Lyndon Johnson shared when reminding the audience in his 1965 inaugural to remain true to their "covenant" rather than succumb to civil unrest.

> Ours is a time of change—rapid and fantastic change—bearing the secrets of nature, multiplying the nations, placing in uncertain hands new weapons for mastery and destruction, shaking old values and uprooting old ways. Our destiny in the midst of change will rest on the unchanged character of our people and on their faith. They came here—the exile and the stranger, brave but frightened—to find a place where a man could be his own man. They made a covenant with this land. Conceived in justice, written in liberty, bound in union, it was meant one day to inspire the hopes of all mankind. And it binds us still. If we keep its terms we shall flourish. First, justice was the promise that all who made the journey would share in the fruits of the land. . . . Justice requires us to remember: when any citizen denies his fellow, saying: "His color is not mine or his beliefs are strange and different," in that moment he betrays America, though his forebears created this nation. (Lott 1969, 275)

Johnson suggests here that in a world of dizzying movement ("rapid and fantastic change," "shaking old values and uprooting old ways") the safety of the United States lies in its people's ability to unite in shared, unchanging beliefs. What is essential to the American people (their "unchanged character") is in fact "character" and "faith"—attitudes empowering them to resist the atavistic pull of allegiances to ethnic groups or social classes. To stray from this belief system (by using racist or otherwise prejudicial language, as in Johnson's example) is to "betray" America and its ultimate promise that "a man could be his own man."

Most other presidents from 1885 through 1992 also named similar beliefs and habits of mind (most commonly faith, loyalty, love of equality, and, for Wilson when the nation was entering war, "calm detachment") as the quintessential characteristics of American identity. Furthermore, they often contrasted these feelings with more common (and quintessentially human) reactions: the irrational impulses of nationalism, the stubborn suspicions of racism, the overinvolved hypersensitivities of victimization, and so on. True Americans control these urges, presidents have repeatedly proclaimed, preferring instead to love philosophical ideals.

This principled self-restraint reinforces the American people's self-image as "God's chosen people" in keeping with the nation's civil religion, making them both unique and united before the rest of the world, much like the picture painted in John Winthrop's classic *City upon a Hill*. Presidents at times have evoked this exact imagery, perhaps to underscore the Creator's special designs for the nation, as was the case when Benjamin Harrison explained in his 1889 inaugural that "God has placed upon our head a diadem and has laid at our feet power and wealth beyond definition or calculation" (Lott 1969, 162) or to explain how these gifts came with international responsibilities, some of which Theodore Roosevelt foreshadowed in his 1905 inaugural: "Much has been given us, and much will rightfully be expected from us. We have duties to others and duties to ourselves, and we can shirk neither" (Lott 1969, 185).

At other times, presidents have focused inward on careful descriptions of the American people themselves, as Herbert Hoover did when telling his American audience that its unprecedented "faith in government by the people" itself had created "a new race . . . great in its attainments" (Lott 1969, 223). Similarly, John Kennedy told the American people that they were "heirs of that first revolution" who must "pay any price, bear any burden, meet any hardship, support any friend, oppose any foe to assure" *not* the dominance of the United States, as one would have supposed during the cold war years, but instead "the survival and the success of liberty" (Lott 1969, 269). Like "the people" painted by the other presidents mentioned here, Hoover's and Kennedy's Americans were "a new race" whose sustenance depended on "the survival and the success" of their uniquely American *ideas*.

IDENTITY AND PEDIGREE

Yet there have clearly been many times in American history when the American people have not been eager to see themselves as members of the same race at all. When I examined speeches given to national audiences during specific crises of diversity between 1885 and 1992, I found a second and more subtle set of messages about American character, messages that reveal additional constraints placed on presidents and their speech by American diversity.

During immigration panics, for example, when feelings of nativism have run high among the nation's citizenry, presidents could not easily ignore their constituents' fears. But they also could not abandon the more inclusive, ideational model of citizenship just delineated. Some presidents managed these tensions by continuing to assert that American citizenship was open to all who accept American ideas, while simultaneously suggesting that some newcomers were incapable of understanding these ideas. This rhetorical juggling meant that Benjamin Harrison could, in the same address, talk about "the spirit of fraternity and love of righteousness and peace" that so uniquely belonged to "our people" and then, just a few moments later, warn of the "ignorant classes" of newcomers whose mob mentality and lawlessness necessitated the development of stricter naturalization laws (Lott 1969, 155).

Likewise, presidents have suggested that certain Americans must be given additional tutoring in the beliefs that come so naturally to others. In examining multiple messages given by various presidents on the "Indian problem" and "Negro problem," for example, I found repeated calls for governmental assistance to help such individuals on the path to proper citizenship. Grover Cleveland asked Congress for exactly this when seeking recognition of the federal government's "guardianship" of Native Americans and the realization that it "involves, on our part, efforts for the improvement of their condition and the enforcement of their rights" (Israel 1966, 1545). This is not an altogether different rhetoric from the one used by Dwight Eisenhower in 1956, when he spoke in earnest about "the progress our people have made in the field of civil rights."

> In executive branch operations throughout the Nation, elimination of Discrimination and segregation is all but completed. Progress is also being made among contractors engaged in furnishing Government services and requirements. Every citizen now has the opportunity to fit himself for and to hold a responsibility in the service of his country. . . . It is disturbing that in some localities allegations persist that Negro citizens are being deprived of their right to vote and are likewise being subjected to unwarranted economic pressures. I recommend that the substance of these charges be thoroughly examined by a bipartisan commission created by Congress. It is hoped that such a commission will be established promptly so that it may arrive at findings which can receive early consideration. (Israel 1966, 3066)

Like Harrison, Eisenhower suggests that it would take governmental assistance to help African Americans act like citizens. I mention this not to suggest that either Harrison or Eisenhower was wrong to promote such interventions but to point out that, against the backdrop of an ideationally based rhetoric of citizenship, such entreaties to teach or assist other groups could have created a kind of citizenly hierarchy where some people naturally "get it" while others do not (unless properly tutored).

IDENTITY AND PARADOX

In this respect, then, the popular fears and prejudices that Gunnar Myrdal referred to as "the American Dilemma" also write themselves into presidential discourse, even in some of its most actively benevolent moments. Here we have the second sense in which presidential rhetoric becomes oddly pluralistic. Within the texts I studied, the tensions between inclusive, egalitarian American ideals and the exclusionary practices of everyday life were comfortably intertwined, even as they tend to be within social relations in the United States writ large.

The paradoxical brand of "inclusive exclusivity" to be found in presidential rhetoric may reflect some of the sociological realities that have persisted throughout the history of the United States. That is, the contradictions and tensions so central to the democracy itself ultimately became imprinted on these texts. Rather than leading American democracy, U.S. presidents are, in a sense, led *by* it (or so their discourse suggests).

One almost has to marvel at the rhetorical genius of the U.S. presidency. It is as if an automatic, institutional impulse forces itself on the presidents, regardless of their circumstances, party affiliation, or specific legislative agenda, to respond similarly to wildly divergent social and political needs. Having inherited, in Skowronek's sense, a perpetual state of *disorder*, the presidents respond by creating an inclusive, nondeterministic rhetoric of ideational citizenship, thereby at least partially ignoring the ever-present disorder around them and inviting their constituents to do the same thing.

They have issued such invitations strategically, to be sure, and their attempts to do so might be described by some critics as predictable or even oppressive. Yet their discourse seems to have worked thus far, at least from a functional vantage point. It may be that, in capturing both the need for belonging and the exclusivist fears of the American people, presidents have somehow managed to balance the felt needs of the *demos,* keeping it from acting upon the unbridled impulses of racial and ethnic nationalism that continue to plague so many countries.

Some of the individual presidents studied here, however, were ironically constrained by their rhetorical inheritance to respond to the implicit needs of a diverse democracy. Even when presidents sought to move the American people toward more inclusive civil rights policies, for example, they were trapped within a logic created by the ideational rhetoric. If African Americans needed help on their way to full citizenship, didn't that mean that they were thus inherently inferior to other citizens who were already sufficiently

"American" without such assistance? Such unanswered questions among non–African Americans often translate into resentments over programs such as affirmative action and welfare. In these moments, it is as if the discourse, like the nation itself, is being challenged by a constant state of negotiation, an ebb and flow consistent with the growing pains of a maturing democracy.

IDENTITY AND BEYOND

From 1885 through 1992, U.S. presidents have responded to the American people's diversity by crafting a schizophrenic rhetoric of inclusive exclusivity. This discourse is both responsive to and responsible for the sharply ambivalent approaches the American people themselves have taken when confronting their own diversity.

Heretofore, the study of presidential rhetoric has featured either the individual or the institutional choices made by "great men" (and, increasingly, their advisers). Within the rhetorical negotiations of American identity, a president's words, and thus part of a president's power, are influenced by institutional tradition and his or her individual circumstances, and also by the presence of a diverse *demos* in the United States. These tendencies have implications that go beyond the study of the presidency and touch on larger questions about the nature and future of American democracy itself. At least three different sets of questions come to mind in this regard.

Comparative Studies

Is the case of the U.S. presidency unique? How are democratic leaders in other countries constrained by the backgrounds and beliefs of their constituents? How do these elected officials describe "the people" in their rhetoric, for example? How have they done so across time? And in cases where democracy has not been as stable as it has been in the United States, can we find *rhetorical* explanations for this lack of stability?

The United States' relative democratic stability has made it an exception rather than the norm within international politics. Arthur Schlesinger Jr. has called attention to the *Economist*'s recent warning that "[t]he virus of tribalism . . . risks becoming the AIDS of international politics—lying dormant for years, and then flaring up to destroy countries" (1992, 14). Indeed, as Schlesinger and other observers have noted, even countries that are home to relatively mature democratic institutions, including France, Spain, Canada, and Great Britain, have faced "rising racial and ethnic troubles" during the twentieth century. Although many factors presumably contribute to such problems, a comparative analysis of their leader's discourse could yield fruitful insights into whether or not leaders' public words have helped solve or exacerbated such troubles. Although there are always systemic and cultural obstacles within comparative research (Almond and Powell 1966), a kind of rhetorical anthropology might help us learn more about the roles elite discourses can play in managing democratic tensions within specific ideological climates. Such analyses might help us learn more about what works and what doesn't within the top-down management of a diverse democracy.

Deliberative Models of Democracy

Increasingly, scholars of political communication are also becoming interested in nonelite-driven models of American politics in the bottom-up processes that can drive political psychology and influence popular perceptions of social cohesion or social capital. Among these studies are inquiries into deliberative democracy or what happens when people come together to think and talk about their own democratic power (see Fishkin 1991, 1).

At first glance, these deliberative exercises seem an ideal enterprise for a diverse democracy, and there is evidence that citizens can indeed participate in rewarding, beneficial deliberation under certain conditions (Fishkin 1991). Many critics, however, have suggested that such circumstances rarely occur in real life (see Walzer 1999). Others have suggested that even if they did, such conversations would inevitably reinforce existing power relationships rather than alter or even question them (see Mansbridge 1980). In general, as Maurice Meilleur has summarized, many of the critiques of deliberative democracy charge that its theorists are "insufficiently aware of the actual practices of deliberation (or its absences)" (Meilleur, 2000, 1).

Given what we have seen about how presidents have tried to manage the American people's differences, one wonders if these insights can help us understand more about the "actual practices or their absences" in public deliberation. Is there a popular equivalent of the democratizing processes reported here, a tendency for ordinary people to show an awareness of competing groups' needs and/or purposefully try to elide their own differences in order to create solidarity? Or is popular deliberation necessarily something different, an undemocratic game of assertiveness based on assumptions of zero-sum stakes? I suggest that we conduct a more detailed rhetorical analysis of what actually happens when citizens deliberate, especially when their fellow deliberators are highly diverse. Does one find truly democratic deliberation about busing, for example, or affirmative action? And even if such candor is found, is it a desirable candor? In an age in which sharing one's innermost feelings about difference is seen as a "talking cure" for racism and other social ills (for example, Bill Clinton's race initiative), closer analysis of *what people actually say* when they try to talk to each other in such emotionally and politically charged moments might help us learn more about the potential limitations of public deliberation within a radically diverse democracy.

Studies of Political Culture

Presidents, when democratizing their discourse, somehow tap into the attitudes, beliefs, and values of their constituents. This locus of popular sentiment is remarkably close to what Gabriel Almond and others have labeled "political culture," the "underlying propensities" that can be found within any political system (Almond and Powell 1966, 23). Indeed, in their influential comparative work *The Civic Culture*, Almond and his colleague Sidney Verba (1965) might have been writing about exactly the type of ambivalence reported here when they focused on "the need for democratic systems to balance governmental power and governmental responsiveness, the involvement and indifference of its members . . . and the consensus and cleavage of their political beliefs and values" (Brint 1991, 113).

In the decades since Almond and Verba's study, many scholars have studied political culture by trying to find exactly that: empirical examples of governmental agents or institutions attempting the sort of balancing act which is apparently so important to the health of a democracy. Here I have done the same, using what presidents have said to record and study such accommodations to the diverse *demos,* but we have also seen something else in this study. So significant are the institutional forces acting upon the presidents that, when it comes to questions of American identity, it appears that presidents have had little choice but to adopt certain types of maneuvers. Rather than assuming that presidents have written their culture, what might it mean to say that their culture—or more specifically, its language itself—had written them?

This latter question evokes the poststructural stance of thinkers like Michel Foucault, who has wondered if discourse produces subjects (rather than vice versa). As a follow-up to my study, we might ask questions about how established patterns of discourse continue to produce certain imperatives for U.S. presidents. Instead of asking how presidents use rhetoric, we might ask the more interesting question of how rhetoric uses presidents. What would such a thought experiment mean for our traditional notions of culture and political agency (Archer 1996)? What would it mean to suggest that some of the most powerful people on Earth are quite powerless over their own talk?

This last question gets us back to the questions about power asked at the outset of this chapter. Presidents have used their considerable rhetorical influence to get the American people to think of themselves as essentially similar. At the same time, people have power over their presidents because of their histories of difference as well as their senses of perceived inequality. This negotiation of power and constraints provides us with a new way of thinking about the relationship between the leader and the led in the United States, but it also prompts us to ask if a thoroughly democratized discourse is good for us.

In order to accommodate their heterogeneous audiences, presidents have made compromises necessitated by cultural logics, by the facts of history, and by public opinion. Some critics warn about the potentially negative consequences of such compromises and adaptations, and so it seems useful to recall a few of these warnings (Tulis 1987; Hart 1987).

Within the realm of race relations, for example, it may become increasingly important for presidents to invent new ways of acting outside the norms of the policies and rhetorics they have inherited. Perhaps there is now an urgent need for the types of bold leadership that Jeffrey Tulis and others have called for, the type of thinking, acting, and speaking that conjoins eloquence with moral leadership (Hart 1987, 205–210). Edwin Hargrove has similarly called for nothing less than a new type of presidential leadership, one that would "appeal to the better angels of our nature" (Hargrove 1998).

My new agenda calls for such imagining as well. The more we learn about democratization, the more we may want to investigate how the American people wish to be written. Perhaps their desires in this regard are manifested in the reasons why moviegoers and television watchers have seemed so interested in "watching" the presidency in recent years. Viewers may enjoy learning about *The American President*'s everyday desires for companionship and they may laugh at *The West Wing*'s all-too-human foibles, but they might also wish to ensure that the presidency is, at least every now and then, grander than they are themselves.

NOTES

1. From 1995 to 1999, the titles were *The American President* (1995), *Nixon* (1995), *Independence Day* (1996), *Mars Attacks!* (1996), *My Fellow Americans* (1996), *Absolute Power* (1997), *Air Force One* (1997), *Contact* (1997), *Executive Power* (1997), *Executive Target* (1997), *Deep Impact* (1998), *Primary Colors* (1998), and *Austin Powers: The Spy Who Shagged Me* (1999). From 1990 to 1994, they were *JFK* (1991), *Dave* (1993), *In the Line of Fire* (1993), and *Guarding Tess* (1994).

2. On February 2, 2000, Bush gave a campaign address at Bob Jones University, a nondenominational fundamentalist Christian university in Greenville, South Carolina. Although Bush's aides characterized the address itself as a "standard stump speech," the event made national news because of the university's ultraconservative policies, which include a ban on interracial dating, and its historically anti-Catholic stance. Bush's appearance at such an institution angered many observers who felt that this particular campaign stop reflected his lack of sensitivity to diversity issues within the United States.

3. Gerald R. Ford, "Address before a Joint Session of the Congress Reporting on the State of the Union," *Public Papers of the President* 31, January 19, 1976.

3

Prometheus Chained: Communication and the Constraints of History

David A. Crockett

Ever since Richard Neustadt wrote *Presidential Power,* much scholarly work has implicitly treated presidents as though they were competitors on a level playing field. The parlor game of presidential ratings is the most obvious example of this phenomenon. For example, a recent C-SPAN poll of historians ranked all presidencies, including the unfinished term of Bill Clinton. This poll is similar to a host of works that compare presidents along various lines much as one might compare teams in major league baseball. The tacit assumption is that everyone starts play on the same day and that everyone plays the same number of games, on similar fields, according to the same rules. All we need to do is determine which presidents were most skillful at selling their agendas to the political community and the public and we will be able to determine who was the more effective leader.

Scholarship in political communication has done much to explain the tools used by presidents to sell their agendas, from Woodrow Wilson's philosophical redefinition of the "rhetorical presidency" (Tulis 1987) to the more recent phenomenon of "going public," in which presidents appeal directly to the public for support of their programs (Kernell 1997). A host of scholars have pointed to the potentially negative aspects of these tools (Tulis 1987; Hart 1987; Kernell 1997; Bessette 1997), but it would seem that the use of such techniques is here to stay. Recent scholarship has even explored the extent to which tools of popular leadership have been developing from the beginning of the republic (Ellis 1998).

Most of these studies perpetuate the idea that all presidents, or at least all "modern" presidents, are created equal, when in fact presidents do not come to power on level playing fields. If they are not playing different games, they are often playing under different rules or conditions, and their relative ability to achieve their goals through the use of communication is in large part determined by their reaction to the broader historical context in which they come to power. Attempts to compare presidents without taking into account that broader historical context tend to obscure more than they reveal.

THE TYRANNY OF HISTORY

Machiavelli once argued that, in addition to good fortune, the leader must match his "modes of procedure" to the "needs of the times" (1940, 92–94). Neustadt updated Machiavelli, arguing that we can evaluate presidents by examining their purposes and determining whether they run with the "grain of history" (1990, 167). While presidents have only marginal control over fortune, all have some freedom to match strategy to context, but it is a conceit to imagine that skillful use of political communication will inevitably save the day for a president. History demonstrates that presidential success is contingent on forces well outside the president himself.[1] The dynamics of successful political dialogue very much depend on the president's ability to match his skill—his rhetoric, his strategy for "going public"—with long-term historical forces, partisan relationships, and his power situation. A president's ability must be placed on a foundation of larger forces already established when he takes office. In order to be successful, he must be "stubbornly realistic" and "reflective" in understanding his position in the larger governmental structure (Jones 1994, 294). Indeed, Hargrove and Nelson argue that the central task of the president is to understand the possibilities for action permissible in the politics of his time (1984, 78).

What is the best way to think about historical context to gain some understanding of the constraints presidents face in communicating their agenda? For over forty years scholars have struggled to describe the periodicity evident in American politics. Despite many variations on a theme, there is a rough consensus that American politics can be described as a series of political eras that favor one party over another, eras bounded by critical realignments or punctuated change (Key 1955; Lubell 1965; Campbell et al. 1966; Burnham 1970; Kleppner 1979; Sundquist 1983; Rockman 1984; Chubb and Peterson 1985; Carmines and Stimson 1989; Burnham 1991; Skowronek 1993). The advantaged political party in an era can be considered the "governing party" and the disadvantaged party the "opposition party." The principal advantage enjoyed by the governing party is the power to define the terms of political debate in its favor. Schattschneider argued that the supreme instrument of power was the definition of alternatives, for he who determines what politics is about runs the country (1960, 68). The "great" presidents have been those who understood the possibilities for action in their time, and redefined politics for the long term. Whether it was Jefferson redefining the Federalists as monarchists and sending them into oblivion (Hofstadter 1969, 85–87), or Reagan delegitimizing the word "liberal" and forcing Democrats to search for a new identity (Skowronek 1993, 415), these dramatic changes constituted "redefinitions of the universe of voters, political parties, and the broad boundaries of the politically possible" (Burnham 1970, 10).

Opposition parties operate at a disadvantage because they are in a defensive posture; that is, the governing party has been able to fashion the long-term political debate on its own terms. Nevertheless, opposition party candidates have been successful in winning the presidency. They have been able, at times, to take advantage of temporary weaknesses in the governing party—whether due to war, economic crisis, or internal dissent—to achieve political success, even if they have not ultimately been successful in redefining the broader terms of political debate in their favor. It is in this sense that we can begin to understand how different historical contexts affect presidential communication.

The experience of the GOP during the New Deal era illustrates this dynamic. Roosevelt was successful not only in criticizing the old power relations but also in generating enthusiasm for his own governing philosophy. He created a new type of politics that favored the Democratic Party, and the Democratic Party became the new governing party because its governing philosophy defined the terms of political debate. The GOP became the opposition party. Although successful in criticizing the governing party in 1952 and in gaining control of the White House and Congress, Republicans were not able to achieve long-term victory. Eisenhower did not redefine the terms of political debate or establish a new Republican era. The GOP attempted to accomplish that feat with Barry Goldwater in 1964, and the defeat was resounding. When another Republican tried again with a similar message in 1980, the party was more successful. Ronald Reagan was the "Great Communicator" not simply because he had the necessary skill but because the times were ripe for the change he advocated.

The time has come, then, for scholars to take more seriously the constraints of history. Stephen Skowronek has explored the contextual nature of presidential leadership and his analysis can be applied to political communication. Skowronek argues that different leadership projects are associated with different situations. "Reconstructors" are the "great" presidents who redefine politics by condemning a bankrupt past and presenting a consistent alternative (1993, 28). Such presidents include Jefferson, Jackson, Lincoln, Franklin Roosevelt, and Reagan. "Articulators" follow the reconstructors, continuing their work and attempting to adapt the new politics to changing times (41). Such presidents include Monroe, Polk, Theodore Roosevelt, Lyndon Johnson, and George H. W. Bush. "Preemptive presidents" (I prefer the term "opposition president," since they come from the opposition

party in a specific era) desire to "preempt" the received agenda of the reconstructors and articulators, but take office during a time when the governing party remains robust and resilient. Thus, the opposition leader is
forced to operate at a time when he cannot hope to transform politics in his
favor. Such presidents include the four Whig presidents, Cleveland, Wilson,
Eisenhower, Nixon, and Clinton. For the purposes of this project, I accept
Skowronek's breakdown of political eras. Since the notion of legitimate opposition did not gain credence until the Jacksonian age (Hofstadter 1969), I
limit my examination to the modern party era that began in the late 1820s.

My principal argument is that studies of political communication must take
account of historical context. Presidents facing different political contexts experience varying constraints when it comes to communicating an ideal
agenda or pursuing a preferred policy outcome. They cannot be divorced
from the era in which they take power, any more than they can be divorced
from the parties that nominate them. They are bound by context and do not
have unlimited discretion in choosing their own strategies. All presidents are
not equally able to "go public" or employ a populist rhetoric. The fact that
American political history has a cyclical pattern allows us to examine presidents from different contexts to see what they have in common, what separates them from other types of presidents, and to determine if there are any
lessons to be learned that can be passed on to other presidents in similar circumstances.

The simplest way to illustrate this dynamic is to graphically place each
president in his contextual home. In table 3.1, I list each president from Jackson to Clinton, with years matched to his associated congresses. The table is
divided along two axes, one delineating whether the president was a member of the governing or opposition party during his era (according to
Skowronek), and the other delineating whether the president experienced
united or divided government. I also place in each box the total number of
years and the percentage of the total 172 years surveyed that each box represents. Some interesting data emerge from this table. While the governing
party has enjoyed united government 50 percent of the time, the opposition
party has experienced it only 8 percent of the time. Both types of parties
have endured divided government in nearly equal proportions, but for the
governing party that time amounts to less than half that of its united control.
By contrast, the 38 years of divided government experienced by the opposition party is an amount nearly three times greater than its united control.

From a different perspective, we can see that 100 out of 172 surveyed
years saw united government, but 86 percent of that time the united government was controlled by the governing party. The opposition party enjoyed united government during only fourteen of those 100 years. Periods of
united government are also much longer for governing party presidents than
for opposition presidents. The lengthy reigns of Jackson to Van Buren,

Table 3.1. Presidents in Historical Context

United Government	
President of Governing Party	*President of Opposition Party*
Jackson–Van Buren 1829–1841	Harrison–Tyler 1841–1843
Polk 1845–1847	Cleveland 1893–1895
Pierce 1853–1855	Wilson 1913–1919
Buchanan 1857–1859	Eisenhower 1953–1954
Lincoln 1861–1865	Clinton 1993–1994
Grant 1869–1875	
Garfield–Arthur 1881–1883	
Harrison 1889–1891	
McKinley–Taft 1897–1911	
Harding–Hoover 1921–1931	
Roosevelt–Truman 1933–1946	
Truman 1949–1952	
Kennedy–Johnson 1961–1968	
Carter 1977–1980	
86 years–50%	14 years–8%

Divided Government	
President of Governing Party	*President of Opposition Party*
Polk 1847–1849	Tyler 1843–1845
Pierce 1855–1857	Taylor–Fillmore 1849–1853
Buchanan 1859–1861	Johnson 1865–1869
Grant–Hayes 1875–1881	Cleveland 1885–1889
Arthur 1883–1885	Cleveland 1895–1897
Harrison 1891–1893	Wilson 1919–1921
Taft 1911–1913	Eisenhower 1955–1960
Hoover 1931–1933	Nixon–Ford 1969–1976
Truman 1947–1948	Clinton 1995–2000
Reagan–Bush 1981–1992	
34 years–20%	38 years–22%

McKinley to Taft, and Roosevelt to Truman are not atypical. By contrast, the opposition party has experienced much shorter periods of united government, Wilson being the only one who experienced it for more than two years. Finally, while both types of parties experienced nearly equal amounts of divided government, governing party experiences tend to be scattered and brief, the exceptions being the post-Reconstruction and Reagan eras. The opposition party tends to experience much longer periods of divided government. In fact, as much as divided government is typical of our current political era, it is far more typical of opposition party control of the presidency across time.

Table 3.2 demonstrates that divided government is a more common artifact of oppositional status—an example of the constraints under which this type of president operates. Governing party presidents have been in power for 120 of the 172 years, spanning Jackson's inauguration to the end of Clinton's second term. In that time, governing party presidents have experienced united government for 72 percent of their terms, and divided government for 28 percent of their terms. That is the mirror image for opposition presidents, who experienced united government for only 27 percent of their terms, and divided government for 73 percent of their terms.

Divided government is only one of the constraints that affect opposition presidents differently from governing party presidents. Four of the five presidents who have won elections without taking at least one house of Congress (Taylor, Eisenhower, Nixon, and Clinton) were opposition presidents (George H. W. Bush was the governing party exception). The only three presidents to face at least three successive congresses controlled by the other party (Eisenhower, Nixon, and Clinton) were opposition presidents. The only twice-elected presidents never to win a majority of the popular vote (Cleveland, Wilson, and Clinton) were opposition presidents. Opposition presidents tend to underperform when trying to win both a strong popular vote mandate (see Taylor, Cleveland, Wilson, Nixon, and Clinton) and a strong electoral vote mandate (see Taylor, Cleveland, Wilson, and Nixon). They tend to have weaker coattail effects during elections and experience heavier party losses during midterm elections. They also tend to leave their party weaker in Congress by the time they exit compared to the party's position when they arrived.

All of this demonstrates that the playing field of power is not equal. If a president has a policy agenda to communicate, it matters when he takes office. Opposition presidents lack the ability to define the long-range terms of political debate in their favor. They are forced to play by rules established by the governing party, which in turn affect the ideological context of their administrations. Their political capital is constrained from the day they enter office, and their ability to communicate their agenda to the public and to Congress cannot help but be affected by that dynamic. Thus, it is imperative for presidents to recognize the larger context of their administrations so that they can pursue appropriate communication strategies. The implication here is that opposition presidents should probably employ different strategies in pursuit of their goals than governing party presidents. For the rest of this

Table 3.2.   Divided Government as Institutional Constraint

	President of Governing Party		President of Opposition Party	
United Government	86 of 120 years	72%	14 of 52 years	27%
Divided Government	34 of 120 years	28%	38 of 52 years	73%

chapter, I focus on opposition presidents in an attempt to understand how presidents can adapt their communication strategies to fit their context. I do this because opposition presidents seem to have the most constrained circumstances. Understanding what makes such presidents more or less successful at communicating their goals will help us better understand how *all* presidents adapt to context.

A TALE OF TWO PRESIDENCIES

How can presidents best communicate their message in a complex world? For an initial exploration of this question, I examine the presidencies of Eisenhower and Clinton. At first glance this might appear to be an odd choice. However, both presidents were two-term opposition presidents, both were "modern presidents," and both experienced identical institutional dynamics—they began their presidencies enjoying united government and permanently lost that status at the first midterm election. While Eisenhower's stature as a war hero might appear to give him an advantage in terms of communicating his message, I point out that other war hero presidents have not been treated kindly by Congress (Taylor) or history (Grant). My objective is to use these case studies to examine the intersections of political communication with ideology and historical context. In pursuing this examination, I take a rather expansive definition of political communication, looking at both the rhetoric of words and the rhetoric of actions. What presidents do—what they choose to support and how they choose to support it—communicates as much about their intentions as what they say. Roosevelt's decision to "purge" his party in 1938 and Reagan's choice to pursue the Strategic Defense Initiative are as much aspects of communicating an agenda as "going public."

Given the need for all presidents to address the issue raised by Machiavelli and Neustadt—matching strategy to context—what strategies are effective for opposition presidents in communicating political goals?

The Natural Route: Frontal Assault

By definition, opposition presidents are presidents whose governing philosophy runs counter to the regnant power. Such a president's natural inclination is to do precisely what Skowronek's term calls him to do: preempt the agenda of the governing party. The word "preempt" implies a forcible seizing or appropriation, in this case of the dominant agenda of a political era. Andrew Johnson attempted to do this by obstructing Republican-led Reconstruction policy, and the result was impeachment. Wilson attempted to do this through extremist rhetoric during the debates over the Treaty of Versailles, and the result was colossal failure (Tulis 1987). Even Watergate can be viewed as an attempt by Nixon to preempt the governing party's agenda through clandestine means.

The first two years of Clinton's presidency are a classic example of frontal assault. The target was the conservative and minimal-government philosophy of the Reagan era. Although Clinton was a member of the moderate Democratic Leadership Council, he retained a vision of government as the "engine of social progress" whose mission is "to create genuine opportunity for all" (Reich 1997, 9). Indeed, after the 1994 midterm elections, the DLC said that "while Bill Clinton has the mind of a new Democrat he retains the heart of an old Democrat" (Aberbach 1996, 184). Clinton sought to reverse and undo the previous twelve years, and his earliest actions as president sent that signal to the public and the political community.

Clinton began his assault with his appointments. He made identity politics his primary focus, promising a cabinet that "looks like America" and allowing various interest groups to campaign for their own slots. He appointed as assistant secretary of housing and urban development lesbian activist Roberta Achtenberg, who opposed United Way funding for the Boy Scouts because the organization barred gay scoutmasters and who introduced her lover at her confirmation hearings. He appointed as surgeon general Joycelyn Elders, who spent the next two years infuriating social conservatives with statements that pro-life activists should get over their "love affair with the fetus," and suggestions that legalization of drugs should be studied and that masturbation should be taught in school. He attempted to appoint, as his civil rights chief, law professor Lani Guinier, who advocated equal outcomes in public policy, not simply a fair process, and who questioned whether certain black leaders were "authentic" representatives of the black community (Drew 1994, 24–25, 198–211, 385; Radosh 1996, 220, 224–226).[2] Clinton also communicated his desire to attack the reigning governing philosophy through his use of executive orders. On his second day in office, Clinton used this power to change federal policies concerning abortion by lifting restrictions on abortion counseling, research on the medical use of fetal tissue, and the use of federal funds for United Nations population programs. He allowed overseas military hospitals to perform abortions paid for with private funds, and ordered a review of the ban on the French abortion pill RU-486 (Drew 1994, 41–42). Clinton then attempted to reverse the military's ban on homosexuals, thus drawing significant opposition both from the military and from fellow "New Democrats" (Drew 1994, 41–42; Radosh 1996, 220–221).

What was distinctive about these early moves was not that Clinton took them but that he made them his first and very visible order of business. The political message he communicated to the country with these actions was not a centrist one but the undoing of the Reagan legacy. Given Clinton's history concerning the draft and the reportedly antagonistic attitudes of some in his administration toward the military, his efforts to reverse personnel policy can be seen as a direct challenge to a military culture greatly nourished by Reagan and Bush. Religious conservatives saw many of these early moves as an assault on traditional values. Republicans quickly became convinced that Clinton's larger agenda was to repudiate all they had achieved. The result was that Clinton enjoyed no honeymoon period even while setting the stage for a series of partisan battles that culminated in the loss of Congress.

This is not to say that Clinton lacked victories during his first two years, but even in his victories he was forced to compromise. He abandoned his investment plans in favor of deficit reduction. The fact that chairman of the Federal Reserve Alan Greenspan sat next to the First Lady at Clinton's first annual message telegraphed to Washington the larger constraints of Clinton's presidency (Reich 1997, 71–72; Woodward 1994, 135–144). A Congress controlled by Democrats defeated Clinton's investment plan because it was labeled Democratic pork, the GOP defined his energy tax as a tax-and-spend measure, and Clinton achieved victory for his economic plan only after promising spending cuts and a commission to examine middle-class entitlements (Radosh 1996, 230–231; Drew 1994, 80–83, 267–269; Woodward 1994, 291–302).

The objective that best demonstrated that Clinton did not understand his historical context was health care reform. In his speech to Congress rolling out his plan, Clinton rhetorically linked himself to Roosevelt, the New Deal, and the Social Security Act, holding up a card that he called a "health security card that will guarantee a comprehensive package of benefits over the course of an entire lifetime." Thus, social security became health security, and the social security card the health security card. However, whereas Roosevelt's achievement came in the context of the Great Depression, Clinton came to power in an era defined by antitax sentiments, tight budget constraints, and distrust of government. The two periods were not at all comparable. Clinton's 1,342-page bill constituted a complete overhaul of the nation's health care system, and Clinton quickly lost control of the definition of his plan, allowing it to be branded a big-government program.

During his 1994 annual message, Clinton issued a veto threat on the issue of universal coverage, saying "If you send me legislation that does not guarantee every American private health insurance that can never be taken away, you will force me to take this pen, veto the legislation, and we'll come right back here and start all over again." In closing the door to compromise, Clinton unleashed what Skocpol called a "thunderous juggernaut" of opposition. Senate Minority Leader Bob Dole called the plan "a massive overdose of government control." Clinton faced an integrated assault from all the elements of the reigning governing philosophy, including conservative think tanks, media outlets, grassroots organizations, and partisan groups. One bumper sticker said the plan possessed "the efficiency of the post office and the compassion of the IRS," while another branded it "another billion dollar bureaucracy" (Skocpol 1997, 1–2, 134–157, 171; Drew 1994, 302–303; Johnson and Broder 1996, 267, 328).

Health care reform never even came up for a vote. The defeat was so total that consultants advised Democratic candidates to stay away from it as an issue for the midterm elections. At a time when success was possible, when he enjoyed united government, Clinton failed to recognize the limits of his position. Believing he was free from historical constraints, Clinton's health care reform battle was his loudest cannon shot against the Reagan era, and his most consequential defeat. The day after health care reform died, House Minority Leader Newt Gingrich gathered 367 GOP House candidates to sign his "Contract with America," a party platform that presented a clear contrast to Clinton's agenda. Using the Contract to mobilize the GOP base, Republican candidates ran ads morphing their opponents into Clinton, thus associating them with his policies. The election cost Clinton control of Congress for the rest of his presidency. In a sense, Clinton had communicated his agenda all too well—it simply did not match what was possible for his time.

The Effective Route: The Indirect Approach

Effective opposition presidents adjust their strategies to what can be accomplished, usually through moderation or some form of deference toward the governing party. Such a president recognizes the futility of a frontal assault on the reigning governing philosophy and instead pursues a more tempered agenda. To the extent that the opposition president does attack the governing party, the attack tends to involve trimming the edges or restraining further advances of the governing party's larger agenda. Purists excoriate such a strategy as "me-tooism," but this subtler approach is the most effective way for the opposition party to gain ground. From Fillmore's support of the Compromise of 1850 to Cleveland's adherence to the gold standard to Nixon's Family Assistance Plan, opposition presidents have tried to achieve success by communicating a moderate agenda.

Eisenhower is the perfect example of this strategy because he was so successful at it. Eisenhower was personally conservative on domestic issues, had no love for the New Deal, and no desire to ratify its principal tenets. He once expressed his hostility to New Deal programs by saying that he saw it as his duty to "unseat the New Deal–Fair Deal bureaucracy in Washington." At the same time, Eisenhower was aware of the GOP's precarious position in the New Deal era. Like Clinton, Eisenhower came to office enjoying united government. Unlike Clinton, Eisenhower never assumed that united government gave him a mandate to repudiate the governing party. He understood that the New Deal was a permanent part of the American system, its policies too deeply embedded for a counterrevolution to succeed. Instead of attacking the New Deal with words and actions, Eisenhower decided to make incremental changes, tinkering at its margins and restraining its extension. He knew that any attempt by the GOP to abolish popular programs like social security would be foolhardy. His brother once chastised him for continuing liberal policies, prompting Eisenhower to respond, "Should any political party attempt to abolish social security, unemployment insurance, and eliminate labor laws and farm programs, you should not hear of that party again in our political history." Eisenhower consciously moderated his own stand for political reasons, avoiding a frontal assault on the New Deal even when he enjoyed united control of government, choosing instead to communicate a more tempered agenda (Leuchtenburg 1983, 53–54; Ambrose 1984, 219; Milkis 1993, 162–163; Hamby 1992, 118–122; Sloan 1991, 62).

It would have been an easy matter for the president to go along with his congressional majority, but Eisenhower signaled his willingness to tame his party's impulses from the beginning. Conservative Republicans sought, through the Yalta Resolution, to repudiate all secret agreements that resulted in the subjugation experienced by Eastern Europe following World War II. The measure constituted a direct attack on foreign policy conducted by Roosevelt and Truman. Eisenhower fought his own party to a deadlock. Continuing the assault on such agreements, conservative Senator John Bricker proposed a constitutional amendment that would place limits on the president's power to make treaties and executive agreements. Facing opposition from a majority in his own party, Eisenhower received enough Democratic support to win the day. In later years, Eisenhower chose to meet with the Soviet Union in summits, raising fears in the GOP Old Guard of another Yalta (Ambrose 1984, 66–70, 260–267; Parmet 1972, 197–201, 305–312; Milkis 1993, 168–169; Pach and Richardson 1991, 59–62, 108–112).

Eisenhower's moderate approach was not limited to foreign policy, an area where he was more internationalist than the Republican core. Greenstein details how Eisenhower strove to conceal the political side of leadership through the "hidden-hand approach" (1982), and Eisenhower certainly worked to communicate an image of nonpartisan leadership. During his first annual message he talked of pursuing a "middle way," referring at various times to his vision as "dynamic conservatism," "progressive moderation," "moderate progressivism," and "New Republicanism." In 1954 Eisenhower said, "When it comes down to dealing with the relationship between the human in this country and his Government, the people in this administration believe in being what I think we would normally call liberal; and when we deal with the economic affairs of this country, we believe in being conservative." At a time when Republicans controlled Congress, Eisenhower succeeded in expanding social security coverage, and raising the minimum wage and unemployment benefits. Some commented that the administration was "New Dealish in its welfare program." In fact, Eisenhower placed a conservative tint on New Deal programs, but his actions

and rhetoric made it appear as though he were less partisan, more consensual, and "above politics" (Sloan 1991, 16–17, 54–56; Reichard 1975,
119–135; Ambrose 1984, 157–158).

As with Clinton, Eisenhower's party failed to maintain its majority in Congress at the midterm election. Knowing that he would need Democrats Sam
Rayburn and Lyndon Johnson to get legislation passed, Eisenhower played
up his nonpartisan image, claiming he stood above politics, and that his programs were "in the best interests of all Americans." The governing party
viewed his 1955 annual message as correctly stating "a Democratic premise,"
and Eisenhower met regularly with Rayburn and Johnson in the White
House for drinks to smooth the way for legislation. As Congress became
more liberal, Eisenhower was forced to use his veto more often, but the administration also supported civil rights legislation, public housing, school
construction, a higher minimum wage, further expansion of social security
coverage, and interstate highway construction. Eisenhower's biggest battles
with Democrats tended to be in the area of fiscal policy, for he had a strong
commitment to a balanced budget. Even in that area, however, Eisenhower's
budget battles were less direct attacks on New Deal programs than pruning
their excesses and restraining their growth. Eisenhower even toyed with the
idea of replacing Nixon on the 1956 ticket with the Democratic governor of
Ohio (Pach and Richardson 1991, 105–106; Mooney 1970, 213–315; Divine
1985, 78; Parmet 1972, 495; Ambrose 1984, 294).

The GOP saw an opportunity in 1953 to attack the foundation of the New
Deal. Eisenhower understood that the party had not campaigned against the
core of the New Deal, and that such a course would be disastrous. In adapt-
ing his strategy to his context, Eisenhower drew criticism from his own party.
Some said he "could not seriously be distinguished from a conservative
Democrat" and that he had "put a Republican stamp of approval on twenty
years of Democratic legislation" (Hughes 1962, 336–338; Ambrose 1984,
624). Eisenhower was self-consciously aware that the repudiation of the
New Deal system desired by the Old Guard would not work, so he targeted
the most vulnerable aspect of that system—money—and sought progress on
that front through the mechanism of a balanced budget. Unlike Clinton in his
first two years, Eisenhower used his resources carefully, proclaiming moderation and nonpartisanship in his public statements and ensuring that his actions matched his rhetoric. Contemporary criticisms of Eisenhower argued
that he "could not lead because he would not lead," complaining that he did
not "shake history," despite his consistently high popularity (Rossiter 1960,
182–195). The truth may be that Eisenhower did not "shake history" because
he knew any attempt to do so would bring disaster. Eisenhower adapted his
communication strategy to the temper of his times and in that way remained
effective throughout his presidency.

Learning the Indirect Approach: Clinton's "Second Term"

In the early, chaotic days of Clinton's presidency, he is reported to have complained that "We're all Eisenhower Republicans. We're Eisenhower Republicans here, and we are fighting the Reagan Republicans. We stand for lower deficits and free trade and the bond market" (Woodward 1994, 164–165). It was not a happy admission but Clinton proved to be prophetic. Once he faced a Republican Congress committed to furthering the Reagan Revolution, Clinton underwent a remarkable metamorphosis, choosing to end his frontal assault on the governing party and instead pursue a more tempered and indirect approach. Clinton learned the lesson Eisenhower had known from the beginning; in so doing, Clinton salvaged his political fortunes.

The rhetorical comparisons with Eisenhower are fascinating. Where Eisenhower sought a "middle way," Clinton pursued a "third way." Where Eisenhower preached "New Republicanism," Clinton claimed he was a "New Democrat." Where Eisenhower placed himself "above politics" and removed from the typical liberal–conservative battle, Clinton and adviser Dick Morris proclaimed the virtues of "triangulation." Morris believed that Clinton should "create a third position, not just in between the old position of the two parties but above them as well. Identify a new course that accommodates the needs the Republicans address but does it in a way that is uniquely yours." After his 1994 thrashing, Clinton adjusted his strategy. Facing a conservative Congress, Clinton became, in essence, a moderate Republican. Clinton's liberal faction did not approve of the transformation. Secretary of Labor Robert Reich even called Morris "Mephistopheles, the corrupter of all means to an end that is never fully realized." But Clinton's shift toward the center—his adoption of the indirect approach, late though it was—saved his presidency (Morris 1997, 80–81; Reich 1997, 325).

Clinton's actions and rhetoric clearly communicated a new understanding of his contextual constraints. In 1995, he acknowledged the ghost of Ronald Reagan, saying that "the ticket to admission to American politics is a balanced budget." He responded to the GOP plan to balance the budget in seven years with his own plan to do so in ten. In the ensuing budget battle and government shutdown, Clinton deftly positioned himself to claim the middle, painting the GOP as extremists. He gave the impression that he sought what the GOP sought, but that he would do so more responsibly. Even while attacking the GOP, Clinton moved away from his ideal program of investments in the poor, education, and job skills toward an agenda of budget cutting, eventually adopting the GOP's timetable. In his 1996 annual message, Clinton announced that "the era of big government is over," a line that could have come from Reagan's own lips. Clinton contested the 1996 election partly by focusing on the issue of moral decline, a traditionally Republican strength. Contrary to the interests of one of his core interest groups,

Clinton signed the Defense of Marriage Act, placing into federal law a definition of marriage as "a legal union between one man and one woman as husband and wife." Finally, after twice vetoing GOP versions of welfare reform, Clinton defied his Democratic congressional leadership and cooperated with Republican Speaker Newt Gingrich in ending sixty years of domestic policy, turning over control of a core element of Roosevelt's New Deal to the states. In his second inaugural address Clinton said there was "work that government alone cannot do," and by May 1997 he made a deal with the GOP to balance the budget by 2002 (Morris 1997, 160–170, 207–214, 221–231; Drew 1996, 232–237, 376; Reich 1997, 336–337; Drew 1997, 130–137, 159).

By 1998 the pattern of success was clear. A *New York Times* article aptly summarized the truth about Clinton, labeling him an "incremental president" who was "accomplishing piecemeal some of what he cannot do all at once" (Bennet and Pear 1997, A1). His goals were certainly more tempered than they were in 1993. Reich argued that to date Clinton's legacy was "primarily a Republican one" of balancing the budget, getting rid of welfare, cutting capital gains taxes, and widening global trade. Other Democrats talked of "a second Eisenhower era," with a limited federal role and a president "willing to accept smaller, incremental victories" (Berke and Broder 1997, A1). One study even suggests that support for Clinton remained high during his impeachment crisis, not only because of peace and prosperity but because his moderate and centrist policies appealed to the ideological center (Zaller 1998, 182–189).

In retrospect, Clinton's impeachment is partly attributable to his early misunderstanding of context. By failing to understand the constraints under which he operated, Clinton also failed to understand his vulnerability to attack by the governing party. From Whitewater to "Filegate," scandals gave the governing party ammunition to attack a president who communicated an abhorrent agenda. Clinton's attempt to redefine politics emboldened the GOP to attack him where he was weak. His management of his agenda in his first two years helped bring about the very GOP majority that impeached him. And, although Clinton adjusted his political strategy after 1994 to deal effectively with the governing party, that party had already written him off. In that sense, Clinton came to moderation too late. Then, by vigorously fighting the investigations, Clinton continued to give the governing party an incentive to attack him.

Clinton's communication skills escaped him at various points during the Monica Lewinsky crisis. From his assertion that he "did not have sexual relations with that woman" to his disastrous television appearance following his grand jury testimony, Clinton communicated disdain for a process controlled by the governing party, making his impeachment no mystery. What saved him was his ability to communicate a moderate image while defining his opponents as extremists. In the midst of the crisis, he claimed the first balanced budget and budget surplus in thirty years, signed a bill to overhaul the IRS, and spoke openly about the possibility of privatizing part of social security. Clinton remained supremely malleable, demonstrating a remarkable ability to transform himself. He came to the strategy of the indirect approach too late to enable him to construct a healthy dialogue with the governing party, but he made the change in time to salvage his popular support and communicate an image of success that sustained him when he most needed it.

EXPLORING CONTEXT

I have called this chapter "Prometheus Chained" and the reference is deliberate. The image of the president is often that of the superman whose tools for communication place other political actors at a great disadvantage. Given such an image, it is no wonder that so many fail to understand how best to communicate their agendas—or adjust their agendas to match the constraints and possibilities of their time. Instead of being supermen, presidents are chained to the rock of context, with minimal power to affect the direction of its movement. This chapter is a first attempt to make clear that political leadership and political communication are multilayered phenomena that merit exceedingly complex treatment. There are questions that need to be examined in future research, from the specific to the more general.

First, we need to become more precise when it comes to thinking about political context. It should be evident that all presidents are not created equal, but in what way are they not created equal? What skills are most important when it comes to communication in a complex political environment? The "context" of a presidency can mean many things, after all. It can refer to economic conditions or to the presence of warfare. It can refer to the partisan makeup of Congress or to popular opinion. It can refer to random events like assassinations or personal scandals. No doubt, all of these elements are important in understanding the context of a presidency, but all are not necessarily equally important to understanding the broader question of a president's freedom or constraints in selling his agenda. It may be that different aspects of political communication should be treated differently depending on what aspect of "context" is being examined.

Second, it is important to understand more fully the dynamics involved in opposition leadership. How is a president to know that he is an opposition party president? All presidents are elected because in some way they have been successful at defining the electoral contest in terms that favor them. Thus, it should be no surprise that any newly elected president believes he has a mandate for change. The Whigs certainly thought so in 1840, and Bill Clinton believed the same thing following his election in 1992. A fine line separates the president-as-preemptor and the president-as-reconstructor. Both would like to transform the political dialogue in their favor. The reconstructor is able to do that, and thus win great freedom of action. The preemptor cannot, and if he tries he will reap the whirlwind. Getting elected and governing equally involve political communication, but is it communication of the same sort? What made the situation faced by Eisenhower different from that faced by Roosevelt? What made the situation faced by Clinton different from that faced by Reagan? How was Clinton to know that he could not, in fact, reverse "the last twelve years"?

Third, are there drawbacks to pursuing the indirect approach to presidential communication? An opposition president who consciously communicates a more moderate agenda will inevitably create friction with the core of his own party, but in a sense his unusual position allows him a degree of freedom that other presidents do not enjoy. It has become a maxim that "only Nixon could go to China"—and perhaps it is true that only a virulent anti-communist could retain the credibility to make that move. In the same way, perhaps only Clinton—only a Democratic opposition president—could reform welfare.

On the other hand, there may be political constraints even in the pursuit of moderation. Was Eisenhower placating his GOP right wing by appearing to tolerate Joseph McCarthy when he could have used his position to rebuke him? Did Clinton retreat from a serious attempt at entitlement reform because he thought he would be going too far? It may be the case that the task of political communication becomes doubly difficult for opposition party presidents as they attempt to walk that delicate ideological line. It is important to understand why presidents sometimes attempt to become "Nixon in China," while at other times they take a more timid posture.

Fourth, if we are going to take seriously the question of political communication in historical context, we will need to look at presidents in all contexts. I have merely scratched the surface of the problems associated with one type of context here, but there are many other scenarios to explore. I have hinted at one—the similarities in incentives between presidents-as-preemptors and presidents-as-reconstructors. What is it, exactly, that makes communication different for these two types of presidents? At the same time, there appears to be some similarity between successful opposition presidents and moderate governing party presidents. This should be no surprise, since the successful opposition president uses a rhetoric of actions and words that moves in the direction of the governing party. Because there can be only one "great redefiner" in an era, his followers cannot help but appear more moderate. Thus, governing party presidents and opposition presidents appear quite similar. This is one explanation for why the 2000 GOP mantra "compassionate conservative" sounds to some like an attempt to claim Democratic ground, to moderate the governing party. Indeed, this may be one explanation for the relative stability and moderation of American politics throughout much of this century's history.

Fifth, just as we need to examine presidents in all contexts, so we should examine communication in all contexts. The model of presidential communication I have laid out here can be applied to other political offices. For example, if the president is an "opposition leader," then the leader of the governing party may be the Speaker of the House or Senate majority leader. He may even be a minority leader in Congress, if the opposition president enjoys united government. All political leaders desire to be effective spokesmen for their party's agenda, and it stands to reason that the task of political communication is probably different for the governing party leader or opposition party leader depending on whether they control one or both elected branches of government, or operate in an "official" minority party status. A strong argument can be made that Newt Gingrich was the governing party leader during much of Clinton's presidency, a time when the locus of power seemed to reside in the House and not in the presidency itself. This project calls for us to examine the possibilities and constraints of the presidency when power becomes thinly distributed.

Finally, how communication works best in the current era deserves closer examination. Many scholars would dispute the notion that we currently operate in a "Reagan era," arguing instead that we are either still in a New Deal era or in a postpartisan age in which neither party can claim majority status, an argument reinforced by the fifty-fifty split in the 107th Congress. The latter scenario presents an interesting dilemma for political leaders intent on selling their agenda. If nothing else, partisan majorities in American politics prior to the late 1960s gave presidents clarity about how to organize their communications strategy. If we now live in a postpartisan age, then presidents may have lost some important decision-making cues and hence some of their ability to communicate an integrated agenda to the public. If there is no reigning governing philosophy and no truly governing party, perhaps every president becomes an opposition leader in a postpartisan age. If so, do such presidents have an opportunity to redefine politics in their favor, if only they can figure out how to reconnect the public to its politics? Is communication different in an age that has no partisan context? Does each president become a rhetorical "free agent"? Whatever the truth, it seems clear that context governs government far more than is usually recognized, and that evaluations of presidential performance are only valid when context is taken into account. Powerful though it is, political communication only begins the task of political leadership and it can be successful only to the extent that a leader is aware of his place in history. As we have seen here, those places can be both multiple and complex.

NOTES

1. Nothing mandates that "success" be determined from the president's perspective, but for the purposes of this chapter I assume that presidents come to power with some desire for ideological success. They are affiliated with political parties with agendas that more or less correspond with their own, and in an ideal world they pursue a significant portion of those objectives.

2. While it is true that Clinton's support of Elders and Guinier proved in the end to be tepid, his eventual retreats do not diminish the symbolic importance of his initial support, which communicated important information about his goals to his enemies.

4

The Presence of the
Past in Public Discourse

Jill A. Edy

An important theme recently developed in studies of communication and political science is the work being done to understand how the public and political worlds are made meaningful for all types of political actors, from legislators to citizens. Early research on mass media and mass political behavior typically emphasized straightforward connections between communication and behavior. This new perspective encourages us to think beyond persuasion and manipulation—to contemplate unintentional effects of political communication, to consider both short-term and long-term outcomes of media campaigns, and to develop an appreciation of the communicative "ground" upon which specific persuasive campaigns are built. All such studies have opened the door to the study of political culture.

At the same time, much research on media and politics lacks any sense of history. Many key theories are formulated in timeless terms suggesting that the behavior of elites, citizens, and media remain constant. Many studies assume that discourses among political actors, elites, and especially citizens are written on a nearly blank slate, subject only to ahistorical stereotypes. While we may sometimes speak of a "democratic tradition," in reality we know very little about how any of our political traditions affect everyday political reality. Surely, these traditions constitute a form of cultural capital that strongly influences how we understand our social world. Further, it seems highly likely that the media play a critical role in the creation and dissemination of such cultural capital in large and diverse nation-states.

Political culture is a broad and diffuse concept, but one relatively concrete aspect of it is collective memory. People who share a culture share a past, although the nature of that sharing is not well understood. Thus, one way to analyze political culture is to study collective memories as they emerge and develop in the media and are used, or not used, to make sense of subsequent public events. How we talk about our past affects how we understand and respond to our present. Collective-memory research begins with the fundamental assumption that political discourse does not exist ex nihilo. Rather, it draws on existing cultural capital, previously created and dynamically shared understandings of the social world.

The relationship between collective memory and public discourse is rich and complex, and my early research on the development of mediated collective memories for controversial events has raised a number of critical questions that cannot yet be completely answered. The underlying premise I have adopted is that the mass media render aspects of the past as stories. As White (1987) suggests, they are stories with morals, and they seem to influence both journalists and political elites as they attempt to make sense of current events. Here, I develop a working definition of collective memory, describe some of my research, and suggest key research areas, questions, and perspectives with the potential to expand our understanding of how the remembered past plays a role in the political present.

COLLECTIVE MEMORY: THE STORY EVERYONE KNOWS

The study of collective memory goes on in a number of disciplines, each of which has its own definition of the phenomenon. Sociologist Barry Schwartz's may be the most concise: "Collective memory is a metaphor that formulates society's retention and loss of information about its past in the familiar terms of individual remembering and forgetting" (1991, 302). However, this simple first cut glosses over a number of important issues: Who is implicated in the term "society"? Are we talking about political elites? Journalists? Average citizens? All three have been the focus of particular studies, in addition to the more amorphous society that is apparently defined by the creation and reception of cultural products such as poetry (Schwartz et al. 1986) and holidays (Bodnar 1992). Further, in the context of a collectivity, who, exactly, has to remember for the memory to be a collective one? If 51 percent of the relevant group recalls a person or event, is that a collective memory? How similar do their memories of that person or event have to be?

Moreover, what do we mean by a memory? Psychologists refer to at least three kinds of memory: short-term, long-term, and process. Short-term memory does not seem to hold much allure for collective-memory scholars, and long-term memory takes on a whole new meaning when the relevant "long term" can mean dozens of generations and thousands of years. Process memory, memory for how to do things, was largely ignored in collective memory research until Michael Schudson (1992) considered the legal structures constituting the residue of "Watergate." Although he does not describe his findings in this way, cultural practices like the special prosecutor law represent a process memory—a memory for how to keep a president honest—however flawed it may be.

My work has defined collective memory as a narrative about the past that is conveyed and negotiated in public spaces. This definition draws on the work of George Herbert Mead, who argues that pasts are entirely imaginary (1929). Once a moment is gone, its passing must be reconstructed. Physical traces of the past may exist, but in order to make a past meaningful, perhaps even to recall it at all, we must tell stories about it. Hayden White's work contains the most famous and well-thought-out discussions of the relationship between history and narrative. His definition of narrative is a story in which the facts appear to "speak for themselves." Narration and narrativity are "instruments by which the conflicting claims of the imaginary and the real are mediated, arbitrated, or resolved in a discourse" (1987, 4). White argues that we take comfort and pleasure in assigning to real events the coherence of a story.

Thinking about collective memories as stories has a number of advantages. For one, this narrative approach highlights the essential role of communication in collective memory. Stories must be told, and they must be public, for collective memory to develop, survive, and have an impact on social life.

A narrative approach to collective memory also underscores the importance of structure and context for remembering. Psychological research has demonstrated that the short-term memory for disconnected facts (such as nonsense lists of words or numbers) is quite limited without the aid of powerful mnemonic devices. To understand how stories aid us in recalling the past, consider how Fentress and Wickham (1992) describe the enfolding of a past into a narrative.

> Information that is context-dependent . . . will tend to be lost whenever that context changes. . . . In narrative memory, stories themselves can serve as internal contexts, fixing the memory of images and links in a properly consequential order. . . . In this sense, a plot functions as a complex memory image, and learning a repertoire of plots is equivalent to learning a large scale mnemotechnique that permits the ordering, retention, and subsequent transmission of a vast amount of information. (72)

Further, a narrative approach emphasizes the dynamic relationship between people and the past by reminding us that in the process of making the past meaningful, we necessarily distort it. Although narrative aids the retention of facts, distortion is likely to occur while encoding facts into a narrative as those facts that are not essential to the narrative are lost. It is also possible that "facts" may be invented in support of a narrative. According to Novick (1999), while the figure of six million Jews murdered in the Holocaust is based on the existing historical evidence, the widely cited figure of eleven million death-camp murders overall appears to have been invented by Simon Wiesenthal and then incorporated into public discourse. My own work suggests that it is the meaning of the past that is malleable within a relatively unchanging understanding of "what happened," yet it is the meaning we give to facts that is so socially powerful. Without it, what would we make of the facts?

The past is also socially powerful to the extent that we collectively remember it. What makes these narrative memories collective? Defining what is meant by *collective* memory has been especially critical for me because I have been studying memories of controversial pasts. Relative to such matters, we should not expect to see, to use Hall's (1982) term, perfect "closure"—an emergent single story that never changes again. Collective-memory research has revealed that any story about the past is not fixed; it is responsive to current events. The nature of narrative also makes perfect closure unattainable. White (1987) points out that any narrative involves choices and implies the possibility of other narratives. He argues that if there were not more than one way to tell the story, there would be no point in telling it. Thus, narratives are created in order to forestall the creation of other narratives. Even if they are never told, the presence of these phantom stories suggests an absence of closure. It also seems unreasonable to demand that every individual in a community be able to recall a past in exactly the same way in order for a memory to be called "collective." Far-less-than-perfect agreement about the nature of the past is needed to make a narrative about the past socially powerful.

A collective memory has much more in common with what the Popular Memory Group (1982) and Bommes and Wright (1982) would call a dominant memory. A dominant memory is the memory that is broadly available in the public sphere. However, a dominant memory may be imposed on people, whereas the idea of a collective memory implies an element of legitimation. A collective memory is accepted by people, whether this constitutes false consciousness or not.

Ultimately, collective memory is the story about the past that people are familiar with. It is the common cultural currency, the story one must know in order to communicate about the past with others. Even those who disagree with this narrative of the past are at least aware of it. It shapes their experience, and perhaps even their resistance.

Collective-memory researchers and psychological-memory researchers alike emphasize that remembering takes work. How is this work accomplished, and what does it achieve?

SOME EARLY FINDINGS

My research on the phenomenon of collective memory has focused on how collective memories are negotiated in public discourse. How is this cultural currency created? I argue that journalism plays an important role in the development of collective memory because it provides discursive public space for negotiations between a variety of actors who have an interest in how a past is remembered. Those actors may include local, state, and national political elites, journalists (see Zelizer 1992), interest group leaders, and average citizens. Journalism is also public in that the struggle between these participants is enacted before an audience; as Schattschneider (1975) points out, the reaction of the audience is a key element in any social conflict. However, journalism is not a neutral discursive space because reporters and editors make choices and embrace practices that influence the memories that emerge in this social discourse. Often, it is not possible to ascribe the construction of the collective memory to any single social actor. Public officials and other sources offer information and interpretation to reporters who pick and choose among what is available according to their professional norms and practices and who may interject their own interpretations into the story. The resulting narrative cannot be said to be the product of any one actor but of the interaction among several individuals. To say that an understanding of the past emerges in the press is to invoke all of these complex processes at work. In this sense, the narratives of past events emerging in the press are truly *collective* memories.

The cases I examine, the 1965 Watts riots and the 1968 Democratic National Convention, involve dramatic public controversies and for that reason highlight the processes of negotiation that go into the creation of collective memory. My findings (Edy 1998) show that conflicting narratives do tend to resolve themselves as they are told and retold in the media, and there is a tendency for one principal story to become dominant. In the case of the Watts riots, the collective memory developed through a process that winnowed out some stories told at the time of the riots and blended others. The emerging story of the Chicago convention, on the other hand, required the creation of new narrative elements as well as the disappearance of some stories told in 1968 in order to reconcile competing stories about the past.

The development of these stories is not well predicted by the principles of hegemony theory that dominate scholarly explanations of news about social controversy. Instead, a complex mix of journalism practices, elite hegemony, and simple chance drive the process. Further, whether or not an aspect of the past becomes important to political discourse depends on the shape of the story that emerges. Some stories encourage using the past to understand the present; others don't. Either way, there is no guarantee that the past will be used appropriately or well. It is, however, used often. The *Chicago Tribune* referred to the 1968 convention an average of once every two weeks between 1981 and 1995, more than thirteen years after the event. The *Los Angeles Times* referred to the Watts riots nearly as frequently between 1985 and 1991, more than twenty years after the event (Edy 1998).

In the sections that follow, I draw upon my empirical findings and the wisdom of other scholars to illuminate some of the major questions that must be addressed for us to understand the role the past plays in contemporary political and social life. I begin with the question I have most directly addressed in my own research: *How are stories about the past created?* There is still much to learn about how meanings for the past are negotiated, and whether and how stories about the past are constrained by what actually happened. Second, I turn to the ways in which the past is used to make sense of the present. My research shows that in the news media, creating stories about the past and using those stories to make sense of the present are fairly distinct processes. Negotiations about the meaning of the past do not usually take place when the past is being used to make sense of a more recent event or crisis (Edy 1999). However, little is known about how a past is chosen as a way to help us understand the present. Third, I address a classic issue in collective-memory research that is rarely considered by scholars of media and politics: why are some pasts remembered and others forgotten? While specific cases of remembering and forgetting have been addressed at length, little work addresses general principles that might govern these processes. Yet these processes of remembering and forgetting may be essential to the development of political culture and tradition as well as directly influencing how we make sense of contemporary public life. Finally, I consider some of the technical research issues that must be addressed in studies of collective memory.

HOW ARE STORIES ABOUT THE PAST CREATED?

Understanding how stories about the past are created is important in and of itself. In the often-quoted words of Santayana, "Those who cannot remember the past are condemned to repeat it." Santayana may be right, but he does not go far enough. When we argue over the "lessons of history," we acknowledge that it is important not just to know the past but to understand it, and our understanding of the past develops as our stories about it do.

My research demonstrates that creating collective memory requires work, but this work is not performed continuously, nor is it performed whenever a past is recalled. In journalism, commemorations, moments when we recall the past for no other purpose but to remember, offer the best opportunity for negotiating contradictory visions. When the past is used as an analogy or as a context for the present, contradictory aspects of collective memory are not typically addressed (Edy 1999).

Research into the development of collective memories also contributes to the broader projects of political science and communication research by enriching existing theory. Current theories about the relationship among media, citizens, and public life often lack a temporal component. They are generated by scholars using empirical evidence from the here and now and formulated in presentist terms. When temporal elements are developed in political communication research, they are often simple and mechanical (for example, trust in government has declined since Vietnam and Watergate; the length of soundbites has declined over time).

In order to understand the process of collective-memory development, I have applied some of these theories, familiar to scholars of media and politics, to discourse about the past. Applying these theories to collective memory is harder than it might appear. This is not to say that the insights developed by researchers examining the present are useless to scholars interested in the past; it is only that the application of these concepts to the study of collective memory produces unique insights of its own.

Take, for example, one of the most basic truisms of journalism scholarship—the relationship between journalists and sources. Sigal's (1973) demonstration that journalists rely heavily on official sources has become a fundamental component of a variety of important theories about how the media report political events and issues to the public (see also Tuchman 1978; Fishman 1980). Sigal and the others are absolutely right. Journalists reporting on current events turn to official sources and often adopt their preferred narratives for ascribing meaning to events. This was true in 1965 during the Watts riots and in 1968 during the Chicago convention. But as events slip into the past, the relative prominence of official sources declines, sometimes precipitously. To understand why, we must discover why journalists rely on official sources in the first place.

Entman and Page (1994) argue that journalists turn to sources who have the power to affect policy outcomes, but for the past, outcomes have already been largely determined, so this incentive is nullified. Further, presentist perspectives are not required to deal with the dual identity of officials as representatives of public institutions and as individuals. When looking at coverage of the past, this dualism quickly becomes apparent. Officials retire, are not returned to office, and die. They are not "officials" any more, and their relative attractiveness to journalists fades.

Another explanation for why journalists turn to official sources stems from ideas about the relationship between journalists and the public. Journalists derive some of their authority from their status as eyewitnesses to history (Zelizer 1992). From this perspective, officials are good sources because the next best thing to being a witness to history is interviewing a witness to history, and government officials are often eyewitnesses to or participants in important events and decisions. However, they share that status with a wide variety of citizens, including people who were living in the affected area and those who were arrested, injured, or otherwise affected by the course of events. Further, officials are often much older than any other group involved in an event. Today, all of the major city officials involved in the Watts riots are dead, but journalists can still find and interview neighborhood residents who recall the events.

Does all of this mean that the relative hegemony of official interpretations of past events declines over time? My own work suggests that sometimes it does, but Frisch (1986) points out that unless nontraditional sources are allowed to interpret as well as to describe events, official hegemony often persists. Existing theory cannot tell us under what conditions average people are permitted to give meaning to their pasts in the media.

Existing evidence does show that citizens' power to resist official constructions of the past can be considerable. Several scholars have documented struggles over the meaning of the past that involved organized citizens who were authorized as eyewitnesses. A notable recent example was the controversy over the Smithsonian's plans for displaying the *Enola Gay,* which dropped the atomic bomb on Hiroshima. Resistance to the officials' narrative was so great that the exhibit metamorphosed into one that had no narrative at all (see Hogan 1996).[1] But the process may be subtler still. Memories contained in the public may act as a constraint on the possible narratives news media can construct to the extent that journalists rely upon their public credibility to give their stories authority.

Testing prevailing theories about the media, politics, and citizenship in the context of collective memory clearly has the potential to promote the development of communication theory as well as theories of collective memory. Adding a temporal element changes the relationships between the public, the media, and the government in many ways that have implications for public policy and public life. More work should be done to examine when and how these changes occur. Researchers must further consider how these relationships are tempered by national culture. Elements such as the relative freedom of the press; levels of citizen education, interest, and involvement; government cohesiveness; and national history almost certainly affect these processes.

HOW DOES THE PAST INFLUENCE THE PRESENT?

Understanding how collective memories are constructed is a fundamental first step to appreciating their role in public life. Understanding how the past is used is the second. Several scholars have documented how memories of the past form the foundation of a civilization. Commager (1965) describes how national identity is founded in part upon collective memories. Zerubavel (1995) and Bodnar (1992) explain how the past is used in nation building in Israel and the United States, respectively. Smith (1985) explains how collective memories promote political action. Yet there is still much to learn.

Here again, lacking a sense of time leaves scholars of media and politics vulnerable to misanalysis. Appreciating that the present is to some extent derived from and in dialogue with the past can help scholars avoid a key pitfall in the comparisons they often make between "like" events. To escape the problems of case-study research, scholars often take comparative cases or analyze a collection of cases. What they almost never do is consider how these cases are temporally related to one another. When we analyze aggregations of presidential elections, we often treat them as if each election were an independent event rather than one in a series of sequential events. Even scholars who recognize that they should not compare, say, elections from the "pretelevision" era to those of the "television" era often treat all of the elections in the latter era as events apparently unaffected by the experiences parties or voters had in the elections that preceded them.

In another example, a number of scholars are currently interested in explaining why it was that Bill Clinton survived his impeachment experience with his job approval rating largely intact when "the same" experience destroyed Richard Nixon's approval ratings. According to Fackler (1999), one likely looking culprit is the economy, which was outstanding for Clinton and poor for Nixon. His study of the relationship between revelations of corruption, the state of the economy, and public support for the president considers the relationships between these variables from 1953 until 1996. However, his study considers only covariance, not temporality. Do citizens apply their memories of presidential scandals to current claims of corruption? Faced with Clinton's impeachment, did people who remembered Watergate say to themselves, "I don't want to go through that again"? Could these memories help to explain the public's reaction to more recent scandals? Understanding how people remember the past may be critical to understanding their reactions to the present.

One of the most intriguing questions is why a past is remembered in some contexts but not others. For example, nearly half of the references to the Watts riots in the *New York Times* between June 1980 and September 1992 appear in the context of the civil unrest following the trial of the Los Angeles police officers who beat Rodney King. However, very few references to the Watts riots were made during the riots in Miami in the 1980s (Edy 1998). Why? The easy answer may be "geography," but one should not gloss over the element of choice in making reference to the past. Both the Miami riots and the 1992 unrest in Los Angeles involved several racial groups, including relatively large proportions of Hispanics. Almost everyone arrested during the Watts riots was African American, and for that reason the Watts event continues to be constructed as an incident of black/white racial tension. So why is geography more important than other aspects of the event that might be more relevant in the construction of comparisons? And what is the impact of recalling the Watts riots in the context of the 1992 multiracial civil unrest in Los Angeles?

In a similar vein, the 1968 Chicago convention protests are never mentioned in coverage of anti–Gulf War protests. As Gitlin (1980) and Farber (1988) have pointed out, the 1968 protests in Chicago were extremely complex events. Protest targets included the Vietnam War, poverty, racism, and the nomination procedures of the Democratic Party, among other things. Contemporary coverage, as Gitlin notes, did not assign any sort of broader social meaning to the protests but treated them as criminal activity. However, by the 1990s, the *New York Times* was painting a much clearer picture of the Chicago convention. The protests in Chicago were now regularly identified as antiwar (Edy 1998). So as some of the most famous antiwar protests in twentieth-century American history, why are they not applied by reporters to help us understand the scope and import of more recent antiwar sentiments? And did this help the cause of the Gulf War protestors, or hurt it?

In thinking about the influence of the past upon the present, it is useful to consider the relationship between collective memory and framing. My findings suggest that a story about the past can perform all of the functions Entman (1993) ascribes to a frame: defining a social problem, identifying the cause of the problem, identifying the agents responsible for the problem, and providing a means to evaluate solutions. Further, collective memory seems to influence both journalists and political elites as they attempt to make sense of current events. Like a frame, it highlights some elements of the present and makes others inconspicuous. However, the precise connection between collective memories and frames remains elusive. In its current state of development, framing research has examined the broad outlines of frames (see for example, Iyengar's [1991] specification of episodic and thematic frames) and has ascribed to the media and political elites broad powers to frame events (see for example, Entman 1991). In contrast, media mentions of collective memory are usually tied to a relatively specific set of facts that cannot be selectively referenced (Edy 1999) and often assume a shared understanding of the past that is far more detailed (Edy 1998) than what is described by framing theory.

More work is needed to develop the relationship between memories and frames. Research on collective memory also has the potential to address questions that framing theory may not be ready to ask yet, such as where the limits of elite power to frame events lie. My research shows that when a story about the past is used as an analogy for the present, the story about the past rarely changes (Edy 1999) and is typically recalled as a whole rather than as selected parts. Thus, when the Watts riots are recalled during the 1992 civil unrest in Los Angeles, the white/black racial violence of the 1965 riots remains part of the story (Edy 1998), even though this would seem to disqualify the analogy given the multiracial character of the later unrest. Reporters and officials have a good deal of power to reference the past, but their choices constrain them in many ways.

The past may influence reporters and editors in ways that are not entirely visible in the stories they produce. Neustadt and May (1986) examined how the past influenced the decisions of political elites faced with perceived crises. For example, they explain that Truman viewed North Korean incursion into South Korea in 1950 through the lenses of similar incursions by Axis powers prior to the outbreak of World War II. He considered what might have been done by other powers in the face of these incursions to prevent world war. According to Neustadt and May, Truman's reasoning was never made apparent to the public; indeed, it was never clearly articulated within his own administration, and they argue that this omission prolonged the Korean War.

Similar work needs to be done to understand how the past is influencing journalists' search for information as well as their construction of meaning for contemporary events. Of course, journalistic practices for covering ritualized public events such as political elections and conventions have been analyzed with great success by many scholars (see, for example, Patterson 1993). This coverage could, in some ways, be thought of as a product of collective memories of past conventions, campaigns, and other regularly scheduled rituals. Media sociologists have documented the day-to-day procedures reporters and editors use for managing information and making it meaningful (see, for example, Tuchman 1978; Gans 1979), and these, too, could be associated with a kind of process memory. However, there are tantalizing hints that when journalists use the past to structure information gathering and processing, they rely on more than scheduled rituals and process memory. For example, Erna Smith (1993) has shown that contemporary media coverage of the 1992 unrest in Los Angeles overemphasized African American participation in the violence and underemphasized the roles Hispanics and Asians played in the disturbances. Could this have resulted from reporters and officials using the Watts riots as their thinking tool? More important, did memories of the Watts riots guide their very search for factual information? More research is needed to appreciate the full extent of the past's influence on how journalists, political leaders, and citizens understand current events.

The possibility that journalists use the past to help them structure narratives about present events has important implications for scholars who subscribe to hegemonic theories of news production. Collective memories may be a double-edged sword for elites attempting to manage the news. To the extent that memory or cultural expectations deflect potential criticism or lead journalists in a direction elites would prefer them to go, collective memory can make the task of managing the news much easier. Schudson (1992), though not considering hegemonic aspects of news production, notes that journalists and political elites failed to hold the Reagan administration accountable for its behavior during the Iran–Contra affair because the memory of Watergate led them to ask administration officials the wrong questions about the affair. Alternatively, it is possible that the presence of a powerful historical analogy may make it extremely difficult for elites to reframe a political problem in more congenial terms. No leader contemplating military intervention seems to be able to avoid dealing with a Vietnam analogy, symbolic shorthand for citizens' reluctance to risk American lives in foreign adventures. Memory of Vietnam is one factor directing both the search for and the interpretation of information. A third possibility, suggested by Novick's (1999) examination of Holocaust analogies in the Bosnian conflict, is that governments may exercise a good deal of control over when historical analogies are presented in the news, deflecting them as they become inconvenient. Newsroom ethnography exploring how journalists use the past to help them tell stories about current events could enrich our understanding of how cultural capital is produced and reproduced in news practices.

HOW ARE PASTS REMEMBERED AND FORGOTTEN?

One of the most pressing questions for collective-memory scholars has always been why some "pasts" seem to disappear entirely from public discourse, essentially forgotten. An equally important question, and one little researched, is why some pasts that individuals and governments work diligently to destroy refuse to disappear. Both questions are relevant to scholars interested in the relationships among politics, media, and citizens.

Political leaders have long known that the public memory is short. Ask George H. W. Bush, who lost an election just two short years after prosecuting a war in the Persian Gulf that was a public relations triumph. But public memory can also be long. Ask the leaders of the Soviet Union. They executed the last Russian monarch and his family in an effort to abolish any nostalgic longing for tsarist Russia, but their efforts foundered on romantic stories of a titian-haired princess who allegedly survived the massacre. Her story lasted longer than their regime. But why? Is it pure luck? Is each case unique? Or can general principles be discovered that will help us understand and predict when and under what conditions stories of the past endure even in the face of dedicated efforts to eradicate them? Much more work needs to be done to understand why some important events are not publicly recalled while others survive concentrated attempts to obliterate them. My own research shows that pasts can be rendered inert, irrelevant to contemporary public life, even though they are remembered. Even more mysterious is why long-forgotten pasts may reemerge in public memory.

Michael Schudson (1992) offers a catalogue of nine reasons why the past is hard to kill. Among the most important are living memory and the presence of multiple versions of the past. Schudson argues that it is difficult to revise the past where such revisions contradict the memory of other living individuals, and this problem is compounded by a kind of "cognitive conservatism" in which past experiences structure our understanding of the present. Schudson's list might provide some insight into critical moments in the process of collective remembering when the whole enterprise could be saved or lost. For example, many of Schudson's safeguards depend on pluralistic assumptions: there should be multiple authorized storytellers and they should have access to a means of disseminating their tales. These assumptions will hold better for some cases than for others. The experiences of totalitarian nations suggest that institutional attempts to control collective memory may be relatively unsuccessful, at least in the short term. This may be because even in authoritarian regimes, recent pasts conform relatively well to pluralistic assumptions. Distant pasts, on the other hand, are more dependent upon the social norms of professional historians to maintain their integrity and may be more easily managed by political elites even in pluralistic societies. However, to date no research has taken as its central question the necessary conditions for the survival of a particular past.

The possibility of forgetting a critical past has driven much excellent work on collective memory, and the case that is the subject of virtually all of this research is the Holocaust. However, Holocaust research is prone to confounding two important but separate collective memory problems: forgetting and "erroneous remembering." A sufficiently distorted collective memory may be the functional equivalent of not remembering at all. However, "erroneous remembering" is a touchy issue. The work of scholars like Hayden White (1987) reminds us that the "truth" about the past may be unknowable, or at the very least, inexpressible. The relationship between the true past and the stories about it bears some similarity to the concept of Platonic forms. The most perfect representation of the past falls far short of the past itself. As White points out, whenever we tell stories of the past, we make choices that preclude other options. Accusing someone of "erroneous remembering" is often a critique of those choices. Irwin-Zarecka (1994), for example, criticizes Holocaust museums that emphasize the national identity of those who died in the camps rather than their Jewish identity. She does not argue that framing the Holocaust in these terms is factually inaccurate but rather that it misses the most important point—the genocide. Since there is widespread agreement about the most important aspect of the Holocaust, her critique of erroneous remembering seems on point. However, the most important aspect of a past is not always easily identified.

Neustadt and May (1986) developed a series of case studies that provided convincing evidence that political elites often "remember erroneously" when trying to apply the past to contemporary policy dilemmas. Their criterion for "erroneous" is a use of the past that produces poor policy outcomes when used to think about a present problem. Their advice to leaders is to keep in

mind that the past is more complex than it seems and is never a perfect analogy for the present. Their analysis of cases suggests that leaders often miss
the critical element of the past that would have made it useful in thinking
about the present.

My own work on collective memory of controversial events has not allowed me to be complacent about what constitutes erroneous remembering.
In my work I have tended to draw attention to the consequences of choices
rather than to label choices as right or wrong. However, my study of the 1968
Democratic National Convention in Chicago revealed a developing narrative
of that event that, to paraphrase Ettema (1994), is closer to forgetting than remembering. Rather than recalling the enduring critiques of the American political system that emerged both inside and outside the convention hall, the
convention is recalled in the historically exceptional context of the Vietnam
War. While it is true that collective memory about the war in Vietnam is still
contested, the Chicago convention is negatively contrasted with more recent
events in ways suggesting that the event has been consigned to history and
could not be repeated in our more enlightened times. What are we to make
of memories that are preserved under glass, as it were, disconnected from
the present? Is this the final stage before oblivion?

Perhaps the most mysterious phenomenon of all is recovered memory.
Not nearly as controversial for sociologists as it is for psychologists, it is nevertheless fascinating that long-lost pasts reappear. Recent attention to a turn-
of-the-century race riot in Tulsa, Oklahoma, provides a good example. Previous scholarship has examined the recovery of the Masada story (Schwartz
et al. 1986) and pre–Islamic Egyptian history (Lewis 1975).[2] Much of this
scholarship suggests that pasts are recovered because they are needed for
some reason. Schudson's (1992) list of means by which the past is preserved,
even when most people do not want to remember it, suggests where the past
hides itself. However, the recovery process is poorly understood. Indeed, the
concept of a "recovered collective memory" presents definitional problems
for the concept of collective memory itself. There seem to be important conceptual differences between individual memories coalescing into a group
narrative (even when that group narrative outlasts individual memories) and
presenting a group with a prefabricated story of its past. Further, the line between a recovered past, such as Masada, and an invented past (see Hobsbawm and Ranger 1983) is a fine one. To date, scholars have been primarily
interested in how recovered memory is disseminated into, and why it is embraced by, the community that had lost it.

Questions about remembering and forgetting the public past should interest scholars of politics and media at least as much as they interest scholars of
history. As we have seen, the past can play an important role in our interpretation of the present, and which pasts we have available for making sense
of the present may be critically important to understanding why social prob-

lems are perceived as they are and to fully explaining the process of political decision-making.

STUDYING COLLECTIVE MEMORY: RESEARCH ISSUES

Researching collective memory has the potential to produce insights into political discourse, political culture, and the underpinnings of public life. However, this type of research comes with a unique constellation of methodological and conceptual problems that investigators must address, even if they cannot fully overcome them.

While collective memory is a concept less diffuse than political culture, it is far from well defined. One key problem researchers are immediately faced with, regardless of whether they are interested in remembering or forgetting, is what sorts of pasts have the potential to become incorporated into the collective memory. Existing research focuses primarily on the memory of real events, such as Masada or Watergate, or of people, such as Lincoln or Washington. However, Hobsbawm and Ranger's (1983) edited volume documents traditions that are wholly or in part invented. Collective memories that form around people or events, real or imagined, make convenient targets of research because they are finite. However, Schudson's (1992) brief exploration of process memory in the case of the special prosecutor laws suggests that a broader operational definition of collective memory is feasible, that collective memory studies could also embrace social processes from how to run an election to how to make it rain.

Theories about public memory and public life are not currently rich enough to draw bright lines between what is "in" and "out" with regard to the universe of collective memory. However, the definition of collective memory as a *story* about the *past* does offer some useful limits. Stories, however rudimentary, should be a required element of collective memory because without them pasts are meaningless. Even the simplest of chronicles (White 1987) can give meaning to the past, but rituals, practices, and monuments can lose their historical meaning. Artifacts that lack meaning for the social group that created them probably should not be considered collective memories unless that meaning is somehow recovered contemporaneously. Collective memory also crucially involves the past. Timeless practices or those that have contemporary rather than historical meanings (regardless of their age) are not collective memories, although they, too, may form the raw material for recovered memories. For example, social norms probably should not be considered collective memories unless, for the relevant social group, they derive directly from a story told about past practice.

A closely related problem is how to define the boundaries of a particular collective memory. For example, I have analyzed the development of a story about the Watts riots but have subscribed to the prevailing understanding of the events that constituted that conflagration. That is, I accept the predominant (and largely uncontested) definition of the Watts riots as the violent events occurring in neighborhoods in south central Los Angeles that began with the arrest of Marquette Frye and that ended with the curfew on south central Los Angeles being lifted. This choice enabled me to focus on the question of how this public controversy developed into a collective memory, but it slights the potential narratives that might have emerged had the media and officials circumscribed the event differently. All research suffers to some extent from this problem. In examining an aspect of the empirical world we necessarily blind ourselves to its other aspects. Developing the boundaries of cases must be done self-consciously, keeping in mind the research question being asked and what aspects of the case will become invisible as the result of borders being created.

Defining what constitutes a case and the boundaries of that case are only the first problems to confront researchers interested in collective memory. Research in collective memory is founded on case studies because they are the only practical way to get at many of the critical processes involved in the creation, use, and destruction of collective memory. The most studied case is the Holocaust, but Watergate and the John F. Kennedy assassination are also frequent subjects. The best scholarship, of course, does not claim explanatory power beyond the case. Indeed, Holocaust scholars often actively resist generalizing from their case in point, arguing that it is a unique and incomparable event. However, the case-study approach does make it difficult to develop an appreciation of general principles. The principles that seem to develop in one case are often refuted by another. For example, Michael Schudson's (1992) analysis of the Watergate story determined that four narratives of the story had survived to present times, including two fundamentally incompatible tales: "the system worked" and "the system almost didn't work." My analysis of the 1965 Watts riots revealed that a common narrative of that controversial event *had* evolved over the course of a quarter century and that a common narrative of the even more controversial 1968 Democratic National Convention might be on the horizon (Edy 1998). It seems entirely plausible that we are both right in the context of our separate cases, and we might leave it at that, yet there is a more productive way to think about the differences in our findings.

For scholars working in this sort of case-study tradition, it is critical to engage in dialogue with other researchers working with other cases. Contrasting findings may be the result of critical differences between cases that can form the foundation of broader theories about phenomena like collective memory. Watergate and the Watts riots may produce different outcomes in part because of the nature of the reputations implicated in the collective memory. Comparing the characteristics of various cases can give us insights into the key aspects of historical events and the processes of remembering them that influence collective-memory outcomes more generally. Thus, one of the most pressing needs in collective-memory research is research that explores more cases, places them in dialogue with existing research, and enables us to derive more general principles about collective memory.

CONCLUSION

Studying how collective memory is created, used, and destroyed has great potential to help us understand political culture and the processes of meaning-making in public life. Collective memory provides a conveniently concrete entry point to the complex, amorphous body of social knowledge we might call political culture. It offers a way of studying the foundations upon which specific political messages are built and the contexts in which they are interpreted.

The meaning of the past is made and has the potential to be remade, but it often cannot be unmade or remade on the spot. The past plays an important role in the present, influencing the development of meaning for current events and potentially directing the search for information about our social world. Political discourse does not take place in a vacuum but draws upon common understandings of what the past means.

Collective-memory research takes existing theories about the media and mass political behavior where they have never gone before and returns them better for the experience. Currently, most theories regarding media and politics lack a temporal component. Scholars have been primarily interested in processes of political persuasion as they happen. Collective-memory research, by applying what we think we know to cases where the temporal element is central to the research agenda, enriches the theories that have been developed to explain mediated political phenomena. For these reasons and many more, collective-memory research promises lively and interesting contributions to what we know about political discourse and public life.

NOTES

1. Smithsonian officials originally planned an exhibit narrative that would describe both the bombing and its aftermath. Veterans' groups, among other organizations, objected to portraying the Japanese as victims. Ultimately, curators decided to simply put the *Enola Gay* on display.

2. The Tulsa race riot had largely disappeared from community memory. It was not publicly discussed or taught in local schools, and contemporary newspaper accounts had disappeared from the archives of the local newspaper (Kenworthy 2000).

Jill A. Edy

The memory of the fall of Masada, one of the last strongholds resisting Roman occupation in the first century A.D., was not preserved in traditional Jewish texts and was only recovered in the Palestinian Jewish community in the early years of the twentieth century (Schwartz et al. 1986). The expansion of the Islamic faith into Egypt promoted among its people a restructuring of that region's history to focus on its Muslim heritage rather than the traditions of the pharaohs (Lewis 1975).

5

Rights Talk as a Form of Political Communication

Amy Bunger

The words *public opinion* in today's "teledemocracy" evoke images of polls and surveys. Media, politicians, and academics all turn to polling data to monitor America's policy preferences and feelings about governance, and how they change in form or strength over time (Page and Shapiro 1992). The accuracy of these polls is frequently contested. Nonetheless, they must measure something important since they absorb much public and scholarly attention. There are other forms of political communication that we do not measure in the same systematic or empirically rigorous way. These forms should be empirically mined as another piece of evidence that can illuminate America's attitudes towards governance and provide genuine insight into the diffusion of ideas.

Lawsuits, ironically enough, have become a form of political communication. Previously, litigation had focused on disputes between two parties over private matters and had a clear and definable solution. An example would be two neighbors fighting over the placement of a fence, with a survey of the property to determine where the fence should be placed. Americans' focus on rights has been essentially constant, but the use of lawsuits has substantially increased. However, the actual number of lawsuits isn't nearly as important as their content. In lawsuits today, the aggrieved party may be amorphous, the topic of the lawsuit may be an actual public policy, and the solution may involve a continued relationship with the courts (Chayes 1976). Prisoners' rights litigation serves as an example of this newer form of litigation, where a lawsuit may be about inmates in a particular institution claiming "unacceptable" or "cruel" conditions, and the courts may appoint a special master to regularly report on the progress made to ameliorate these concerns. It is a sweeping overgeneralization to argue that "Americans have become more litigious," but it is not an overstatement to say that Americans are now highly accustomed to using the language of rights. Further, litigation and rights talk have evolved from a concern for private issues to topics of social policy, from a focus on economics and property to expectations of privacy. The consequence of these new topics is that citizens are now asking questions that may result in large-scale social change via lawsuits. Thus, rather than focusing on the actual numbers of lawsuits, we need to examine Americans' attitudes about their various social and economic representations and how the law, not unlike the initiative and proposition movements, has become a new forum of direct democracy.

The decade of the sixties was a period that witnessed the clash of "old" and "new" values, making an obvious public or consensual opinion hard to pinpoint. This period was seminal in changing how Americans thought about their rights and how to secure them. *The Politics of Rights* (Scheingold 1974) argues that the civil rights movement created a new model of effecting social change—"policy making by lawsuit"—a strategy later adopted by many contemporary social movements such as environmental interests groups and welfare rights advocates. Mid-twentieth-century governance was also illuminated by the advent of television and by the passage of "sunshine" laws. The 1960s were host to various forms of cultural transformations, from social integration to increased mobility to testing norms and rules (Heclo 1996). Many contentious social issues, particularly in the area of civil rights, were ripe for legislation that never reached the decision agenda. It has been argued that the legislatures of the time "couldn't take the heat" and were unresponsive to public demand for legislation. Thus, the courts became an alternative way for citizens to get a response, and ultimately, to follow along the path to power. My assumption here is that there is some precursor to lawsuits, some type of discussion that makes pursuit of a legal strategy more likely (Felstiner, Abel, and Sarat 1980). Rights talk is one such precursor.

In *Rights Talk: The Impoverishment of Political Discourse* (1991), law professor Mary Ann Glendon asserts that rights occupy a large part of the public conversation, often at the expense of others topics (such as responsibilities). It is hard to measure conversations about rights, for that quickly becomes a highly subjective procedure, and some might argue that almost all human conversations, to some degree or another, are about rights. Glendon argues that we phrase much of our societal conflict in the language of rights, and scores of scholars now debate the degree to which an overabundance of rights talk has resulted in excess litigiousness (Friedman 1980; Galanter 1986; Lieberman 1983; Manning 1977; Olson 1991).

This work argues that rights talk isn't new to Americans. Quite the contrary, it is a part of our national identity. What have changed are the types of topics sharing sentences with the words "right to." Why have our conversations about rights changed from a focus on negative rights (freedom from) to positive rights (entitlement to) (Berlin 1969; Currie 1986)? Why were discussions of rights in the early part of the twentieth century predominantly about economics and property while they are now focused on social policy and privacy? By choosing not to focus on case law, the de facto frame used by political scientists to analyze changes in rights, we can "hear" more of what Americans are really saying when they speak the language of rights.

Echoing Foucault, this chapter examines a "macrodiscourse," a wide-ranging discussion among a populace about a particular topic (Foucault 1977; Conley and O'Barr 1998). My research traces how the discourse of rights has come to encompass many different variations. Three major thematic categories emerge from my research: first, "rights" is used interchangeably with the terms "privilege" and "liberty." Second, positive rights (entitlements) are now being more frequently discussed. This represents a change from what is generally agreed to be the basis of the U.S. Bill of Rights, at minimum a document of negative liberties that frames restrictions on what the government cannot do and how citizens can maintain freedom from government intrusion. Third, the data show the roots of this growth in the debate over positive rights, including the actual "right of the government to act" and the "obligation to set standards, and promulgate regulation."

METHODOLOGY

This work provides an empirical, thematic content analysis of rights as expressed over ninety-six years (1900–1996) in four premier law reviews from Harvard University, Northwestern University, the University of Virginia, and Columbia University. Each law review was analyzed every fourth year; that is, all issues of the *Virginia Law Review* in 1900 were examined, *Harvard Law Review* in 1901, *Northwestern University Law Review* in 1902, and *Columbia Law Review* in 1903, returning to the *Virginia Law Review* in 1904. Every article meeting inclusion criteria was "interviewed" using a survey instrument. Articles which specifically identified "due process" were included.

A methodological word of caution is in order. Law reviews, particularly the ones chosen for this study, are surely "elitist," and this was a conscious trade-off in my work. Law reviews are clearly not a perfect substitute for popular opinion although, as public opinion scholars tell us, elites often help to prioritize popular opinion (Iyengar and Kinder 1987) if not define it. Nevertheless, it is clear that to push litigation or public law issues onto the governmental agenda, if not the decision agenda (Kingdon 1995), lawyers are going to be involved in the process. Rights talk therefore, isn't new, but the topics of rights talk are. The mechanism used to get these rights recognized has increasingly become the lawsuit, the very haven of the legal elite. Lawsuits, after all, cannot happen without plaintiffs and plaintiffs typically have lawyers.

Lawyers, particularly those engaging in large-scale social issues, read law reviews. Law reviews help create fertile soil for plaintiffs' constantly evolving questions. Law reviews, therefore, are only one way to understand perceptions and assertions of rights, but they are a forum read by both legal scholars and jurists as well as by practitioners looking for new ways of refining political strategies.

Choosing which law reviews to examine is also problematic; the four chosen here are obviously the cream of the crop. Balancing issues of representativeness occurred where possible, and consideration was given to issues like geography (Northwestern as a Midwestern school; UVA as a Southern school); state (UVA) versus private schools (Harvard); and, notable legal intellectual philosophies (Columbia and legal realism) but, admittedly, the sample is somewhat skewed. Like much historical work, my study is limited by the data made available during the time period chosen—there weren't a large number of law reviews at the turn of the century, for example. But law reviews do give us a sense of the intellectual scope of a given period while case law, for example, gives us a much more limited glimpse of the diffusion of ideas.

The elitist slant to my sample is diluted by several factors. While case law is used by political science scholars to study and analyze changes in rights, it only tells us what cases and issues are successful in getting before the court—generally less than a couple of hundred cases per year. Case law tells us the *outcome* of a given rights orientation, but it doesn't explain what combination of factors came together for an assertion of rights to begin with, and it doesn't tell us why particular cases were put forth at a given time.

"Due process" was chosen as a special focus here because it is an amendment that attaches to others via incorporation of the Fourteenth Amendment, including such issues as civil rights and civil liberties. Due process was also the vehicle used to provide state-supported defense to indigent defendants in *Gideon v. Wainwright.*

Law review articles are therefore an interesting forum for tapping public discourse. Law reviews provide a forum where people debate ideas about rights and how those rights should be secured. Law reviews are also more representative of the wider range of societal conflict in a given period than are actual court cases, which often have more to do with legal issues (that is, standing and justiciability) than with the range of ideas about which people are debating. Rights talk, in short, is "old"—the United States is known for it. What is new is what Americans are now talking about and how these topics are being incorporated into lawsuits and thereby becoming a de facto mechanism of governance.

While the topics analyzed here varied widely, they can be thematically organized into the overarching category of negative and positive rights. The data demonstrate the growing prevalence of discussions of positive rights. In the discussion of "the rights of government," one finds a change in the type of issue or entity said to possess a positive right. Regarding positive rights, one also finds significant discursive changes across time. The data illustrate a conscious attempt to reframe positive rights into negative ones, a frame that is much more familiar to American political philosophy. The creation of minimum standards is a good example of this discussion, because the failure to adhere to a newly created minimum standard is often talked about as a deprivation. The data also show that many key phrases became associated with securing positive rights, in particular, actions pursued "in the public interest."

NEGATIVE AND POSITIVE RIGHTS

Liberty is often confused with the term "right" and is interpreted in one of two ways—"freedom from" government intrusion or "freedom to" explore one's own pursuit of happiness. American law has frequently wrestled with the degree to which positive rights (entitlement to something) were guaranteed by the Constitution. Generally, the data suggest that rights connected to social issues are more often positive rights, where criminal procedure is seen as a negative right. The controversy in the law reviews was not whether the Bill of Rights secured negative or positive rights—it was universally agreed that the Bill of Rights was a charter of negative liberties. "No general constitutional principle is as accepted in theory yet so often violated in practice than that the Bill of Rights is a bulwark against majority tyranny. In theory, the Bill of Rights shields particular spheres of human affairs from majoritarian intercession" (Faigman 1992). Instead, the contested issue in the data set was whether, and to what degree, the Bill of Rights gave protections to positive liberties as well. The distinction between negative and positive rights was treated at both theoretical and practical levels

No scholarly consensus emerged from the law review culture regarding positive and negative rights, demonstrating a balance that remains debated (and perhaps one that always will be). There was a significant rise in the appearance of articles referring to positive rights starting around the time of the New Deal, an era marking the beginning of the growth of a large administrative body that conferred benefits to persons in need. References to positive rights, particularly in the form of duties (as opposed to entitlements), were present in the early portion of the century but they were much less common in the data set.

Commentary on the Bill of Rights in the late 1940s was solidly rooted in the negative rights interpretation: "These amendments [the first ten known as the Bill of Rights] *were based on a fear of tyranny*" (Clark 1947, emphasis added). In this post–New Deal period, author Tom Clark explained the organizing notions of the Founders as "distrusting all government, they set forth what their newly created government must not do to them and included amongst these the freedom of religion, freedom from unreasonable search and seizure and *due process of law.*" Unlike many of his contemporaries in more progressive midcentury thought, Clark attempted to pair due process, often used as justification for the recognition of positive rights, with negative liberty. Clark added that our forefathers "aimed the Bill of Rights against the federal government only, by giving it no power to protect *fundamental personal rights* against infringement by either the states or individuals" (Clark 1947, 176 emphasis added).

Negative rights highlight protection from an intrusive government and enshrine the idea of a private, protected sphere. "The protection of private rights from governments' wrongs and the maintenance of a federal system and a strong federal government have been important objectives of the Court at every period of its history," said Malcolm Sharp (1933, 366). Sharp's interpretation was quite typical. Throughout the twentieth century, discussions of negative rights never lessened. To the contrary, positive rights were frequently disguised as negative ones (an interesting development to be explored later).

Scholar Isaiah Berlin was an influential thinker in this distinction between positive and negative rights and was cited by many authors included in the data set. In his noted article "Two Concepts on Liberty," he explained that there were two persistent questions concerning liberty. The first, or negative question, is "How many doors are open to me?" which is about the obstacles that prevent an action. The second form of liberty is positive and asks, "Who is in charge here?" or "By whom am I governed?" Berlin, who was an ardent supporter of negative liberty, nonetheless called both types "central and legitimate" (Berlin and Jahanbegloo 1991). Berlin wrote, "The concept of positive liberty, which is of course essential to a decent existence, has been more often abused or perverted than that of negative liberty. . . . Negative liberty must be curtailed if positive liberty is to be sufficiently realized; there must be a balance between the two, about which no clear principles can be enunciated. Positive and negative liberty are both perfectly valid concepts, but it seems to me that historically more damage has been done by pseudo-positive than by pseudo-negative in the modern world" (Berlin and Jahanbegloo 1991, 41).

To Berlin, fighting over a positive or a negative interpretation of rights was unavoidable. The resolution of the fight ultimately determined the character of a society, affecting that nation's form of governance, and whether it became democratic, authoritarian, despotic, theocratic, individualistic, or communitarian. Such questions have heightened resonance in an individualistic, representative democracy like the United States. Today, this debate is one of public policy, and more notably of case law, because the former is increasingly stemming from the latter, as Archibald Cox has observed. "The Court is responsible for protecting individuals and minorities in their relations with government, chiefly against governmental aggression but *increasingly against failure to perform affirmative obligations* of sufficient importance to rank as constitutional" (Cox 1978, 1 emphasis added).

The discourse of rights, in particular that of due process, will undoubtedly continue to capture discussions of positive rights. The due process clause of the Fourteenth Amendment in particular remains the most common avenue for the judiciary to promote such discussions. David Currie has argued that the due process clause was originally phrased as a prohibition and *not* as an affirmative declaration. The key concept here was the notion of deprivation—"states are forbidden to 'deprive' people of certain things, and depriving suggests aggressive state activity, not mere failure to help" (Currie 1986, 865). There are places in the Constitution, says Currie, where affirmative duties of the government were explicitly delineated, as in the duty to conduct a census or to guarantee a republican form of government, but these were clearly the exception rather than the rule. Nevertheless, positive rights continue to force their ways into the public forum.

THE EMERGENCE OF POSITIVE RIGHTS

Positive rights were articulated from the beginning of the data set, but such focus dramatically increased throughout the century. Early on, such notions were explained by their relation to conditions in society, in contrast to an assertion of a right. More contemporary discussions, however, focused on the right of government, particularly in the name of the public interest, to set minimum standards and to engage in state action.

In 1907, Walter Wheeler Cook explained police power as both a positive and a negative right. That is, police power is the administration of civil and criminal justice, which obviously involves the prevention of wrongful acts by the state. Yet it is also the enacting of positive regulations constructed for the promotion of the public welfare (Cook 1907). In 1910, progressive legal scholar Louis Greeley expanded the discussion of positive rights, declaring them a necessary benefit for citizens. In doing so, Greeley illustrated the importance of *rights being perceived as duties of the state*. He felt that societal changes were making it necessary for the state to expand its power and that it was now the duty of the state to promote and protect society. In 1910, significantly before the New Deal but at the pinnacle for the Progressives, rights were seen to be a function of the times (witnessed by Greeley's support of the right of public welfare). He applauded courts that were more sympathetic to public regulation, particularly relative to the individual right to contract in the name of public welfare. The positive rights referred to by Greeley were actually discussed in terms of *policy preferences*—as opposed to

constitutional mandates. That is, a right to welfare was framed more as a societal need than as a human right. The Progressives actively pursued policy
making with respect to social engineering, particularly in reaction to an
emerging regulatory state. The law itself was seen as a social actor in this
arrangement.

In 1932, an explicit reference to positive rights emerged again in the data
set. The change in rhetoric was concurrent with the growth of the administrative state, which is both supportive of, and expects, action on the part of
the government. Noted contemporary legal scholar Cass Sunstein explained
the popular view in that time period. "The rise of the modern administrative
state is based largely on a perception that aggressive governmental action,
repudiating the common law, has become necessary" (Sunstein 1987b, 902).
A 1932 article (Barry 1932) explicitly advocated an increase in such notions
of duty. Demonstrating a casual, ready willingness to deem things as matters
of right, Barry presented a classification scheme for the rights of children,
somewhat intermingled with references to duties. Barry reinforced Greeley's
earlier call for public welfare in his discussion of five types of rights: *citizenship*, where he viewed both rights and duties being conferred; *political
rights* such as the right of suffrage and of eligibility for office; *deferred rights*
of a child, consisting of voting and holding public office; *civil rights* guaranteeing freedom from physical restraint and the right to control property; and,
the largest category, *parental rights* and duties. Like Greeley before him,
Barry saw issues of child welfare and public education as "concerns of the
day," evidenced by the fact that many states had passed minimum standard
laws. Thus, the macrodiscourse of rights at the beginning of the century was
particularly sensitive to changing times. In essence, the data show that rights
were always part of our public conversations but they were often keyed to
changing, situational needs—far from the original Lockean conception of
"absolute" or "essential" rights.

Between 1930 and 1960, many articles referred to positive rights in passing, unlike Barry and Greeley who explicitly advocated the recognition of
positive rights. For the most part, positive rights were largely distinguished
from negative rights. Elder (1934), for example, discusses a positive right to
employment versus the negative right of protection of private property. He
asked, "If price fixing for homes and places of business after the war was justified because of the social emergency," then why can't policy support fixing
prices for labor if there is a shortage of work? He justified his view by arguing that if a society can provide welfare for those out of work, why wouldn't
furnishing employment be appropriate?

Law review scholars also debated the contemporary records of seminal legal minds, particularly where positive rights were concerned. Authors Louis
Jaffe and Francis Allen, for example, examined the legal philosophy of two
midcentury Supreme Court justices, Justice Frankfurter and Justice Vinson.

Justice Frankfurter, explained Jaffe, opposed "fashioning a positive code" because this should be produced by the legislature, not the judiciary (Jaffe 1949). Conversely, Allen reviewed Chief Justice Vinson's frustration that liberty was seen solely as *freedom from* government. Allen wrote, "Any view which conceives of liberty simply as the absence of restraint could not have appeared adequate to the Chief Justice. Rather he tended to think of the problems of freedom largely in terms of the affirmative use of political power to create and preserve such conditions as are favorable to freedom" (Allen 1954, 19).

Former Supreme Court Justice William Brennan (although a sitting associate justice in 1965 when the article was written) commented on the scholarship of one of his contemporaries who had voiced a similar idea. Alexander Mieklejohn had written that rights were not just freedoms but that they had a deeper or more comprehensive essence as well. "The freedom that the First Amendment protects is not, then, an absence of regulation. It is the presence of self-government" (Brennan 1965; Meiklejohn 1961). Another author illustrated how a statement of negative rights can be transformed into one embracing positive rights. In "*Roe v. Wade* the United States Supreme Court held that the constitutional *right of privacy* guaranteed a woman the right, within certain limits, to choose whether or not to have an abortion. Opponents of the *right to abortion . . .*" (Emerson 1982, 129 emphasis added). The former is a negative right—a freedom from government—while the latter is a positive right to have something guaranteed or secured. Here, Emerson used the concept of rights rhetorically, on behalf of policies supporting state-subsidized abortions. The discourse of positive rights usually surpassed the Court's recognition of such matters, for the Court had surely explicitly recognized abortion as a right. Thus, abortion serves as a good illustration of how discussions of rights are sometimes translated into case law or policy simply by the turn of a phrase. This is the power of rights talk.

THE RIGHTS OF GOVERNMENT: IN THE PUBLIC INTEREST

Discussions of positive rights took some important discursive turns over the years. Actions said to be "in the public interest" began to appear in combination with discussions of public welfare and the right of the government to act. Phraseology was crucial here because there is a difference between the *duty of the government to provide something* and *the right of the government to engage in an activity*. Throughout the years studied, rhetoric about *rights possessed by the government* clearly increased. The main turning point of the argument was whether the government had pursued a course of action or inaction. The main portion of the Constitution (as opposed to the Bill of Rights) delineates the power structure built into the American form of government, and yet one finds numerous examples of scholars discussing the "rights of" a governmental entity to pursue a given course of conduct. It is possible that these scholars were offering a defense of *delegated* power associated with the rise of the administrative state. What is significant, however, is that the authors frame such powers in terms of rights. For example, sometimes a legislature's capacity to legislate is discussed in terms of rights rather than in terms of justifying a particular policy. Thus, for example, government interest is translated into language like the "government has a *right* to action," although a contemporary scholar has taken issue with the practice of "using government interests at the right definition stage as contrary to the fundamental operating assumptions of the Constitution" (Faigman 1992, 1525).

Such phraseology—"the right of the government to do something"— existed early in the century although it was used sparingly. This line of reasoning quickly picked up both speed and advocacy, however. Victor Morawetz, early in the century, focused upon the *right of the Congress to regulate* in the best interest of the general welfare and the right of companies or individuals to not have their due process rights infringed upon (Morawetz 1905, emphasis added). Pairing personal and state rights represented an interesting, but not unusual, twentieth century phenomenon. The source of the rights differed as well—the power of Congress to regulate comes from Article I, whereas the individual protection of due process stems from the Fifth Amendment to the Constitution. The power of regulation by Congress is asserted here as a right instead of a function granted to the body.

In 1910, the noted progressive Louis Greeley was complimentary of the Supreme Court for actively endorsing regulation in the name of the public good, while de-emphasizing the importance of contractual or property rights. Data from this time period shows the emergence of a spirited defense of the "right" of the public good and of the notion that it be placed on equal footing with individual rights. Greeley quoted from *People v. Strollo* that "under a judicial system which has for centuries magnified the sacredness of individual rights, there is much less danger of doing injustice to the individual than there is in overlooking the obligations of those in authority to organized society."

This defense of governmental action demonstrated how a mixture of due process became integral in the developing rights rhetoric. According to that rhetoric, the right to regulate hinged on the interpretation of due process. "The cornerstone of regulation is the 'governmental interest' concept of due process," said Richard Speidel (1958). Louis Henkin, a preeminent liberal legal philosopher, advocated the link between positive rights and government interest when writing about past offenses to American Indians. Henkin argued that reparations to victims may be part of a "seamless general welfare," which may stem from "a sense that such particular welfare is the moral responsibility of all" (1975, 490). Henkin's rhetoric underscores the movement away from a purely individualistic notion of the law to a system concerned with communitarian goals or public values. The rise in such discussions of public interest graphically illustrates the expansion of rights rhetoric over the years.

Such discussions of positive rights also reflected a more philosophical, moral approach to what "rights" meant. Philosophically, the discussion moved away from Locke and more toward Kant and Rousseau. Golding (1963), for example, was the most specific in his explanations of positive rights, particularly their justification and goals, but he also shed light on their philosophical underpinnings. Seeing Kant as a model of moral reasoning, Golding noted that Kant disagreed with the view that an action's correctness can be determined by its consequences, arguing that all moral decisions make a universal claim for all similarly situated persons.

There were many references in the data set to the role of morality in legal decision making, again underscoring the shift from rights perceived as tools of law to tools of social justice. Golding, for one, argued that infusing morality into decision making was a requisite element of the concept of social justice. Equally important, and reminiscent of Rousseau's social contract, was the notion that rights belonged to society, to collectivities or groups of persons, thereby replacing Locke's ideas of the individual as the unit of analysis.

Next, Golding argued that Kant's philosophy, when coupled with his view of principled decision making, would mandate that "principled moral decision-making must not only be 'impartial' with respect to persons, but also must be 'impartial' with respect to similar circumstances" (Golding 1963). This, too, reflects a change reminiscent of the latter portion of the twentieth century—a call for less individual case-by-case reasoning and a focus on notions like mandatory sentencing guidelines where people in "similar circumstances" were treated uniformly. Golding's article also furthered an understanding of how notions of social justice were transferred from discussions of rights into discussions of law. Administrative and legislative tasks, he argued, must take values into account despite the complications thereby posed for the courts. Thus, if the legislature takes values into account when enacting legislation, so must the judiciary, for the intentions of the legislature should be a central element in the court's decision-making process. "A court *does* decide *only* the case that is before it. But if a tribunal is to be principled, what it must do in essence is to anticipate the kinds of criticism that might be made of its decision" (Golding 1963, 50).

The time period from the mid-1950s to the mid-1970s witnessed a new focus on "public consciousness." The public interest cannot be excised from the discourse of positive rights, the feeling went, and justification for regulation and various forms of positive rights was the result. In defending its regulatory activities, for example, the government is essentially arguing that it has the right to do something (similar to an individual's right to do something). That something, however, is the government's right to act, even if its action is flawed. "Fallible wisdom produces fallible legislation. To deny government the right to act except with omniscience and pre-science is to deny it the right to act at all. The right to act is evolving empirically and waveringly" (Frankfurter 1939, 103). This assertion of the right of government to act foolishly or wisely was couched in the language of the public interest, including the terms, "government interest" and "public welfare."

"Public interest," therefore, came to be seen as a source of positive action for the government. Further, the public interest became a justification for interfering with the rights of individuals. Alternatively stated, the right of the government to act in the name of the public interest was contrasted to the right of the citizen to avoid governmental interference. Both are seen as rights and the contest becomes one of "My right is bigger than your right." Debates about such matters spanned the course of the twentieth century, and a recent article criticized this tendency to "constitutionalize" political ideas, arguing that "identifying the 'public interest' is a question not of constitutional interpretation, but of debatable social policy" (Chang 1991). Conversely, in 1927, in an article written prior to the New Deal, Maurice Finkelstein commented on *Tyson v. Banton,* which declared unconstitutional a regulation on the resale of theater tickets. Finkelstein questioned which industries were "clothed with the public interest," and defined the public interest as a right—to further competition between two "rights" if an individual's rights abuts society's interest (Finkelstein 1927). Finkelstein also discussed the right of a governmental body, or the balance of power as a right, but downplayed it. Notably, Finkelstein's article was written just prior to FDR's New Deal, which significantly shifted the balance of power among the branches of government.

The data set contained many more discussions of whether a particular action was supported by the "public interest" and of how recognition of government interests and rights may change the status of preexisting rights—that is, those of the individual. "The search for meaning of the constitutional text often includes a review of the government interests at stake. Because the threshold question regarding the existence of constitutional rights has become infected with the government's countervailing interests, those individual rights have lost much of their vitality, if not their very existence" (Faigman 1992). The notion of the government having a "right" to act in the public interest, as well as the government's interest as a public right, were increasingly viewed as more important than individual rights. Until Faigman's 1992 article, the interests of the government remain counterpoised to those of the individual.

MINIMUM STANDARDS AND POSITIVE RIGHTS

The discourse of positive rights developed into the idea of a guarantee of "minimum standards" with a consideration of how much of something—protection or services—the government must provide. Actions of the legislature, and regulations in the name of the public interest, went a long way toward arguing for the development of minimum standards. Once minimum standards are made law, of course, they can become positive rights and part of the discussion of due process. Due process, after all, is a citizen's guarantee against deprivations on the part of the state. If minimum standards are developed, then the absence of minimum standards can be claimed as a deprivation.

The data set contained many articles discussing the establishment of minima, most of which were clustered in a thirty-year period from the mid-1940s to the late 1970s. None was more articulate or more fervently argued than a 1969 article by Frank Michelman. A detailed analysis of Michelman's view of positive rights, particularly his argument of minima, reveals him to be an exemplar of the other data. Michelman's work was also an excellent example of the changing rhetoric of positive rights. Written during President Johnson's "War on Poverty," Michelman's article specifically sought to redefine the parameters of intellectual and political debate with his notion of "minimum welfare." Three themes common in the development of rights discourse can be found in Michelman's work: the notions of *minimum* acceptable levels of living, the charge that such unfulfilled minima constitute *deprivations* by the state, and thus, a requirement of *action* to fulfill minima (Michelman 1969, 7–59).

Michelman, in the name of social justice, argued for "minimum protection against economic hazard." To him, minimum protection "meant that people are entitled to have certain wants satisfied . . . by government, free of any extra charge beyond the obligation to pay general taxes (and perhaps free of conditions referring to past idleness, prodigality or other economic 'misconduct')." Michelman specifically explained why the due process clause has such a strong connection to positive rights. "The due process clause inveighs only against certain 'deprivations' by the 'state,' occurrences which seemingly cannot occur by mere default." The criterion for minimum protection, argued Michelman, is not the presence of inequalities. It is for "instances in which persons have important needs or interests which they are prevented from satisfying because of traits or predicaments not adopted by free and proximate choice."

Michelman relied on Americans' sense of egalitarianism and he applauded like-minded thinking by the judiciary. He wrote that "the judicial equality explosion of recent times" is not out of deference to equality but rather to a "minimum welfare" which would help protect "poor persons from the most elemental consequence of poverty: lack of funds to exchange for needed goods, services, or privileges of access" (Michelman 1969, 9). In true egalitarian spirit, he opined that "classification of 'the poor' as such may, like classification of racial minorities as such, be popularly understood as a badge of inferiority."

Michelman's article demonstrated a shift from rights as a mechanism of law to rights as a tool of social justice. He explained his purpose as redefining the factors central to legal decision making, arguing that a legitimate claim or right was one which would "have a specific existing want provided for, rather than to have a generally larger or more equal income." Rhetorically, his definition of wants—"wants to which this claim applies we shall call 'just wants'"—is important, for his phrasing was more suggestive of justice than of entitlement.

Guided by John Rawls's theory of social justice, Michelman conceded that true justice need not produce equal outcomes. In other words, social justice can still be "achieved" even if a range of disparate outcomes results—a premise similar to the distinction between equality of opportunity and equality of outcome. However, while it is acceptable that just practices produce disparate outcomes, it is not acceptable for legal processes to produce inequality. Michelman concluded his plea for the establishment of minima by advocating for an expansion of justiciability: "But this 'advantage' of the minimum protection hypothesis (if we would so regard it) remains utterly theoretical until (if ever) we can develop a 'justiciable' standard for specifying the acceptable minimum and the acceptable gap."

In the decade of the *Brown v. Board of Education* decisions, which declared the segregation of schools to be unconstitutional, Michelman drew an analogy between educational inequality and educational deprivation. "It happens that educational inequality and educational deprivation are so closely intertwined that minimum protection thinking about the educational–finance problem may lead to a statement of grievance in a justiciable form resembling that of more conventional equal protection disputation." Retreating from his "equality of opportunity is sufficient" position, Michelman shifted toward equality of outcome as the appropriate measure, thereby using "just wants" and "severe deprivations" interchangeably. Here, a transformation of "wants" into rights can be seen occurring, a move that is necessary to constitute actual deprivations by the state.

Michelman offered his opinion about how to provide "minima" based on "deprivation," arguing that "the equal protection clause is the constitutional text which most naturally suggests itself to one who would claim a legal right to have certain wants satisfied out of the public treasury." Arguing for action on the part of the state, Michelman used terms connoting obligation—particularly "duty." According to Michelman, it is a state's "duty to protect against certain hazards which are endemic in an unequal society, rather than vindication of a duty to avoid complicity in unequal treatment." In an interesting passage about action taken by the state to protect against inequalities, he wrote, "differences of consequence may ensue from a theoretical distinction between a duty to protect against certain severe consequences of economic inequality and a duty to avoid hyper-offensive inequalities of treatment." While both "duties" were saying something different, Michelman largely ignored the distinction between "duty" and "obligations." For him, both terms connoted action—affirmative measures taken by the state.

In sum, Michelman's arguments on minimum deprivation and state action contained discussions transforming positive rights into ones that, on the surface, were discussed as negative. Michelman made explicit arguments about how to insure positive rights, but some of his implicit ideas were also consistent with the other rhetoric found in the data. First was his argument that some negative rights were conversely positive—"that the negative right not to be officially subjected to unfavorable treatment by reason of poverty does not encompass the positive right to be educated at public expense." Michelman also discussed the constitutionality of economic inequality, arguing that such a condition was repugnant to constitutional values.

The Michelman article set the tone for many articles that would follow in the data set, many of which advocated minimum guarantees in a variety of areas, areas traditionally focused on negative rights, particularly with respect to protections against the accused. Minimum standards were discussed most often in areas of social policy and procedural rights, particularly with regard to labor law and trade unions. The ability to join a union, which deals with the right to participate, was one example of such rights. In 1947, one legal scholar argued that "the right to obtain work is far more important than the right to a particular job" (Summers 1947). Intertwined with the right to work, that is, is the right to participate and join a union. "The right to work includes also the right to work on equal terms free from all unreasonable discriminations. But beyond the right to work on equal terms is the element almost uniformly ignored—*the right to participate in making decisions"* (Summers 1947, 73 emphasis added). Summers's article demonstrated an escalation of the rhetoric, the emergence of a constitutional recognition of a positive right. The author recognized that the Constitution is silent about the right to join a union, but he defended the declaration of the right as being constitutional. Arguing that unions needed to be identified as "economic legislatures engaged in determining the laws by which men work, eat, and live," for then it would be clear that "guaranteeing workers the right to share in making those laws is self-evident. The right to join a union involves the right to an economic ballot" (Summers 1947, 73).

A 1969 article recommended a "uniform requirement of full written notice" for union disciplinary proceedings (Etelson and Smith 1969). Like right-to-counsel cases earlier in the decade, the authors asserted that "the guarantee of lay representation is an important *minimum* safeguard to the right of a fair hearing" (Etelson and Smith 1969, 747 emphasis added). Again, the notion of a minimum underscored a kind of public responsibility or obligation, the absence of which would result in a deprivation.

Discussions of minima were also present in the area of social policy, such as abortion. Laurence Tribe, for example, wrote, "If the developing concept of *minimum protection were thus shaped so as to reflect an underlying governmental duty,*" and if there were a failure to meet such a need, "it would appear to follow that no woman could be denied public assistance for a lawful abortion which she says she cannot otherwise obtain" (Tribe 1973, 49 emphasis added).

Cass Sunstein, in 1987—fourteen years after Tribe—illustrated how equating rights with "minima" had gained ground throughout the course of the century. "Claims for 'positive rights' cannot be dismissed," he said, "by reference to the 'negative' character of constitutional guarantees of the word 'deprive' in the Fourteenth Amendment." Sunstein notes that were there to be a preexisting right to welfare, the failure to deliver it would be a deprivation and thus it could be claimed "that *in the modern era the right to a minimal level of material goods,* like the right to protection against trespass, has constitutional status" (Sunstein 1987b, 890 emphasis added).

STATE ACTION

The scope of state power clearly expanded during the twentieth century. The ability of the state to act has always been discussed in American governance, but the words and motifs used in these conversations have changed over time. In the late 1960s and throughout the 1970s, for example, discussions surrounded the duty of the state to act. Discussions also centered on the obligation of the state to enforce laws. In discussing positive rights, Tribe asked, "Why should some needs be singled out as justifying a constitutional demand for positive state action while others are relegated to governmental discretion and the impersonal verdict of the market?" (Tribe 1973, 45).

In the 1970s, the egalitarian mood of the nation was high, and so was the idea that a state had a "duty" to act. The authors I reviewed often asserted the "right of non-discriminatory application" (Weissman 1974). These arguments gave a "legal voice" to contemporary aspects of criminal justice that were subject to allegations that prosecutorial or sentencing policies targeted specific classes of offenders (such as crack–cocaine charges leveled excessively at one racial grouping). One author reviewed here reversed this argument, contending that if no person had a right to not be targeted by law enforcement, was there a corresponding "right to compel" the police or prosecutor to respond similarly and have laws "enforced with equal vigor"

(Weissman 1974, 513)? Even if pursuing prosecution was justified based on the evidence, Weissman argued that if such an act would not be pursued in *all* cases, prosecution should be prevented. "The right to prevent unjustified law enforcement discrimination should be generalizable *into a positive right to demand equal law enforcement* efforts by state prosecutorial officers on behalf of all classes of citizens" (Weissman 1974, 514 emphasis added).

In the purely legal sense, these questions have been largely answered by case law. Yet it is important to detect the degree to which these discussions of rights depart from prevailing law. The most notable case in point is *Jackson v. City of Joliet* (1983). The Joliet case centered on the deaths of several people in a burning car, where the first policeman on the scene began directing traffic away from the car before checking to see whether people had been trapped inside. A suit was filed against the city on behalf of the deceased, claiming a deprivation of life or liberty without due process of law. The family argued that the officers had failed to save the lives of the persons in the car, implying that they had a "duty to rescue."

Judge Richard Posner wrote the opinion for the Court of Appeals in what has become one of the most quoted decisions arguing against the Constitution being a charter of positive rights. Posner wrote that the concern of the Founding Fathers who wrote the Bill of Rights wasn't that the government would fail to meet the needs of all citizens, but that it might do too much to them. He argued that the goal of the Fourteenth Amendment, adopted in 1868, was to guard against oppression by state government, not to obtain basic governmental services for people. The effect of the opinion was to declare that the city had no constitutional duty to take action. In this same case, Posner explained the difference between positive and negative liberty. "The difference between harming and failing to help is just the difference . . . between negative liberty—being let alone by the state—and positive liberty—being helped by the state" (*Jackson v. City of Joliet*). Therefore, if there is no duty to provide something, an argument of deprivation does not exist. The concept of deprivation nonetheless emerged as a critical concept in the course that rights discourse has taken throughout the twentieth century.

Several articles have claimed that state action should be pursued as a right, preceding the decision in *Joliet*, but there has always been disagreement about whether inaction, or the absence of a specific policy, is an extreme position. Sunstein, for example, has argued that if the government doesn't protect people against private racial discrimination, it has not become involved in a state action and therefore isn't involved in a constitutional question. Sunstein wrote, *"All of these issues are resolved by the choice of a Lochner-like baseline of government 'inaction,'* one that appears neutral and natural. Neither enforcement of the trespass law nor repeal of laws forbidding private discrimination is taken as state action—*a conclusion that relies upon common law notions about the role of government*" (Sunstein 1987b, 887 emphasis added). Sunstein acknowledged arguments about the Constitution being a charter of negative liberties and therefore concluded that affirmative rights exist either rarely or not at all. In citing *Harris v. McRae* (448 U.S. 297 [1980]) as his example, Sunstein wrote, "It is said that government may not intrude on private rights, but there is *no claim against the government if it has failed to act.* The basic position has resulted in rejection of claims to various public services, ranging from police protection to welfare" (Sunstein 1987b, 888 emphasis added). Discussing the contract clause, he wrote that it is, in practice, a right to state enforcement of contractual agreements, for a violation of the contracts clause would exist if the state declined to enforce a contract, thus failing to protect (Sunstein 1987b, 889).

Sunstein argued against the Constitution being viewed solely as a guarantor of negative liberties. At issue, he argued, is whether the status quo is equated with "neutrality" or "inaction." In other words, if the Constitution permits a particular change, must that change be considered a positive right? We should be wary, says Sunstein, of seeing constitutional doctrine as what defines "neutrality in terms of the perpetuation of current practice, and that treats government conduct tending to sustain it as inaction invariably escaping legal sanction, and government conduct proposing change as action tending to raise legal doubts" (Sunstein 1987b, 919). In essence, Sunstein believes that the concept of inaction and status quo is more judicially palatable, an interesting parallel to arguments in the political arena where the status quo, or "no action," is seen as the most stable sector of public opinion (Lippmann 1922).

Quite clearly, rights discourse becomes intertwined with public policy and public opinion here. For example, Sunstein argued that affirmative action should not been seen as a constitutional issue. However, he also posited that the status quo (defined by the current government policies or absence thereof) should not be perceived as a neutral baseline. He contended that the distribution of benefits was the result of a history of legal discrimination and that "efforts to eliminate the subordination of blacks can hardly be regarded in the same way as efforts to perpetuate it" (Sunstein 1987b, 911). Sunstein's choice of words is important in this debate. He noted that words like "affirmative" and "action" echoed the decision in *Lochner*, which struck down the employment laws passed by the legislature. Such terms suggest change that, Sunstein opined, can give a false appearance of bias, or lack of neutrality. He made a similar point with respect to distinguishing between public and private law, arguing that private preferences should be seen as the proper consideration for dictating social preferences. The crux of Sunstein's argument was that a political ordering could exist that was affirmative, or based on state action. Sunstein's position was reiterated in one of the final articles studied here. In 1991, Chang argued that "the proposition that the government may not act because of racial stereotype proscribes reliance on certain factual premises. No Justice denies that equal protection encompasses these proscriptions—each of which can be stated as an individual right: *the right not to be regulated because of racial animus, favoritism, or stereotype*" (Chang 1991, 799 emphasis added).

CONCLUSION

The data gathered here suggest an ongoing struggle to categorize and define rights, as well as confusion when the term rights is used to reflect both "privilege" and "liberty." Confusion has occurred because the Court has held many aspects of procedure to be rights instead of privileges. Definitions of rights have gone from being based in a purely legalistic realm to one featuring strong sociological, political, and philosophical undercurrents. Rights, as we have seen, have been discussed in debates sprinkled with the terms "justice," "equality," "duty," and "morality."

Confusion has also permeated debates about positive and negative rights. For traditionalists, the Bill of Rights was thought to be, at minimum, a charter of negative liberties. Increasingly, though, there has been significant disagreement about the degree to which it also contains or secures positive rights. The distinction between positive and negative rights has been blurred over the course of the century, particularly in the discourses of "minima" and deprivation, where scholars have argued for declarations of minimum standards so that the failure to meet such standards could be declared a deprivation under the Fourteenth Amendment's due process clause. The discourse of positive rights reflects tenets embodied in other twentieth-century constitutions in other Western countries. In the United States, however, the Constitution is largely silent about such matters, thereby giving rise to the public arguments about affirmative welfare or group rights profiled here.

There has also been a continuing tendency to confuse other terms with rights. More commonly, and indeed more importantly, there was a related tendency to label political desires and ideals as "rights." Specifically, references to the "public interest" included the assertion of the right of the government to act. This tendency became more pronounced with the rise of the regulatory state where the conflict between the rights of the individual and the rights of the state has increased. Here the state asserts a right to a particular action (often regulatory) that a citizen then claims to be an infringement of individual rights. There is considerable evidence of a tendency to discuss the powers granted in the first two portions of the Constitution as issues of rights contained in its latter portion, the Bill of Rights. The amalgamation of rights with an idea closer to liberty happened concurrently with the changes

in the structural aspects of the Constitution. The twentieth-century's central-
ization and proliferation of the administrative state also has increasingly con-
flated individual and group desires with the notion of rights, in part because
rights are the language of the courts—the ultimate path to power in a democratic society. To be sure, the categorizations and definitions of rights presented here represent only a portion of the discourse studied. The sources of
rights, be they common law, constitutional law, statutory law, or natural law,
have become a significant portion of this nation's most divisive discourse
and it is not likely that such debates will be resolved soon.

This chapter argues that Americans are not more rights conscious per se
than in previous times—although rights are surely still normal parts of public conversation in the United States. What is different, and what has
changed, are (1) the types of issues now being discussed as rights, (2) what
we mean when we speak in the language of rights, and (3) what all of this
says about the relationship between citizen and state.

Further research should consider whether lawsuits can be seen as a "mass
medium" much like the news. Heretofore, most scholarly focus has been on
case law, which comprises only the cases that have been successful in getting before the courts. If our goal is to understand the range of issues comprising societal conflict, one fairly unmined source would be to look at the
contents of filings to see what issues are uppermost in the minds of Americans. But more than the topics involved, another question is posed. The
American citizenry, when looked at comparatively, is universally supportive
of the rule of law (sometimes in contrast to individual laws). But why? And
to what end? Historically, talking about rights is really not new, but which
type of rights do we most talk about, and more importantly, which rights do
we wish to see action on in the form of litigation? In a sense, litigation can
be seen as analogous to policy making in Congress. That is, while citizens
may agree that certain social issues are problematic, this does not mean that
they want policy made about such topics. Similarly, we may talk exceedingly
about rights, but what creates the momentum for rights to manifest themselves in the form of lawsuits? Do lawsuits, spawned by the legal elite, help
the citizenry prioritize its views, similar to how political elites and the news
media tell us what to think is important? In other words, the rhetoric of rights
may now be setting the agenda for public discussion in the United States. If
that is so, we need to know how, and why, it is so.

6

Defining Events: Problem Definition in the Media Arena

Regina G. Lawrence

On April 20, 1999, Eric Harris and Dylan Klebold strode into Columbine High School in Littleton, Colorado, armed with guns, explosives, and long-concealed rage and alienation. Within hours, they, along with many of their classmates and one of their teachers, were dead. Their murderous rampage scarred the families of Columbine students and seared the national psyche as it dominated headlines and newscasts for weeks to come. The Columbine story became the most closely watched news story of 1999 (Pew Center 1999a), while opinion polls registered a sharp increase in public concern with teenagers and several key influences on them: families, entertainment media, and guns (Pew Center 1999b). The story shaped the early stages of the presidential election as candidates for both parties' nominations searched for ways to address these newly salient issues (Seelye 1999). Meanwhile, the White House convened a "summit" of gun industry executives, Hollywood bigwigs, and experts who identified a number of complex and interconnected forces allegedly responsible for youth violence. Congress responded with a protracted debate on gun control that yielded little except rather weak provisions governing sales at gun shows and an amendment allowing schools to display the Ten Commandments. And all the while, mass-mediated public discourse on Columbine continued to focus on the question of why it occurred and what it meant.

In this chapter, I argue that the shooting at Columbine High School was something more than a sensational, long-running news story. It was the centerpiece of a national conversation about the state of late-twentieth-century America and the causes of and cures for a newly emerging problem (or a newly emerging understanding) of youth violence. More specifically, it was an illustrative example of how dramatic news events are

defined in the news in ways that contribute to the social construction of
public problems.

PUTTING COLUMBINE IN CONTEXT: AGENDA
SETTING, FRAMING, AND PROBLEM DEFINING

News coverage of the shooting at Columbine High illustrates one approach
to thinking about the political dynamics of the news, an approach I call
"event-driven problem definition." This approach views the media as one social arena in which society's understandings of reality take shape, and it analyzes how dramatic news events (like the Columbine shooting) focus public attention on particular issues while becoming objects of struggle among
competing perspectives on reality. As journalists, political leaders, and
publics try to make sense of troubling news events, opportunities are created
for various groups to make claims about societal problems that need to be
fixed. In other words, society's problems are often identified and defined
against a backdrop of single, concrete events.

This approach to the news incorporates three paradigms in political communication: agenda setting, framing, and the social construction of reality. According to the social construction paradigm, problems exist in perception as
much as in reality. *Problems* are those societal conditions which people find
unacceptable, conditions that people believe should be addressed by public
policy (Kingdon 1995, 90–115). At its heart, the social construction paradigm
tries to explain how we perceive and define issues in ways that allow some
to become problems to be fixed while others remain merely conditions to be
endured. This paradigm also explores how problems confer power on certain
societal groups. Although people "take quite different 'realities' for granted"
(Berger and Luckmann 1967, 2), through the process of problem defining,
some peoples' realities become authoritative and widely shared while others'
are marginalized. Finally, this paradigm explores how particular problem definitions allocate resources and responsibility differently. Is poverty, for example, a condition sufficiently serious and widespread to demand large-scale
government intervention? The answers to that question have varied throughout the nation's history. Is poverty a problem of individual shortcomings or
failed social policy? The answers and implications have been different depending upon who has gained the authority to define the problem: When
poverty is viewed as a result of failed social policy, poor people themselves
are less likely to take the blame for their condition, and responsibility for addressing the problem is laid at the feet of government.

Agenda setting is an important component of the social construction of
public problems. The study of agenda setting focuses on "the ability of newspapers, television, and news magazines to focus public attention on a few

public issues" (McCombs, Danielian, and Wanta 1995, 281). More broadly, it analyzes the interaction among the media, the public, and policymakers as different political issues compete for the limited resource of attention. According to one set of authors, "the heart of the agenda-setting process is when the salience of an issue changes on the media agenda, the public agenda, or the policy agenda" (Dearing and Rogers 1996, 1, 8). The Columbine shooting offers several examples of agenda setting at work. The event gained considerable media attention (thus shaping the media agenda), which in turn shaped the issues the public expressed concern about (thus shaping the public agenda), simultaneously goading Congress and the White House into debates about gun control and the entertainment industry (thus shaping the policy agenda).

This ability of dramatic events to turn public attention and political energy to particular issues has been demonstrated in many agenda-setting studies (Dearing and Rogers 1996, 54–71). Agenda-setting studies, however, have generally treated certain events as "natural" catalysts for certain predefined issues and then traced their impact on the media agenda. For example, Dearing and Rogers (1996) showed that the highly publicized AIDS-related deaths of actor Rock Hudson and young student Ryan White triggered a sharp increase in media coverage of AIDS. The focus of their study was the question, "What finally put AIDS on the [media] agenda?" (56). But the crucial processes by which events themselves are defined and used to construct particular problems by journalists, their sources, and the public have not been examined as closely by scholars of political communication. The problem-definition framework invites us to examine the interpretation and communication that go into linking events with problems. It might seem obvious or "natural" that the Columbine shooting should boost public attention concerning gun control or violent media, but it is important to explain how Columbine was linked to the problems of easy access to guns and a violent media culture more decisively than to competing problem definitions—such as the lack of school counseling programs and the state of teen mental health.

This is where another key paradigm in political communication comes in: framing. Framing is often used to analyze how news stories emphasize or deemphasize different aspects of reality, which both shape and reflect the cognitive categories politicians, journalists, and citizens use to make sense of the political world (see, for example, Entman and Rojecki 1993; Iyengar 1991; and Neuman, Just, and Crigler 1992). The fundamental premise of framing is that people generally cannot process information without (consciously or unconsciously) using conceptual lenses that bring certain aspects of reality into sharper focus while relegating others to the background. Frames are the basic building blocks with which public problems are socially constructed. Sometimes explicitly, sometimes implicitly, news frames define problems, diagnose the causes of problems, make moral judgments about problems, and suggest remedies for problems (Entman 1993, 52). In the process, frames suggest who or what is responsible for causing and for solving problems.

The news is a key arena in which framing, agenda setting, and the social construction of public problems play out, and those dynamics can be especially evident in the aftermath of highly newsworthy and troubling news events. It is common for different groups—officials, pundits, op-ed writers, leaders of interest groups and social movements, and regular citizens interviewed by reporters or writing letters to the editor—to compete to define a dramatic and troubling news event by placing it within different frames. Journalists, as managers of the news arena (Gans 1979), decide how news stories about the event will be framed and determine which claims about reality will gain wide exposure. In the process, certain claims makers are empowered (or marginalized), problems are defined (or ignored), and some realities win authority and legitimacy over others.

EVENT-DRIVEN PROBLEMS

The Columbine shooting shares with many other memorable news events its status as an "accidental" event (Molotch and Lester 1974). These events are accidental in that they are not planned by elites as news, often arising spontaneously far from the well-worn path of the standard news beat. Such events, as Molotch and Lester suggest, can create pivotal moments in the news when standard news perspectives on political issues can be challenged.

Events like the Columbine shooting often create opportunities for problem-defining activity in the news, in large part because they do not come to journalists predefined in the way that many "routine" news events do. When the president signs a bill in the Rose Garden or visits a foreign country, for example, the event comes to reporters packaged in its official frame. The president's critics in Congress may offer a competing frame, or journalists may resist the official frame by searching for an underlying "real" story, but those who have staged the event have probably established the basic story line (unless some unexpected gaffe or revelation upsets the official line). In contrast, news driven by accidental events stem from the fundamental indeterminacy of the "real meaning" of those events. Indeed, what events tell us about the problems we face as a society is a matter of social construction, and there is often an interpretive gap between the objective facts of an event and the significance it acquires in the news. A standard journalistic response to dramatic, unexpected events is to fill that gap with the voices of experts, interest groups, and average citizens. As journalists seek to explain and interpret a major news event for their audiences (Graber 1993, chap. 5), they often cast their nets for news sources more broadly than usual.

Moreover, dramatic news events may catch political elites and other standard news sources off guard or throw them on the political defensive. These dynamics can encourage a further broadening of the news net to include critics, activists, and other advocates of change. Thus, accidental events create opportunities for various groups to actively shape public discourse, provide incentives to reporters to admit organized groups clamoring for entrance to the news, and provide incentives for more entrepreneurial reporting, which draws other voices and views into the news.

Most research on the news has focused on institutionally driven rather than event-driven news dynamics (see table 6.1). Institutionally driven news is pegged to the daily activities, conflicts, and debates happening on institutional news beats such as the White House or city hall. Event-driven news often erupts outside these news beats. The predominant frames in institutionally driven news are usually those offered by elites, and the range of debate found in that kind of news is likely to be correlated with the range of debate among key policymakers (Bennett 1990). Event-driven

Table 6.1. Characteristics of Different Problem-Definition Processes in the News

Features of the News	Institutionally Driven Problem Definition	Event-Driven Problem Definition
Impetus for news.	News focused around "routine" events like presidential speeches, congressional committees, campaign strategies, daily crimefighting, etc.	News focused around dramatic "accidental" events. Over time, institutional processing of the event provides additional news pegs.
Key providers of news narratives and frames.	Most likely to be officials.	Likely to be nonofficials as well as officials.
Basis for narrative structure of the news.	Defined by key decision points within institutional processes.	Defined by story developments that are less tightly pegged to institutional processes.
Range of voices and perspectives in the news.	Range of official debate roughly defines range of debate in the news.	Likely to range wider than current official debate.
Kinds of problems that are defined in the news.	Problem definitions more likely to be those that officials want to (or have to) deal with.	Problem definitions more likely to be variable and volatile, and to favor critics of the status quo and advocates of reform or social change.
Direction of agenda-setting influence.	Political institutions set the news agenda.	News organizations set the official agenda.

problem definition arises more sporadically, and the perspectives included in event-driven news may range beyond the spectrum defined by official debate. In the former dynamic (institutionally driven news), officials play the main role in defining the problems appearing in the news, such as welfare or taxes. In the latter dynamic (event-driven news), problems are more volatile and difficult for officials to control and more open to a variety of competing frames.

The categories of event-driven versus institutionally driven dynamics are more useful as a heuristic device than as firm, mutually exclusive empirical categories, because the boundaries of each type of news are permeable. For example, dramatic news events can prompt policymakers to put issues on institutional agendas, which in turn triggers institutionally driven news—a dynamic that is discussed further below. Event-driven news, moreover, is in some cases fairly routinized. Plane crashes and earthquakes, for example, are quintessentially "accidental" events but the news tends to cover them in relatively predictable ways (bodies are recovered and counted, the dead are remembered, families and communities begin to heal and rebuild, etc.). Indeed, as Gaye Tuchman (1978) recognized long ago, news organizations depend for their livelihood on being able to "routinize the unexpected." To the extent that coverage of accidental events is highly routinized, it affords less room for wide-ranging discourse among various voices and problem definitions. Moreover, it stands to reason that events lacking an element of human causation are not likely to generate a great deal of problem defining in the news. It is important to bear in mind, however, that the meaning of events is as much a matter of social construction as of empirical fact. Earthquakes are not humanly caused, for example, but lax building codes may be as much to blame as seismic faults for the deaths that result.

Event-driven news is important to study, therefore, because it reveals how officials, journalists, and other groups construct public understandings of society's problems out of the inherently contestable meaning of accidental events. It is also important to better understand event-driven news because it shows signs of increasing. Technological innovations and mounting commercial pressures on mainstream news organizations have made officially staged events less dominant in the news today than when Molotch and Lester (1974) first identified them as the touchstone of daily news. Audiences can now view news events unfolding in real time (or close to it), with potentially enormous commercial payoffs for news organizations. News sagas built around accidental news events, sometimes events of dubious news value, have become a new industry standard. Indeed, "the imperative to compete for audiences has led to a loosening of commitments to traditional journalistic values and canons of practice, resulting in news that is more sensationalized (in turn, all O. J., JonBenet, and

Elian, all the time)" (Swanson 2000, 3). The commercial dynamics underlying the "tabloidization" of the media should not be overlooked as an important structural influence on event-driven media discourse, for certain accidental events are likely to be heavily publicized based in part on their commercial value to news organizations. But changing journalistic norms and routines are an important cause as well. As one recent study of newspaper news spanning one hundred years discovered, news organizations have become more inclined to treat news events as jumping-off points for thematic exploration of social issues. Indeed, "the basic recipe for news [has changed]: For a story to qualify as news, journalists must link [events] to something bigger" by supplying "a context of social problems, interpretation, and themes" (Barnhurst and Mutz 1997, 27, 51). Indeed, event-driven news sagas, though they may have roots in commercial imperatives, sometimes also produce mediated public discourse exploring issues of serious political substance.

Indeed, so many dramatic news events and event-driven problems seem to vie for our attention these days that the reader can probably immediately think of at least two or three—some examples that seem serious and well grounded, and others that seem more frivolous or based upon questionable premises. They range from the bombing of the Murrah Federal Building in Oklahoma City, which set off an unprecedented national conversation about militia groups and domestic terrorism, to the story of Stella Liebeck, the "McDonald's coffee lady," whose third-degree burns figured prominently in rude jokes, urban myth, and efforts to legislate tort reform.[1] Other examples I have analyzed include the infamous garbage barge *Mobro* that wandered the high seas in 1987 looking for a port that would accept its cargo (Bennett and Lawrence 1995); the beating of African American motorist Rodney King by officers of the Los Angeles Police Department in 1991 (Lawrence 1996, 2000); and the *Exxon Valdez* oil spill in the waters of Prince William Sound in 1989 (Lawrence and Birkland 1999). The research questions and hypotheses presented here draw from those studies and are illustrated with data from news coverage of the more recent case of the Columbine shooting.

A very simple (indeed, oversimplified) model of event-driven problem definition in the media arena would include four stages: the appearance of an accidental event, intense media coverage of the event, an interpretive struggle among various news sources over the meaning of the event, and the emergence of particular problem definitions linked with the event. Though simplistic, this model suggests three valuable research questions: Which events do news organizations "select" as candidates for problem definition? What voices and perspectives get to participate in the ensuing struggle over meaning? And which problem definitions emerge victorious from the struggle?

MEDIA SELECTION OF PROBLEM-DEFINING EVENTS

While the news teems with dramatic events, not all events become occasions for problem defining. Many news events stimulate some degree of mass-mediated discussion about problems in society. Indeed, it is more useful to conceptualize problem-defining responses to various news events as ranging along a continuum (from little or none to a great deal) rather than falling into dichotomous categories (problem defining as either occurring or not occurring). One important research question involves explaining why some events become major problem-defining occasions in the news.

The events that news organizations treat as indicators of public problems will not necessarily be valid indicators, statistically speaking. Singular events having highly newsworthy characteristics may become emblematic of purported public problems quite apart from real statistical trends. The Columbine shooting is one example. Journalists, pundits, op-ed writers, and policymakers all focused attention on the question of what can be done to stop school violence (and youth violence more broadly) precisely at a time when trends in overall crime and in juvenile crime were down and when statistics suggested little if any increase in violence at schools (Bureau of Justice Statistics 1999; Donohue, Schiraldi, and Ziedenberg 1999; Office of Juvenile Justice and Delinquency Prevention 1999). This was not the picture that emerged in the news; indeed, only 2 percent of news articles mentioning Columbine in the *New York Times* and *Los Angeles Times* put the shooting into this statistical context.[2] This example reveals how problems are based as much on perception as on facts, and raises important questions about how the media single out certain events for problem-defining emphasis.

There is no simple formula by which to predict which events will become the most intensely covered and engender the most problem-defining activity. How news organizations determine the newsworthiness of various events ultimately stems from the underlying norms and incentives that drive journalism as a profession and as a business. A thorough examination of the complex norms and incentives shaping contemporary journalism is beyond the scope of this chapter, but we can begin with the simple premise that news coverage of events reflects news organizations' sense of what is "important" to cover and "interesting" to audiences. A more complex and nuanced premise would be the following: The events that engender heavy problem-defining activity are those that appeal to news organizations as storytellers and commercial profit makers (Darnton 1975; McChesney 1999; Schudson 1978), as monitors of societal developments and normative boundaries (Ericson, Baranek, and Chan 1991; Gans 1979), and as the "guard dogs" of established power structures (Bennett 1993; Donahue, Tichenor, and Olien 1995). In other words, major problem-defining events are those that offer journalists plenty of storytelling material that they believe will appeal to their audiences, events that represent important developments in society or violations of shared societal norms and expectations, and events which engender political conflict or promise political impact. Some of the event characteristics most likely to lead to intensive problem-defining activity include:

- *A large scope or magnitude of harms.* Events are likely to become candidates for problem definition when they involve relatively large numbers of victims or high monetary impact (Birkland 1997), or affect a significant geographic or demographic area, or involve particularly egregious violence or other wrongdoing (Lawrence 2000).
- *Similarities to other recent news events.* Events that seem to follow a pattern can be seen by news organizations as particularly newsworthy. When one dramatic event occurs shortly after another similar event, this offers an invitation to journalists and their sources to construct a pattern or "wave" (Fishman 1978), and thus a problem.
- *Dramatic narrative possibilities.* Three kinds of event characteristics seem to evoke intensive problem defining because they trigger journalists' storytelling and monitoring instincts: events that generate particularly evocative imagery, either on camera or in the public mind; events that promise subsequent developments that can be "serialized" (Chermak 1994) into a "continuing saga" (Cook 1996); and events violating commonly shared assumptions about the world that strike journalists and their audiences as shocking, disturbing, or "abnormal."
- *Interest to key demographic audiences.* Events that news organizations believe are particularly interesting to those relatively well-off, upwardly mobile audiences that their advertisers seek may be more likely to get greater play than events that news organizations believe will receive scant attention. Of course, some events are newsworthy enough on other grounds that they become big news even though they might not seem to harm, threaten, or directly affect most middle-class audiences (the beating of black motorist Rodney King by police, for example). But, in general, news organizations respond to the commercial possibilities as well as the narrative possibilities of breaking news events.
- *Public and political reaction.* Events that present political challenges to officials by stimulating widespread public reaction are especially ripe for problem-defining activity in the news. When an accidental event occurs in tandem with a policy debate currently on the official agenda, or when it spurs new or renewed political conflict, journalists are likely to see an important story in the works. Moreover, when officials respond to an event with public pronouncements or new policy proposals, news organizations are "licensed" to pursue problems more vigorously (Lawrence 1996). This is not to say that news organizations necessarily

"take sides" in such political standoffs, but rather that they recognize political conflict as particularly newsworthy and as a green light for more intensive coverage of the issues prompting the conflict.

This list of characteristics, though certainly not exhaustive, can help explain why certain events win the heaviest coverage among all the routine and accidental events the news might cover, and why certain events win the heaviest coverage among similar kinds of events occurring at different points in time. The latter is a particularly interesting question. Why, for example, did media coverage of Columbine far outstrip coverage of other recent school shootings? (See figure 6.1.)

First and most obviously, the unprecedented number of injuries and deaths at Columbine—fourteen students and one teacher killed—made it more newsworthy than previous school shootings, which had involved at

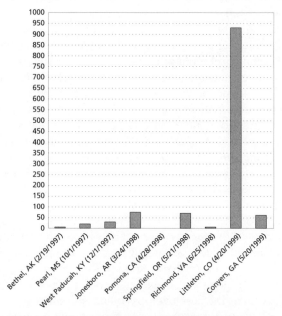

Note: Data are derived from a search of the Nexis database for the number of news and editorial items mentioning each incident (that is, that mentioned the location of each shooting or the name of the shooter in close proximity with the words "shoot" or "shooting" and its cognates) to appear in the *New York Times*, the *Los Angeles Times*, the *Washington Post*, *Newsweek*, and *U.S. News and World Report* for a four-month period following the day the incident occurred; news summaries and sports page items were excluded. The incidents shown here include all known shootings of students by students occurring on school grounds between January of 1997 and June of 1999 that involved more than one victim (see National School Safety Center 1999).

Figure 6.1.   Coverage of School Shootings, Major National Print Media, 1997–1999

most five deaths. Those previous events (seven other school shootings with multiple victims in the previous two years) also made Columbine more newsworthy and more subject to problem defining, for journalists and their sources could easily link Columbine with other shootings to begin defining a purported problem of rising school violence. The commercial and narrative possibilities of the story were also boosted by the vivid imagery of a wounded student trying to escape from a window of the school, captured by a helicopter cameraman, and by a telephone call from a student trapped inside the school to a local radio station; both were broadcast live and aired repeatedly for days thereafter. A continuing saga was promised by political reactions to the event, such as the president's prime-time television address on the evening of the shooting and the quickly rising pressure on Congress to respond with some new policy initiative. Finally, and perhaps more than any other factor, the Columbine shooting was highly newsworthy because it occurred in a largely white, upper-middle-class suburb outside of the South. Previous high-profile school shootings, tragic as they were, may not have seemed as dramatically or commercially promising to news organizations because they more easily fit stereotypes associated with the "rural gun culture." Columbine's solidly white, middle-class suburban setting, moreover, violated standard assumptions about where such violence typically occurs and to whom. The geographic and demographic setting thus rendered Columbine more shocking and disturbing—reflected in President Clinton's observation on the evening of the shooting that "perhaps now America would wake up to the dimensions of this challenge if it could happen in a place like Littleton" (President's Remarks 1999)—and thus more newsworthy. Tellingly, after Columbine, the question of whether the country "really" had a problem of school violence was almost never raised in the media.

SOURCE ACCESS AND THE STRUGGLE OVER MEANING

The sources journalists use to comment on and contextualize news events are central to how events are defined and to what public problems are constructed around them. When societal groups disagree about the existence and nature of problems, the problems the news publicizes are in part a function of which voices and views it amplifies. There are really two dimensions to these interpretive struggles: the "struggle over access" and the "struggle over meaning" (Wolfsfeld 1997). The interpretive struggle over meaning is where the contest among competing frames or problem definitions enters our analysis; it will therefore be analyzed in both this section and the next.

One important variable in the struggle over access is the proportion of nonofficial voices, such as interest groups, activists, and average citizens, who get to participate in event-driven debates. Numerous studies of the

news have demonstrated that political elites—such as politicians, bureau-
crats, police, and others who hold political office—generally enjoy privileged access to the news, while nonofficials gain access more sporadically
(Gans 1979; Bennett 1990; Lawrence 2000; Wolfsfeld 1997). Yet how officials
define events may not always coincide with the implications the public sees.
To take just one example: in the wake of the *Exxon Valdez* oil spill, envi-
ronmentalists claimed that the spill illustrated the oil industry's complacency
and the government's indifference to the environment, and polls suggested
that the public had grown more concerned that the government was not doing enough about environmental protection (Gallup 1999). That perspective
was not shared by the Bush administration nor by many powerful members
of Congress nor by the oil industry, all of whom argued that the spill was
simply an unfortunate accident that did not indicate larger problems within
the industry or with existing environmental protections. Who gets to speak
in such cases—who gets to frame news events—can be a crucial determinant
of problem definition. Indeed, the degree of access nonofficials gain is likely
to be correlated with the number and diversity of problem definitions aired
in the news.

Gaining access does not guarantee the ability to frame the event-driven
debate. Oil industry executives won plenty of access to the news about the
Exxon Valdez spill, for example, often outnumbering their environmentalist
critics, but they did not always succeed in controlling the news frame
(Lawrence and Birkland 1999). Therefore, analyzing event-driven debates
requires us to identify the factors that allow certain voices and views into the
media arena and the factors that allow certain frames to predominate. Certain factors are likely to be relatively constant: some degree of organizational
resources, social status, and political credibility are generally the sine qua
non of media access (Gans 1979; Wolfsfeld 1997), and successfully competing in the struggle over meaning generally requires some degree of fit between the claims a group wants to make and broad cultural values, themes,
and preoccupations (Gamson 1992; Hilgartner and Bosk 1988; Wolfsfeld
1997). Yet within those relatively constant boundaries, different groups may
win differential access and the power to shape the news at different times,
depending upon:

- *The event's impact on a group, or a group's impact on postevent politics.* Whether they enjoy regular access to the news before an event or
  not, groups become more newsworthy after an event to the degree that
  the event directly affects them (for example, minority and anti–police
  brutality groups gained a brief but considerable window of opportunity
  in the aftermath of the Rodney King beating [Lawrence 2000]). Moreover, as suggested above, events are more newsworthy when they
  throw officials on the political defensive. By the same logic, those who

challenge officials become more newsworthy as well (Wolfsfeld 1997; Lawrence 2000). During event-driven debates, nonofficial groups whose moves will "advance the story" arising out of an event are likely to gain greater access to and influence over the news than usual (Cook 1996, 52–57).

- *Degree of "fit" between a group's claims and the particulars of the event.* Even claims that fit within broad cultural boundaries may clash with the imagery arising out of a particular event. Think, for example, of one oil executive's claim that the damage done by the *Exxon Valdez* was simply "the price of civilization," or Los Angeles Police Chief Daryl Gates's claim that the Rodney King beating was purely "an aberration." As television screens filled with imagery of oiled and perishing Alaskan wildlife in the first case, or officers seemingly ganging up on an unarmed motorist in the second case, these claims became difficult to sustain. Event particulars provide resources for some groups—evocative imagery that illustrates their claims—and encumbrances for others.
- *News value of a group's claims.* Some problem definitions will be relatively overlooked in the news not because they violate cultural boundaries or clash with event imagery, but because they don't make for good news. Generally speaking, claims that suggest "new" problems have an advantage over claims about "the same old" problems, as do claims that "democratize the risk" of problems (Best 1999, 22), casting them as frequent, widespread, and threatening to a broad population.

As shown in table 6.2, officials were the most cited group of sources in news about the Columbine shooting, yet they did not dramatically outnumber nonofficial groups such as professional and academic experts, media industry spokesmen, and "average" citizens. Indeed, the post-Columbine debate was remarkably broad, especially in comparison to typical crime news (Chermak 1994; Lawrence 2000) and to other institutionally driven stories like foreign policy debates (Bennett 1990; Cook 1994) where officials generally have an overwhelming advantage.

The relative breadth of post-Columbine discourse illustrates how event-driven news reflects both the clamoring of organized groups for entrance to the media arena and some entrepreneurial initiative on the part of news organizations to bring in a variety of voices. While groups such as the National Rifle Association, Handgun Control Inc., the Motion Picture Association, and other organized lobbying groups did win space for their views on gun control and popular culture, other sources—especially many experts and "average" citizens—were ushered into the debate at the behest of reporters looking for good story angles.

Three key sets of nonofficial sources in the post-Columbine debate—the entertainment industry, experts, and advocates on both sides of the gun

Table 6.2.   Voices in the Post-Columbine Debate, *New York Times* and *Los Angeles Times*

Group	Percentage of Stories Citing at Least One Source from Group
Federal, state, and local officials	38%
Experts	
Psychologists and mental health experts	12
Criminal experts	5
Other academic experts	16
Total experts	33
Citizens, citizen activists, parents, teens, and other unaffiliated nonofficials	24
Media, entertainment, and Internet industries	21
Journalists, editors, and professional pundits	20
Gun lobby, gun-rights advocates, and gun-control advocates	8

Note: Data in this table are based on coding of the full text of a random sample of 135 news and editorial items appearing in the *New York Times* and *Los Angeles Times* that mentioned the Columbine shooting; intercoder agreement was 97 percent. Items chosen for analysis were not "episodic" (Iyengar 1991) reports of details of the Columbine shooting but news articles and editorials that ranged beyond the specifics of that event to explore public reactions, trends, and other broader issues associated with school shootings. Sources "cited" are those that were quoted in their own words or who authored op-ed or other editorial pieces.

control debate—shaped the mediated debate over Columbine in significant ways. The degree of access to the news gained by these groups illustrates the propositions above. Two of these groups, the entertainment industry and gun groups, were influenced directly by the political fallout from the Columbine story and were crucial to the way the story played out politically. Yet gun groups were cited less often than were the other two groups (even though, as we will see below, the gun control debate became a major spin-off story). In part, the greater access won by the media industry may stem from the fact that the *Los Angeles Times* is particularly well connected to Hollywood.[3] The greater access gained by the expert group, on the other hand, reflects its diverse composition. Whereas gun groups were likely to appear only in stories specifically about gun control, experts could appear in virtually any kind of story. These findings also reflect the differential newsworthiness of the three groups' claims. As news organizations searched for the causes of Columbine, psychologists, education professionals, criminologists, and other experts could offer journalists highly newsworthy analysis. In contrast to gun groups, which could only offer "the same old" analysis about the role of guns in societal violence (or the same old rebuttals to those claims), the experts could offer more "interesting" claims about new pressures on teens, new tears in the social fabric, and new malignant media influences. Media insiders, in turn, were well positioned to rebut (or, in some cases, to acknowledge) these newer and "sexier" problems.

As pointed out above, however, gaining access does not guarantee a victory in the struggle over meaning. The diverse experts who gained considerable access to the news were hardly a unified group offering a simple problem definition, and so the various concerns they raised about the social, psychological, and cultural causes of school violence dissipated as the Columbine story played out. As we will see next, the problem definitions that gained the greatest media attention were those that focused on the two other key groups: the media industry and gun groups.

PREDOMINANT PROBLEM DEFINITIONS

The typical case of event-driven problem definition is not one in which who (or what) should be blamed for an event is objectively self-evident (although it will surely seem so to various people viewing the event from different perspectives). Indeed, assigning responsibility lies at the heart of event-driven problem definition. Was it a drunken ship's captain or a greedy oil industry that ruined Prince William Sound? Were a few racist cops or a corrupt police department responsible for what happened to Rodney King—or was Mr. King himself to blame? And what was to blame for the wandering garbage barge *Mobro*: a lack of recycling programs, the *NIMBY*-headedness of residents of Long Island, or an American culture known for its overconsumption and wastefulness?

In more formal political arenas such as legislatures and bureaucracies, particular problem definitions are enshrined in the very act of policymaking. Problem definition in the media proceeds more haphazardly, often with multiple voices in multiple news organizations offering competing problem definitions with little formal resolution. It is therefore often an easier task for the researcher to identify the weapons used in the struggle than to pronounce victors. Indeed, because event-driven problem definition happens within a complex and ongoing negotiation of social reality, it is often difficult to boil events down to a single problem. The 1992 Los Angeles riots, for example, were said to indicate everything from blacks' disgust with the criminal justice system to the failure of 1960s social welfare programs to a continuation of the inequalities that had helped trigger the Watts riots twenty-five years before (Page 1996; Edy 1999). Therefore, the best model of problem definition in the news is not one that visualizes a single problem definition emerging triumphant. Rather, problem definitions will often proliferate before a few achieve relative prominence and longevity.

Two factors seem particularly important in determining the prominence and longevity of competing problem definitions. One is the amount of "new" news certain problems offer: how readily they can be made the subject of news stories that appeal to journalists as storytellers and as monitors of developments on the social and political scene. The other factor is how readily problems are institutionalized. It is not uncommon in the immediate aftermath of a dramatic accidental event for multiple problem definitions to proliferate and then, over time, to narrow down to a few. In part, this reflects the inevitable shifting of media attention as new events draw the media spotlight elsewhere, but it also reflects the basic newsgathering apparatus of the media. The problem definitions that achieve longevity in the news are likely to be those that are taken up in other institutional arenas with corresponding news beats. When Congress responds to an event with a new piece of legislation, for example, the problem definition enshrined in the bill gains extended coverage from reporters stationed on the congressional beat. Problem definitions that are more easily institutionalized thus enjoy an advantage over others. In certain cases, as Best (1999, 69) theorizes, the media become part of an "iron quadrangle" of problem institutionalization—at which point event-driven problems become institutionally driven problems.

The struggle to define the "real" problem represented by Columbine was remarkably rich and protracted. Table 6.3 lists the impressive variety of problem definitions that emerged in news coverage in the aftermath of the shooting.[4] It also suggests how the characteristics of the event provided openings for multiple interpretations. The fact that Eric Harris and Dylan Klebold were white, middle-class suburbanites with only minor criminal records and no known history of illicit drug use defied common stereotypes about who commits such violence and why. Harris and Klebold remained enigmas, especially since they could no longer speak for themselves, which gave politicians, journalists, experts, and the public considerable interpretive license. Indeed, the breadth of post-Columbine debate reflects in part that there were few claims that clearly clashed with the imagery of that enigmatic event. Many claims could be made and were made about what caused the violence at Columbine.

Of these various problems, however, only a small number persisted in the news, particularly gun control and the entertainment media, while others, such as parenting and teen mental health, fell by the wayside. Of all news stories and editorials mentioning Columbine to appear in the *New York Times* and *Los Angeles Times* between April and August 1999, stories about gun control (focusing on the congressional debate; on gun control efforts at the state and local levels; or on other aspects of gun ownership, gun violence, and gun control) became the dominant category of stories (24 percent).[5] Gun control was also a problem definition favored by both newspapers, which published thirty-eight editorials and op-ed pieces on the topic between April and July (over one third of all editorials mentioning Columbine), nearly all of them arguing in favor of tougher gun control. Popular

Table 6.3.   Problem Definitions in News Coverage of Columbine

Guns	Inadequate gun control laws, abundance and availability of guns
Hollywood	Content of television, movies, video games, and pop music
Internet	Internet allows kids to express violent fantasies; information available over the Internet encourages antisocial behaviors
Societal culture	General breakdown of civility, social norms, expectations of responsible behavior, etc. (nonreligious)
Religion	Lack of/hostility to prayer and religion in schools and society
Parents	Parents' lack of involvement with their kids; parents not recognizing signs of trouble; parents not exercising their responsibility to screen social and cultural influences on kids
Adults and community	Lack of community/social cohesion; adults not getting involved with kids
Schools and teachers	Inadequate counseling services, antiviolence programs, etc.; inadequate teacher training to recognize problems
School security	Inadequate security measures at schools
Criminal justice	Inadequate criminal justice system measures: law enforcement; "cracking down" on youth crime; criminal programs to identify problem youths and intervene
Mental health	Poor mental health, depression, mental illness
Alienation	Teen "alienation"
Teen fads	Teen culture fads, such as "goth" dress, heavy metal, industrial, or rap music, or involvement in groups like the Trenchcoat Mafia
Teen life	Social difficulties of adolescence and school: teasing, peer pressure, ostracism, cliques, etc.
Jocks	Jock culture: the dominance of popular athletes, overemphasis on sports, etc.
Racism	Racist beliefs or ideologies; Hitler-worship
Individual dysfunction	Purely individual problems: maladjustment, misguidedness, lack of moral values
Evil	The unexplainable or ineradicable presence of evil

Note: Data in this table are based upon coding of the full text of a sample of 135 news and editorial items appearing in the *New York Times* and the *Los Angeles Times* that mentioned the Columbine shooting (see table 6.2). Problem definitions were derived from statements made by all types of news sources listed in table 6.1.

culture was the second most prominent focus of news coverage in these two newspapers (stories about the content, effects, and industry behind films, popular music, video games, and the Internet), comprising 16 percent of all articles mentioning Columbine. Meanwhile, only 3 percent of stories in these newspapers focused on the trials of teen life, 2 percent on the responsibilities and difficulties of parenting, and 2 percent on the subject of mental health.

The two problem definitions that emerged most strongly in post-Columbine media discourse illustrate the propositions about newness and institutionalization described above, and suggest different routes by which problem definitions gain prominence in media discourse. The gun control problem became firmly institutionalized when Congress debated gun-control legislation for months after Columbine, providing news organizations with plenty of ongoing pegs for news stories. Yet, interestingly, this was not the problem definition to which these news organizations devoted their greatest creative resources (even though, judging from their editorial pages, it was a problem definition they took seriously). Eighty-five percent of news items focusing on guns were standard episodic stories filed from the congressional beat in Washington, D.C., that simply reported the day's developments in the gun control debate, while 14 percent were broader thematic explorations of the gun issue from various angles. In other words, the vast majority of news coverage focusing on the "guns" problem definition took its cue straight from the institutional cues provided by Congress, and very little of the reporting actually examined the role of guns in youth violence specifically or the place and effects of guns in our society more broadly. In contrast, although popular culture got less coverage overall than did guns, 30 percent of all articles focusing on the entertainment media were broader thematic explorations of the content and consequences of popular entertainment media.[6] To be sure, the pop culture problem definition had its own institutional news pegs, such as the White House "summit" of entertainment and gun industry executives, but popular culture apparently provided greater thematic news interest as a "new" public problem around which news organizations fashioned more creative, wider-ranging news coverage. (This finding is noteworthy given that thematic news is more likely to set the public agenda [Shaw and McCombs 1977] and to encourage news consumers to hold government responsible for solving problems [Iyengar 1991]).

Thus, both "newness" (a term that must be used advisedly, since few problem definitions emerge completely de novo from the rubble of accidental events) and institutionalization can contribute to a problem definition's success in the media arena. Table 6.2 makes the power of institutionalization especially clear: While mental health experts and other experts were scattered relatively heavily throughout the coverage, their concerns did not become focused in a piece of legislation or a White House initiative that could sustain them as a spin-off news story. This is particularly interesting for the fate of certain problem definitions: given that one of the Columbine shooters had been prescribed an antidepressant, the possible linkage between the shooting and the problem of mental health never took firm shape in media discourse.

CONCLUSION

Having mapped some of the basic terrain of this research agenda, areas for additional research beckon. One such area lies in the interactions among the public, media, polling organizations, and policymakers in defining and responding to event-driven problems. Future research could explore how opinion polls both draw from and contribute to how the public and the media construct problems. For example, survey data suggest that the public immediately linked Columbine to a few particular problems—at least when prompted to do so by pollsters. A Gallup poll reported on April 23, just three days after the shooting, that the public was most likely to blame guns (60 percent reported they blamed this factor "a great deal" for "causing shootings like the one in Littleton"), parents (51 percent), and the entertainment media (49 percent) (Newport 1999). The policy proposals that strong majorities thought would be "very effective" in addressing school violence were stricter gun control laws for teenagers (62 percent) and increased counseling for teenagers (62 percent). Interestingly, however, in polls in which respondents were asked to identify *in their own words* the problems causing school violence like that at Columbine, guns and Hollywood were much less likely to be mentioned than a more basic American preoccupation: parents and family—topics which, as reported above, were not covered much in the news. These surveys also echo table 6.3 in showing a wide range of problems on America's mind, from parenting and societal breakdown to lack of religious values to the pressures of teen life (Newport 1999). Moreover, while Gallup offered its respondents in closed-ended surveys a mental-health solution to school violence by asking how useful additional school counseling might be, it did not offer respondents a mental health cause for school violence. As these data suggest, pollsters may play an important role in firming up public opinion on public problems—indeed, in constructing it (Bennett 1993)—while the public can be expected to formulate some problem definitions that are based as much on enduring cultural preoccupations as on immediate media content (Neuman, Just, and Crigler 1992).

Another key area for future research lies in the link between problems discussed in the news and the content of public policy. Like all institutional arenas, the media channel public attention and structure social conflict according to their internal norms, rules, and incentives. The media play a key role in determining how popular understandings of problems evolve and, at least sometimes, in the evolution of policy responses. In the media arena, possible "problems" are often vetted long before those same problems are debated in more formal institutional arenas like Congress. Yet, as suggested above, how policymakers respond to an event-driven debate also powerfully influences the construction of problems in the media, pointing to complex and interactive causal relationships. Meanwhile, given the realities of power inequalities in our political system, a problem definition clearly endorsed by both the public and the media can nonetheless fail to become enshrined in public policy. Despite considerable attention to the problem of guns throughout the summer of 1999, for example, Congress declined to enact anything more than minor revisions to the nation's gun laws. To what degree, and how, media definitions influence the ways problems are defined in society will therefore continue to offer intriguing research possibilities for many years to come.

NOTES

The author wishes to thank Tom Birkland, along with Peter May, Stuart Scheingold, Mark Smith, and others at the Center for American Politics and Public Policy colloquium at the University of Washington, where an early draft of this work was presented; thanks are due as well to Walt Amacher and Kim Jasper-Landau for their data-gathering and coding assistance. Portions of the theoretical framework presented here appear in *The Politics of Force: Media and the Construction of Police Brutality* (Berkeley: University of California Press, 2000).

1. While Liebeck's injuries and initial jury award were widely reported, the subsequent adjustment of that jury award was far less well publicized in the media (Aks et al. 1997).

2. This finding is based on my coding of a random sample of 135 news articles and editorial pieces mentioning Columbine in those two newspapers from April through July 1999.

3. Media industry sources appeared in 26 percent of *Los Angeles Times* stories versus 17 percent of *New York Times* stories, a difference that is not statistically significant ($p = 0.125$) but that does suggest somewhat different levels of industry access to the two newspapers.

4. These findings are based on reading the full text of a random sample of 135 news articles and editorial pieces mentioning Columbine in the *New York Times* and *Los Angeles Times* from April through July 1999. These "problem definitions" include statements by journalists, their sources, and editorialists about the causes of the Columbine shooting in particular or school or youth violence in general.

5. The findings reported in this paragraph are based on coding of the citations of all 607 news articles and editorial pieces mentioning Columbine to appear in the *New York Times* and *Los Angeles Times* between mid-April and mid-August 1999. The citations were obtained from the Nexis database. Coding was done by the author, with a sample coded by a graduate student yielding an intercoder reliability score of 93 percent.

6. The distinction between "episodic" news, which focuses on discrete daily events, and "thematic" news, which covers broader conceptual context, is borrowed from Iyengar (1991). Percentages of thematic items about both guns and the entertainment media reported here are percentages of news items only, not including editorials. Examples of thematic coverage of the gun issue include articles headlined "For Those at Home on the Range, Guns Don't Kill," "The Gun Debate Has Two Sides; Now, a Third Way," and "With Guns, a Safer World for Women?" Examples of thematic coverage of the popular culture issue include articles headlined "The Movies: When Violent Fantasy Emerges as Reality" and "The Stresses of Youth, the Strains of Its Music."

7

The Paradox of News Bias: How Local Broadcasters Influence Information Policy

J. H. Snider

In the Telecommunications ("Telecom") Act of 1996, Congress granted existing local TV broadcasters a spectrum the FCC valued at between $11 and $70 billion if sold by auction (Pepper 1995).[1] The grant was controversial.[2] Reed Hundt, the chair of the Federal Communications Commission, said that granting digital channels to broadcasters was "the biggest single gift of public property to any industry in this century" (FCC Begins 1996, 2). The National Cable Television Association, which often lobbies against broadcasters, said in a nationally syndicated AP story that the grant "makes the sale of Manhattan for a few beads look like a hard bargain" (Aversa 1997). William Safire, a nationally syndicated *New York Times* columnist, described the grant as a "rip-off" worthy of "yesteryear's robber barons" (Safire 1996).

In the period immediately preceding passage of the Telecommunications Act and immediately thereafter, major print publications alleged that a major reason for the broadcasters' political success was their control of politicians' gateway into voters' homes. Politicians, they alleged, feared antagonizing their local TV broadcaster for fear of some type of news-related retaliation. By implication, this allegation applied not just to the spectrum clause in the Telecom Act but also to all cases when important broadcaster interests were at stake. I shall call this "the Allegation," capitalizing it for emphasis and easy identification. A front page *Wall Street Journal* article presented a common variation of the Allegation. "Broadcasters control the one thing politicians care about more than money: television time. It is hard to find a member of Congress who doesn't fear that crossing the owner of his or her local broadcast station will translate into an immediate reduction in airtime. So when broadcasters come knocking, members of Congress answer" (Murray 1997, 1).

Between December 27, 1995, and September 29, 1997, the *Wall Street Journal* printed the Allegation four times. It presented the Allegation a fifth time on March 17, 1997, but along with a broadcaster denial.[3] Between February 25, 1996, and July 23, 1997, the *New York Times* printed the Allegation four times. The *Washington Post* printed the Allegation four times, including twice in Herb Block's cartoons. The Allegation was also printed in a diverse group of other reputable publications, including the *Columbia Journalism Review, New Republic, Washington Monthly, Wired, Broadcasting & Cable, Variety, U.S. News & World Report,* the *Washington Times,* the *Boston Globe, National Journal,* and *The Hill.* A variety of respected broadcasting historians from different eras made the Allegation (Krasnow and Longley 1978; Baughman 1985; McChesney 1999; Hazlett 1998, Brinkley 1997; Southwick 1999). Representatives from prominent Washington, D.C.-based think tanks and public interest groups made the Allegation. These included the Heritage Foundation, the American Enterprise Institute, the Media Access Project, and Common Cause. In an advertorial in a leading trade publication, a prominent cable TV industry leader advised cable operators to develop a local news capability so that they could compete in Washington with the local TV broadcasters (Daniels 1998).

In not a single case cited above was verifiable proof offered of the Allegation's veracity. Only in rare cases was a named politician even cited as a source for the Allegation. The most common type of proof offered was to cite an unnamed lobbyist, an unnamed politician, or a named representative from a public interest group.

In part to better assess the validity of the Allegation—the alleged link between broadcaster control of news and broadcaster political power regarding telecommunications policy—I interviewed more than fifty Washington insiders. These included prominent officials responsible for telecommunications policy at government agencies (the Federal Communications Commission and the National Telecommunications Information Administration), Congress (members, personal staff, and committee staff), and lobbyists (for example, the National Association of Broadcasters [NAB], National Cable Television Association, and United States Telephone Association). I asked these individuals a variety of questions, but the two questions I asked most consistently were: 1) what major interest groups lobbied in behalf of the Telecommunications Act of 1996 or the Cable Act of 1992? and 2) why were they politically effective? I concluded from these interviews that the elite print reporters who made the Allegation were accurately reflecting common perceptions by political insiders who were speaking off the record.

Political communication scholars who have studied the Allegation are generally skeptical of claims and evidence that media owners use the media to pursue their public policy interests (Entman 1989; Gans 1979; Tuchman 1978).[4] As Doris Graber sums up the literature, perhaps with slightly excessive conclusiveness: "A number of content analyses of [political] events definitely refute the charges of political bias, if bias is defined as deliberately lopsided coverage or intentional slanting of news" (1984b, 97).

A partial explanation for the failure to find media bias relating to public policy may be the narrow way in which bias is commonly studied. Generally speaking, media bias can be divided into three categories: cross-industry, industry-specific, and company-specific. The vast majority of studies on media bias have focused on cross-industry bias, specifically, whether media have a liberal or a conservative ideological bias (Patterson 1998; Lichter, Rothman, and Lichter 1986; Weaver and Wilhoit 1986; Parenti 1986; Herman and Chomsky 1988; Gans 1985). Another group of studies—much smaller in number, anecdotal in nature, and most often found in journals of media criticism such as the *Columbia Journalism Review* and *Brill's Content*—looks at company-specific bias (Guensburg 1998); for example, whether NBC will objectively report on the affairs of its parent company, GE (Bagdikian 1992). The existence of industry-specific bias, the type of bias potentially illustrated by the Telecommunications Act, has rarely been studied.

There are a number of reasons why industry-specific bias might be unusually common, especially in comparison to cross-industry bias. First, the selective incentives for industry-specific bias are much stronger than for cross-industry bias. For example, a $50 billion tax break for corporations in general must be shared with literally millions of companies. But a $50 billion subsidy for the twenty-five companies that dominate local TV broadcasting would come to $2 billion on average per company.

Second, collective action problems are greater for cross-industry bias because the number of beneficiaries is larger (see Olson 1965). Continuing with the example above, the general corporate tax cut benefits millions of companies, whereas just twenty-five companies divvy up the lion's share of the spectrum grant to local TV broadcasters. Given the relatively small number of beneficiaries for industry-specific bias, the beneficiaries have less incentive to "free ride" on the political efforts of others.

Third, cross-industry bias is generally a lot harder to hide than industry-specific bias. For example, a liberal or conservative slant necessarily cuts across a large number of issues. Since both the political process and news programs are structured around information about competing ideological positions, the public is highly informed about ideological issues and can relatively easily detect ideological bias. In contrast, industry-specific bias cuts across a tiny fraction of total issues and often does not lend itself to an ideological frame. In the case of the primary area of broadcast industry lobbying, information policy, public deliberation suffers from an additional handicap: the issues tend to be technical and therefore intrinsically difficult for the public to understand.

Despite these theoretical grounds for believing that industry-specific bias would be relatively common, I found little direct evidence of such bias, in part because local TV news archives are all but inaccessible in the United States (Snider 2000a). Why, then, the discrepancy between the Allegation and the evidence necessary to back it up? Why have scholars—let alone journalists and even politicians—failed to find direct, verifiable evidence to support the Allegation? Why has no smoking gun been found? Does this mean the Allegation is false? Or does it mean that scholars have been looking for the evidence in all the wrong places?

THE PARADOX OF NEWS BIAS

The fundamental insight necessary to pick a method to study news bias is what I call the "paradox of bias," of which the "paradox of *news* bias" is a special case. The paradox of news bias is a logical implication of principal–agent theory.

In a principal–agent relationship, one person (the principal) delegates a task to another person (the agent) in return for some type of compensation (Lupia and McCubbins 1998). Such principal–agent relationships are prevalent in modern societies because no individual can efficiently produce the thousands of private and public goods he or she consumes. By delegating the production of the great majority of these goods to other individuals, specialization ensues and a complex, prosperous civilization becomes possible. In the context of local TV public affairs coverage, the local TV broadcasters are the agent, the local TV viewers the principal, and accurate, fair information about public affairs the product that broadcasters offer to exchange with viewers in return for their attention, which broadcasters can then sell to advertisers.

The two central problems of delegation are that 1) principals and agents often have conflicting interests, and 2) asymmetric information between principals and agents often cannot be completely eliminated. In the context of local TV broadcasters and the Telecom Act, the conflict of interest is that it is in the broadcasters' interest to pay (in-cash or in-kind contributions) the minimum amount for its share of the public spectrum, and in the public's interest to receive the maximum amount for its property.

Asymmetric information occurs when one party to a transaction has information not available to the other party and that *private information* has a material impact on the outcome of the transaction. *Bias* is the act of selectively changing incentives to acquire information so as to create a condition of asymmetric information.[5] *Opportunistic behavior* is behavior that increases the agent's welfare at the expense of the principals' welfare.[6] *Trustee-like behavior* means behavior that enhances the principal's welfare even if it might mean a reduction in the agent's welfare. The payoff from opportunistic behavior is the motive for bias. Since bias facilitates opportunistic behavior, it can be viewed as a type of opportunistic behavior.

According to principal–agent theory, agents have a strong incentive to hide opportunistic behavior, including bias, because no rational principal would pay someone to harm himself. A corollary is that if bias is discovered, it is no longer useful. The very act of discovery eliminates the motivation for the discovered phenomenon. Since humans can anticipate the act of discovery, they will not practice bias in a way that can be discovered. If by chance an act of bias is discovered, they will find a new method of bias, if one exists, that remains unlikely to be exposed.

The paradox of bias as applied to the news has important—and interrelated—methodological consequences for both scholars and politicians. For political communication scholars, the paradox of news bias implies that merely looking at public data sources (that is, actual media content) for direct and verifiable evidence of media bias is a fundamentally incomplete (if not flawed) method. The method of analyzing such output, sometimes employing highly elaborate statistical analyses, is called content analysis.

Scholars should also not expect broadcasters who engage in opportunistic behavior—or people who depend on broadcasters' goodwill—to go on the record with claims of broadcaster bias. Scholars should accept as common sense that people would not publicly incriminate themselves or others on whose goodwill they depend.

For politicians, the paradox of news bias has similar methodological consequences: politicians should not expect definitive evidence of news bias to be readily available. But there is one vital difference between scholars and politicians: politicians must make decisions even in an environment of uncertainty. Moreover, a politician's entire career may depend on a correct assessment of the consequences of angering his local TV broadcasters. Scholars, in contrast, can reserve judgment until better evidence (which may never arrive) can be found.

These different ways of coping with uncertainty are closely related to different professional rewards. Scholars are likely to be rewarded for rigorous methods as much as for important results; politicians, in contrast, are rewarded only for results.

In this chapter, I look at the world through the eyes of politicians. In particular, I explain how politicians can infer news bias even when they lack direct information about it. I conclude with an assessment of what this means for scholarly methods. I call this approach a "rational choice" approach because of its heavy emphasis on using incentive structures—the anticipated utility (benefits minus costs) of actions—to explain behavior. The emphasis on working out the logic of universal incentive structures (for example, principal–agent relationships) and applying them to a specific domain (for example, the relationship between news director and viewer) is also characteristic of rational choice theories. Contrary to much rational choice work, I eschew formal mathematical analysis here. Such analysis adds little insight given my application of a well-developed rational choice construct—principal–agent theory—to a specific situation. Contrary to much rational choice work, I am also primarily interested in the rationality of belief formation rather than behavior. Specifically, given the evidence, what is it rational for a politician to believe? And if given very poor evidence, how can a politician figure out the causal structure of the situation he confronts?

HOW POLITICIANS REASON ABOUT BIAS

Reasoning is the process of inferring from what one knows to what one doesn't know. Theories (or models) are the primary tools of reasoning because they allow us to make predictions based on limited data.

On what basis do politicians evaluate the news media's claims of objectivity and trusteeship? Let us contrast two types of reasoning: high-information and low-information (Simon 1957; Downs 1957; Popkin 1994; Sniderman, Brody, and Tetlock 1991).

In high-information reasoning, decision makers have all the relevant information needed to make a decision readily at hand. They know all the possible alternatives, carefully weigh them, and choose the best one for their purposes. In low-information reasoning, decision makers have little information directly relevant to the decision at hand. Instead, they use information shortcuts to come to a decision. These shortcuts involve using an indirect piece of information (also called a cue), which triggers a theory (also called a schema, interpretative construct, rule of thumb, or heuristic) that can be used to generate a prediction.

An example of low-information rationality is the way most voters choose their elected representatives for Congress. Instead of relying on extensive information about the candidates for office, voters are likely to rely on simple cues such as the candidate's party label, likeability, gender, ethnic group, hometown, or last name.

An example of high-information rationality might be the way elected representatives choose their chiefs of staff. Since many chiefs of staff are promoted internally or come from other congressional offices with which the representative has had a long relationship, representatives are likely to have highly detailed and relevant information about these candidates.

The decision about whether politicians use high- or low-information reasoning to make decisions about news bias affects the type of evidence considered relevant in analyzing news bias. If politicians use high-information reasoning, then the only relevant information has to do with direct evidence of news bias. However, if politicians use low-information reasoning, then a wealth of indirect evidence becomes relevant.

Of course, there is no sharp dividing line between high- and low-information conditions. Styles of reasoning are not mutually exclusive. For example, both politicians and scholars can combine them to gain confidence in their estimates of the probability of media bias under specified conditions. Snider and Page (1997, 1999a, 1999b) and Snider (1997, 2000b) have presented evidence appropriate for high-information reasoning.

In this chapter, my focus is on explaining how politicians (and thus scholars) can cope with the paradox of news bias, not proving that they do in fact reason that way. Nevertheless, it is useful to provide evidence that at least some people rely on low-information reasoning, especially the variant that concerns us here: the use of conventional lobbying behavior to infer the likelihood of media bias. I leave for other scholars the effort to more precisely assess the relative frequencies of the different reasoning styles.

One type of evidence for low-information reasoning comes from the Washington insiders described above who made the Allegation but who were unable or unwilling to back it up with the type of evidence that would be convincing in a court of law. (Courts don't convict people for murder merely for having a motive for murder; they need actual evidence of murder.) When I pointed out to the insiders I interviewed that the discrepancy between their Allegation and the available evidence made them sound paranoid, I on several occasions received a contemptuous reply that I understood nothing about politics because the reasons for the Allegation were obvious. Unfortunately, when I conducted my interviews, I was not sophisticated enough to ask why the Allegation was obvious because, following the conventions of the literature, I was not interested in indirect evidence of news bias. In fact, when I continued to probe for direct evidence, the interviewee, annoyed with my naiveté, occasionally brought the interview to an end.

Another type of evidence is the broadcasters' own fear of low-information reasoning. A vivid illustration of this occurred in 1986 when NBC's President Robert Wright proposed establishing an NBC political action committee (PAC) financed by employee contributions. Traditionally, newspaper and broadcasting companies had avoided setting up their own PACs because of the appearance of news bias it would create for their news divisions. Wright's proposal caused a furor within the press, including his own company, and he was forced to give it up. Brandon Tartikoff, president of NBC Entertainment, explained why not only news but also entertainment employees couldn't be allowed to contribute: "I wouldn't want . . . somebody in Iowa or Montana or Michigan or someplace else to think that the programming arm of a network had any sort of political debt." He continued that the entertainment division should remain "apolitical" and "not be seen as taking sides on issues" (NBC's *Tartikoff* 1987). A CBS spokesman explained why the CBS corporation, one of the two other TV networks at the time, lacked a

PAC: "We feel that having a PAC would be inconsistent with being a major and significant news organization. . . . We want to keep the political process separate from our job of informing the public" (Wright Ponders 1986). A *New York Times* editorial against NBC's proposed PAC summed up the conventional press view: "The appearances for the network are bad enough. It is a business, but it is also a primary instrument of information and opinion that depends on public trust. Mr. Wright exempts *NBC News* from his contribution program, but try making that distinction to ordinary citizens" (Speaker Wright 1986). Nevertheless, it is important to note that although NBC gave up its proposal for an impossible-to-hide PAC, its conventional, outside-the-public-eye lobbying never abated and arguably became more intense than ever in the years leading up to passage of the Telecom Act.[7]

Broadcasters' fear of low-information reasoning is manifest in the unusual efforts they make to hide evidence of conventional lobbying. An example of this logic occurred on February 8, 1996, when network TV executives collectively refused an invitation to stand next to President Clinton during the February 8 signing of the Telecommunications Act of 1996, a scene widely shown on TV. The network executives were conspicuous in their absence both because they were so actively involved in lobbying for the bill and because they were the only major industry involved in lobbying for the bill that did not appear on the dais with President Clinton.[8]

A common way local TV broadcasters hide their conventional lobbying is to never mention it when reporting their news. For example, TV station management aggressively lobbied members of Congress on the spectrum clause in the Telecom Act. All 535 members of Congress were invited to TV stations and told that this was a life-or-death financial issue for the TV station. Nevertheless, I was unable to find any evidence of the following type of disclaimer: "The member of Congress you are about to see has been lobbied by the management of this station for favorable laws and regulations that have a material impact on the financial well-being of this station." Why has this disclaimer been absent? The stations might answer that it is unnecessary because of a claimed "firewall" between the business and news sides of a TV station. Alternatively, they might simply answer that they would never allow such material considerations to color the news. But another possible interpretation is that TV stations fear that such a disclosure would shed doubt on the objectivity of the news they present. Given the many cracks in the firewall between the news and business sides of media organizations, and given local TV stations' pattern of secrecy regarding many such cracks (Snider and Page 1999a), the latter explanation may be more plausible.

It seems reasonable to infer that if the public can use nonmedia political action to infer media bias, then politicians could do the same, and with a much greater body of evidence, for they are the objects of the lobbying and can observe the discrepancy between what broadcasters do in private and show the public.

A RATIONAL CHOICE MODEL

When politicians lack direct evidence about likely opportunistic behavior in a given situation, they can use the *incentive structure* of the situation to make inferences. The incentive structure facing a political actor is "the full set of costs and benefits of behaving in one way rather than another" (Dowding 1996, 8; see also Goldman 1986). When political actors lack detailed information about a particular incentive structure, they can use their general knowledge of similar incentive structures to predict likely behavior.

When the prediction involves how an agent will interact with a principal, the politician can use a particular kind of rational actor theory, a principal–agent model of behavior. A principal–agent model is simply a general class of incentive structures. If a politician determines he is faced with a principal–agent relationship, he can use his entire experience with other principal–agent relationships, including his own experience as an agent for both voters and special interest groups, as a basis for predicting what will happen in this particular relationship, given his incomplete information.

The phrase "principal–agent model" may sound intimidating and academic, but it is really just a formal way to describe commonsense perceptions about how people interact in day-to-day situations and decide whom to trust. Every adult has personally experienced or observed thousands of principal–agent relationships in his or her life. As suggested earlier, the daily act of one person (the "principal") delegating a task to another (the "agent") is what makes modern civilization possible. Therefore, most people are pretty sophisticated principal–agent theorists, even if only in the narrow sphere in which they live.

Although politicians can use any principal–agent relationship to make an inference about another one, I will use a particular and well-known set of principal–agent relationships—well known to both politicians and the general public—to make my point. In figure 7.1 we see two sets of principal–agent relationships. Each set is named after its "dual agent," the agent that must serve two competing principals. Accordingly, the first set is named the "reporter case"; the second the "legislator case." Arrows points from principal to agent.

The chief reporter I have in mind here is the local TV news director; the chief legislator I have in mind is the member of Congress. The legislator case is the "reference case" because it is used to make inferences about the reporter case, the "test case."

Each case has four elements: 1) an agent that serves two principals with competing interests, 2) a primary principal, 3) a secondary principal, and

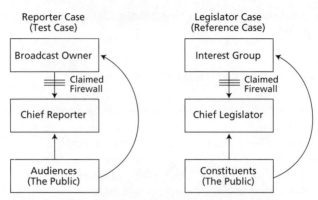

Figure 7.1.   The Common Incentive Structure of Two Dual Agents

4) a claimed firewall that prevents the dual agent from acting opportunistically on his conflict of interest. A primary principal is the one the agent publicly claims to serve. For example, local TV news directors claim to act on behalf of their audiences; members of Congress claim to act on behalf of their constituents. A secondary principal is the one the agent serves in private. For local TV news directors, it is their superiors and corporate owners. For members of Congress, it is special interest groups. The firewall is how the dual agent deals with public knowledge of a potential conflict of interest. For reporters, it is the claimed separation of the business and news sides of their corporate employer. For politicians, it is the claimed separation of the political and public policy sides of their offices.

In both the reporter and legislator cases, it should be extremely difficult for third parties to find verifiable evidence of a breach in a claimed firewall, even when such a breach exists. As argued earlier, this lack of evidence arises because agents (that is, reporters and legislators) have strong incentives to hide opportunistic behavior from principals (that is, the public).

REASONING FROM THE REFERENCE CASE TO THE TEST CASE

The argument here is that members of Congress can use information about the legislator case, of which they have direct and intimate knowledge, to make inferences about the reporter case. For example, let's assume that the two sets of principal–agent relationships described above are structured similarly from a strategic standpoint. If legislators don't believe the claims of interest groups and fellow legislators that campaign contributions are unrelated to policy stands, then it is easier for them to infer, all other things being equal, that the public trustee claims of broadcast owners and chief reporters may not be credible.

Of course, the legislator case is not the only reference case from which members of Congress can draw inferences regarding the reporter case. Indeed, every principal–agent relationship with which a member of Congress is familiar is a potential basis for making such an inference. The legislator case, however, is useful for three reasons.

First, the case is familiar to readers. The possibly corrupting influence of special interests on members of Congress is a staple of the scholarly and popular literatures. Most political scientists also know that it is hard to draw causal inferences from campaign contributions to legislative behavior.

Second, the case is familiar to members of Congress. All members of Congress deal with special interests on a regular basis. They use knowledge of such relationships to attack political opponents, and they expend great effort to make sure that no such influence is traceable and verifiable by their own potential opponents.

Third, as described above, the strategic position of the legislator and reporter is quite similar in both cases. The legislator and reporter each have a conflict of interest. Legislators need campaign contributions to win reelection; reporters need to please their bosses to keep their jobs. Both have strong incentives to claim that a firewall exists that prevents this conflict of interest from hurting the general public, their primary principal. Both have strong incentives to both hide and deny any evidence to the contrary.

A Control for Confounding Variables

One subcase of the legislator case is especially useful as a reference case because it controls for confounding variables. That subcase substitutes one particular interest group, broadcast owners, for interest groups in general, as the secondary principal. The reference case is now a closer approximation of the test case, and the member of Congress can therefore make a more valid inference from the reference case to the test case. In both cases now, the secondary agents and the principals are the same; that is, the conflict of interest in both cases now stems from the same person, the broadcast owner. The new reference case is depicted in figure 7.2.

The use of broadcast owners rather than interest groups in the reference case by no means guarantees a flawless inference, but it does increase the odds of drawing a correct conclusion. An example from day-to-day experience: consider a woman's mistrust of a man's protestations of love. If, all other things being equal, this inference is based on false claims made by former men she has known, the inference is not as good as if it were based on false claims by the man currently making the protestation. In neither case is the inference perfect, but the inference involving the same man, rather than different men, is likely to be more accurate.

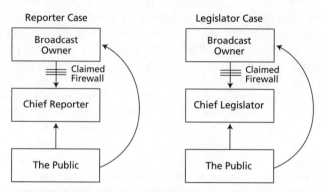

Figure 7.2.   The Reference Case Controlled for the Secondary Principal

An important feature of the more precise reference case is that broadcasters can manipulate it to send signals to legislators. Broadcasters know that legislators will use their own direct experience to make inferences about what they cannot experience. Therefore, if broadcasters simply act like every other interest group in their contacts with legislators, they may well be seen as "closet activists" rather than as objective purveyors of the truth.[9] In other words, conventional lobbying behavior by them may contain an implicit threat to employ news bias. Moreover, because conventional lobbying can be done outside the public eye, such a threat may well be invisible to the general public. Actual news bias, of course, is far riskier to a media outlet's reputation than is an implicit threat carried out in a one-on-one interchange with a member of Congress, an interchange that cannot be documented by third parties.

GATHERING EVIDENCE

How does one go about gathering evidence to substantiate this type of inference? I suggest three steps:

1. Verification

Verify the structure of the principal–agent relationships in figure 7.2. A simple way to do this is by looking at the ethics codes of the agents. These codes are useful because they identify the primary principal and exhort agents to place the interests of the primary principal over all secondary principals. The three agents of relevance here are chief legislators, chief reporters, and broadcast owners/lobbyists.

Chief Legislators

The U.S. Senate is one of two bodies that constitutes the U.S. Congress. Although each body has different ethics codes, the basic principles contained in them are the same. The U.S. *Senate Ethics Manual* clearly identifies a Senator's primary principal, the public. According to Senate Resolution 266, "[a] public office is a public trust" and each Senator "has been entrusted with public power by the people; that the officer holds this power in trust to be used only for their benefit and never for the benefit of himself or a few" (Senate 1996). The *Senate Ethics Manual* is 562 pages long and elaborates on this simple principle in great depth. One section of the manual describes establishing a "firewall of ignorance" as a solution to conflicts of interest created by financial contributions from special interests:

> [A] number of Senators have instituted practices to strictly separate fund raising from substantive legislative or constituent casework activities. . . . If the Senator or staff member does not know if an individual is a contributor, he or she is not required or encouraged to find out. Most Senate staff members are not provided with information regarding contributions and are unaware of whether an individual seeking assistance is a contributor. (234)

Chief Reporters

The Radio-Television News Directors Association (RTNDA) is the primary professional body of local television news directors. Its ethics code includes the following text:

> Professional electronic journalists should recognize that their first obligation is to the public . . .
> Professional electronic journalists should pursue truth aggressively and present the news accurately, in context, and as completely as possible . . .
> Professional electronic journalists should present the news fairly and impartially . . .
> Professional electronic journalists should present the news with integrity and decency, avoiding real or perceived conflicts of interest. (American League of Lobbyists 2001)

Lobbyists

The American League of Lobbyists is the premier association exclusively serving the interests of individual Washington lobbyists, including employees and outside contractors of the NAB. Its ethics code includes the following text:

> The association lobbyist will always deal in accurate, current and factual information, whether it is being reported to the employer or client, government

officials, the media or professional colleagues, and will not engage in misrepresentation of any nature.

The association lobbyist will acquire enough knowledge of public policy issues to be able to fairly present all points of view.

The association lobbyist will avoid conflicts of interest . . . and where conflict is unavoidable will communicate the facts fully and freely to those affected. (American League of Lobbyists 2001)

Other types of evidence could be used to ascertain the validity of the principal–agent relationships depicted in figure 7.2. Research questions could include: Can the secondary principal fire or otherwise harm the agent? What penalties can be imposed when an agent (for example, legislator or reporter) is publicly caught acting opportunistically with regard to the primary principal (for example, constituents or viewers)? How often do the agents publicly admit acting against the interests of the primary principal? When conflicts of interest are obvious to outside observers? Do agents claim that a firewall protects them from the influence of secondary principals?

Space limitations do not permit me to address these questions here. Suffice it to say that one never hears a prominent working legislator, lobbyist, or reporter claim, in a public setting, to be acting against the public interest. But one frequently hears them strongly deny accusations to the contrary. For all of these reasons, the principal–agent relationships depicted in figure 7.2 appear to be quite commonsensical.

2. Conflict of Interest

Find evidence of a conflict of interest between the secondary principal (the broadcast owner) and the primary principal (the voter). In the case of the grant of digital spectrum to broadcasters, it was in the interests of the broadcasters to get the spectrum at least cost (zero dollars) and the interests of the public to get the maximum return on its property (up to $70 billion according to an FCC estimate). For example, if a citizen were to walk out of a congressional building with an old beaten-up chair that the U.S. Congress valued at $5 for its junk sale, this would be considered a theft of public property and the citizen could be thrown into jail. Similarly, if broadcasters were to take control, without payment, of billions of dollars worth of airwaves, the public might feel it wasn't getting fair compensation.

Willingness to Act

Find evidence that the secondary principal (the broadcast owners) were willing to act on their conflict of interest. The information here can be divided into two categories: nonmedia lobbying that is public (that is, disclosed by government mandate and/or reported in the news) and that which is private (that is, is known by broadcasters and/or politicians).

Public Activities

The public portion of the broadcasters' lobbying primarily consists of PAC expenditures, lobbying expenditures, and public comments by Washington representatives of the broadcast industry. According to the Center for Responsive Politics, during the 1997–1998 election cycle the National Association of Broadcasters, the largest lobbying organization of the combined radio, local TV, and network TV companies, spent $456,671 on PAC contributions to federal candidates, $28,196 on soft money donations to political parties, and $9,880,000 on lobbying expenditures (Open 2000). The lobbying expenditures included the paid services of more than forty Washington insiders.

Private Activities

One of the most important private activities of the local TV broadcasters is their grassroots lobbying. Most of this lobbying is orchestrated through the NAB. The NAB's information flow to and from local TV broadcasters signals a lobbying effort of considerable frequency and intensity.

The NAB regularly sends policy information to local TV broadcasters with the intent both to inform and to activate them for lobbying purposes. This information includes the following: 1) *TV Today*, a weekly fax sent to rank-and-file TV station general managers; 2) *Congressional Contact*, a monthly newsletter sent to an elite group of local broadcasters called "LLCs," who are recognized for their interest and prowess in lobbying Congress; 3) *Telejournal*, a monthly satellite TV–delivered policy update, mostly watched by LLCs; and 4) *Legislative Issue Updates*, distributed semiannually to LLCs.[10] All the above publications, with the exception of the *Legislative Issue Updates*, regularly encourage local TV broadcasters to lobby their member of Congress on key issues.

In addition to these periodical publications, the NAB sends a substantial amount of nonperiodic public policy information. Regarding the grant of digital spectrum to broadcasters, for example, the NAB sent numerous special fax alerts to NAB board members, TV group heads, state association executives, and rank-and-file general managers. All of these alerts focused on applying pressure to one or more members of Congress, usually just before Congress was expected to make a key decision.

Whenever a local broadcaster lobbies a member of Congress, a "Contact Report" is filled out and sent to the NAB. One purpose of the contact report is to identify friends and foes, although the results of the contact reports are never released publicly. Nevertheless, the lobbying campaign is largely built around the feedback obtained from these reports.

The NAB frequently sends out lobbying toolkits, which are substantially similar to those used by other special interest groups. They include a call for action, a detailed action plan, and tools to implement the action plan. In early 1996, for example, the NAB sent out two lobbying toolkits, one brief (eight pages) and one long (sixty-five pages), designed to prevent the digital spectrum from being auctioned to the highest bidder rather than simply given to existing broadcasters. The shorter toolkit, sent out during the third week in January 1996, was given the title "A Call to Arms for Television Broadcasters." The toolkits were based on detailed public opinion research.

CONCLUSION

The paradox of news bias suggests that neither politicians nor political communication scholars should expect to find evidence of bias in easily available documents. For scholars, this means that classic methods of researching bias, such as content analysis and interviews with agents (such as chief reporters), are unlikely to yield valid data no matter how sophisticated the statistical apparatus. For politicians, it means that they would be wise to rely on low-information reasoning when making inferences about bias. As noted before, low-information reasoning involves the use of indirect evidence as a proxy for direct evidence.

One type of indirect evidence is conventional lobbying activity. Politicians can use nonmedia (or "conventional") lobbying activity to update their beliefs about the probability of media influence. One of the noteworthy features of most of this lobbying is that it is done out of the public eye but is nevertheless visible to politicians.

From the paradox of bias we thus arrive at a paradoxical conclusion: the most realistic way to study the scope and impact of media bias may be to study its nonmedia counterpart, where bias is defined in terms of a desire to create asymmetric information favoring media owners' interests.

Studying nonmedia lobbying does not preclude studying media content. At some point, one or more powerful politicians or interest groups will have a strong incentive to oppose the broadcasters on an issue of great importance to the broadcasters. The resulting situation will be a "critical test" of the broadcasters' willingness to engage in overt news bias. The politics surrounding the Cable Act of 1992 (Snider 2000b) and the Telecom Act of 1996 (Snider 1997; Snider and Page 1997), for example, provide two such critical tests. Nevertheless, the paradox of news bias and the resulting heavy reliance politicians place on low-information reasoning suggest that the opportunities for such critical tests will be rare.

The media's practical goal of influencing politicians rather than the general public also suggests a crucial change in research design when studying both nonmedia and media bias. The lion's share of the broadcasters' lobbying focuses on influencing a few key senior members of Congress who control what legislation gets introduced and how it gets framed. This suggests that broad-based content analyses of national media are misplaced. What counts is how local TV media portray people like Representative Billy Tauzin (R–Louisiana; chair of the House Telecommunications Subcommittee), and Senator Conrad Burns (R–Montana; chair of the Senate Communications Subcommittee). Unfortunately, due to inaccessible local TV archives (Snider 2000a), this is a daunting undertaking.

Even when a critical test via content analysis is appropriate, careful study of the media's conventional lobbying may be necessary to identify their most important pocketbook issues and potential allies and opponents. Learning this type of information may require skills more often associated with conventional investigative reporting than with conventional political communication scholarship. To assume that accurate information about media incentives, allies, and opponents can be learned by studying the texts produced by trade or mass media may well be a naïve assumption.

Traditional content analysis may be best suited to the study of ideological and cross-industry bias (where bias would be hard to hide) or other types of media behavior (where the "paradox of bias" is not a relevant consideration because the media have nothing to hide). The methods outlined here may be best suited for industry- and company-specific bias where the incentives to create bias and the ability to hide it are greatest. Given the growing importance of the information technology sector and the active role the media play in determining information policy, the effort necessary to study this type of bias is surely justified.

If industry-specific bias is important, then the scholarly literature on "media monopoly" needs to be rethought. The unit of analysis in such studies has conventionally been the individual company (Bagdikian 1992; Alger 1998), but on the basis of the logic presented here, the unit of analysis should be varied with the type of bias being studied. In the case of information policy bias, for example, the unit of analysis should be set at the level of the industry rather than that of the individual company. Studies should focus not on the number of individual media outlets but on the extent to which local TV broadcasters, network TV broadcasters, daily newspapers, cable news networks, and other news outlets have common interests that may be adverse to the public. If the interests of the press and public conflict, then the key research question becomes whether other democratic intermediaries—such as political parties and competing interest groups—are sufficiently powerful to keep the press in check.

NOTES

1. The transfer of spectrum rights from the public to broadcasters actually involved a series of steps culminating in the FCC's grant of digital licenses to the broadcasters in April 1997. The 1996 Telecom Act, however, is widely perceived to have been the crucial step that made the rights transfer a near certainty.

2. Public spokespeople for broadcasters denied the spectrum was a grant in the sense of a gift. Compared to standard property exchanges, the grant appeared to be a gift because it involved no explicit, quantifiable, and legally enforceable quid pro quo. Broadcaster supporters called the new spectrum a "loan," but unlike conventional loans, the loaned property was ambiguously defined (thus providing loopholes to diminish its value); had indefinite duration; and no explicit, quantifiable, and legally enforceable interest payments.

3. The four additional *Wall Street Journal* Allegations: "I-Way Detours," Dec 27, 1995; "Asides," April 26, 1996, A20; "Off the Dole," January 24, 1996, A14; Alan Murray, "Digital TV Giveaway Foils Campaign Reform," March 17, 1997. The four *New York Times* Allegations: Max Frankel, "Digital Castles in the Sky," February 25, 1996, 38; "Another Broadcast Giveaway," June 25, 1997, A26; William Safire, "Broadcast Lobby Triumphs," July 23, 1997; Leslie Wayne, "Broadcast Lobby's Formula: Airtime + Money = Influence," May 5, 1997, C1.

4. Recent exceptions include Sparrow (1999) and Gilens and Hertzman (2000).

5. This definition of bias differs from typical journalistic accounts of bias (for example, Bagdikian 1992; Schudson 1998b), which contrast bias with fairness or objectivity and do not clearly specify an audience (principal) that is harmed by the media's (agent's) act of bias.

6. The principal–agent literature often uses the term "shirking" to describe opportunistic behavior.

7. According to interviews with telecom lobbyists, the breakdown of the rank-and-file broadcaster's inhibition against conventional lobbying is widely considered one of the NAB's greatest triumphs since Eddie Fritts took over the organization in the early 1980s.

8. The intensity of network lobbying is indicated by the following events: On November 30, 1995, the network TV presidents met with Senate Majority Leader Bob Dole to make sure that he didn't oppose the spectrum grant to broadcasters. On January 4, 1996, the day after a New York Times op-ed supported Dole's attack of the spectrum "giveaway," the network TV presidents initiated a direct-calling campaign to senior members of the U.S. Senate.

9. Examples of inconspicuous conventional behavior include making passionate one-on-one pleas for legislation, bundling campaign contributions from nonbroadcasters, and providing highly valued but nonreportable perks (see Snider and Page 1999b).

10. The NAB and the vast majority of its members refuse to make this lobbying material public. However, much of the material is distributed broadly enough that it is possible to find an occasional broadcaster willing to share it for scholarly purposes.

8

Voice, Polling, and the Public Sphere

Lisbeth Lipari

> Vox populi may be vox dei, but very little attention shows that there has never been any agreement as to what Vox means or as to what Populus means.
>
> —Sir Henry Maine, *The Nature of Public Opinion*

The success of democracy is said to rest upon public opinion. As many scholars have recently noted, however, fundamental questions persist about who and what constitutes a public, who speaks for whom, what constitutes an opinion, and how such opinions are best communicated (Bickford 1996b; Fishkin 1995; Fraser 1994). Despite many doubts about the reliability and suitability of polls as a surrogate for public discourse, politicians, journalists, and citizens turn with increasing frequency to public opinion polls as a manifestation of public opinion. The Roper Center's POLL database, which advertises itself as "the most comprehensive, up-to-date source for U.S. public opinion data" (Roper 2000), contains over a quarter-million poll questions asked since 1935. Each year the number of poll questions archived in POLL grows—in 1945 alone, a total of 1,880 questions were added to the POLL database. In 1995, another 13,297 questions were added to POLL. Further, the number of organizations conducting public opinion polls continues to increase. Bauman and Herbst (1994) report that in 1972 two media organizations conducted three polls, while by 1988 eight organizations conducted 259 polls.

The results obtained from public opinion polls serve a variety of political purposes. Politicians make both visible and invisible uses of polls in political campaigns, policy initiatives, and legislative reforms. Journalists turn increasingly to polls for seemingly factual information with which to construct news stories. In addition, public opinion polls also have a less recognized use in the production and maintenance of political symbols. In this chapter I briefly sketch the outline for a new agenda in political communication research that examines polling from three new perspectives: 1) as a symbolic form, 2) as a form of discursive social interaction, and 3) as an ideological form that perpetuates certain dominant beliefs. Each of these perspectives departs from the presuppositions of most polling research, which considers it to be a more-or-less accurate measure of public opinion—at worst a methodologically flawed research tool, and at best a virtual plebiscite that provides citizens an opportunity to express their views on public issues and thereby hold government accountable to their wishes.

In order to situate these arguments in a specific social and political context, this chapter draws on a corpus of poll questions about welfare drawn from the POLL database in 1994, just prior to passage of the Personal Responsibility and Work Opportunity Reconciliation Act of 1996, which dramatically revised the nation's public assistance (welfare) system. In this chapter, I raise and begin to address questions which, while specific to the case study, are capable of broader application.

- How have researchers, politicians, and journalists written, deployed, and interpreted polling about welfare?
- What voices and perspectives are included in and excluded from polling about welfare? What presuppositions are embedded in the poll questions?
- How do these voices, perspectives, and presuppositions influence political discourse in the U.S. public sphere?
- What ethical implications do these conceptual and interpretive practices have for discourse in the public sphere? For democracy?

SYMBOLIC POLITICS

Despite what might appear to be an arbitrary association, public opinion and welfare share, among other things, a common history. Both gained institutional legitimacy in the United States in the 1930s and both shortly thereafter assumed a central role in political life. In fact, the earliest poll question archived in the POLL database is a 1935 Gallup question about government spending on relief (Gallup 1935). But what the institutions of polling and welfare share most is the fact that while both appear to derive their legitimacy from the instrumental power of numbers, both harness enormous social and symbolic influence. For example, since their inception in the 1935 Social Security Act, welfare programs have been a continual source of heated political debate, despite accounting for only about 1 percent of the federal budget. In much public discourse, welfare serves to symbolize indolence and moral failure. For the past six decades it has been repeatedly portrayed by politicians and the media as the province of unwed (hence unfit) mothers, teenagers, and slothful women who mindlessly bear child after child in order to increase their benefits. As governor of California, and then later as president, Ronald Reagan made political capital by referring to welfare recipients as lazy "welfare queens" joyriding around in Cadillacs.[1]

Sixty years after the original social security legislation passed, public welfare programs became, for the first time since the New Deal, subject to attack by a Democratic president. In his 1992 campaign address to the Democratic convention, then-presidential-candidate Bill Clinton struck a historic consensus between Democrats and Republicans by promising to "change welfare as we know it." Two years after he was elected, he fulfilled that promise. The seeming consensus, however, reflected few of the critiques advocated by progressive Democrats and antipoverty and welfare rights activists, such as the provision of offering more generous and less stigmatizing income guarantees for children and poor working families. Instead, Clinton's welfare reform consisted primarily of age-old demonizing and punitive measures advocated by conservative critics of the welfare state who seek to blame the poor for their poverty—such as anti-immigrant eligibility restrictions, temporal and monetary benefit limits, and mandatory work requirements. For several months in 1994, conservative politicians even attempted to resurrect the nineteenth-century orphanage as an instrument of welfare "reform."

Needless to say, audible among the hue and cry for welfare reform issued by politicians and policymakers was the so-called voice of the public, as measured, of course, by public opinion polls. In fact, in much public discourse the twin symbolic evocations of polling and welfare worked together in concert. Consider, for example, the following newspaper lead from a *Los Angeles Times* article on welfare reform: "The welfare reform plan that President Clinton released Tuesday sits squarely in the center of public opinion on this historically divisive issue, according to several recent polls (Brownstein 1994, A14).

According to politicians and journalists, the American public despised welfare, revered work, and had some measure of ambivalence about the poor (Weaver, Shapiro, and Jacobs 1995). These claims are, of course, grounded in seemingly incontrovertible evidence: polling data. In the years prior to the 1994 welfare legislation, poll questions about welfare became increasingly prevalent, if not ubiquitous. As shown on figure 8.1, the number of public opinion poll questions and newspaper reports containing the word "welfare" soared from 1969 to 1994.

Figure 8.2 shows that, in 1994, as many poll questions were asked about welfare as were asked about taxes—purportedly the central political issue of our time—and about defense—a government program that spends roughly twenty times more federal tax dollars annually than does welfare (Herman 1995). Figure 8.2 also illustrates the extent to which welfare functions as a

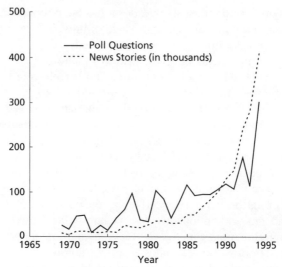

Note: Data for this figure were obtained by an electronic keyword search of the word "welfare" in the POLL and the Lexis-Nexis Major Newspaper databases in March 1996.

Figure 8.1.   Number of Public Opinion Poll Questions and Newspaper Stories Containing the Word "Welfare": 1969–1994

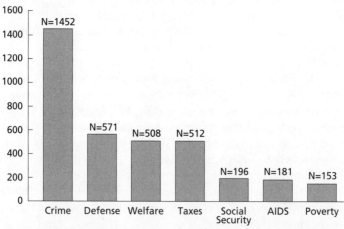

Note: Data for this figure were obtained by an electronic keyword search of the words "crime," "defense," "welfare," and so forth in the POLL database in March 1996.

Figure 8.2.   Comparison of the Number of Public Opinion Questions Containing Selected Keywords in 1994

symbolic political issue (Handler 1995; Schram 1995; Edelman 1977). That is, the amount of public attention given to welfare via polling is disproportionate to the magnitude and scope of the program in any kind of practical or material sense. As many questions were asked about welfare, which serves forty million people (two-thirds of whom are children) and consumes about 1 percent of the federal budget, as were asked about defense and taxes. Further, far fewer poll questions were asked about social security—which spends roughly thirty-five times more federal tax dollars and serves about three times more people than welfare. No topic received as much attention as the highly symbolic issue of crime.

POLLING AS SYMBOL

Like welfare, polling also conjures up tremendous symbolic resonance. It symbolizes all the promise of democracy by ostensibly giving voice to the will of the people.[2] Yet ever since it became widespread in the 1940s, critics have questioned the validity of polling. Blumer (1960) cautioned against mistaking the results of public opinion polls for authentic opinions of the public. His concerns were echoed recently by Carey (1995), who argued that polling simulates, rather than stimulates, public opinion. Other scholars of public opinion such as Bennett (1993), Edelman (1988, 1993), Herbst (1993, 1995), and Zaller (1992, 1994) have questioned the degree to which opinion polls can represent the complex and myriad thoughts, beliefs, and desires of citizens. Still other scholars, such as Bourdieu (1979) and Converse (1964), question whether it is even possible for polls to do so because citizens do not possess opinions in the sense of "formulated discourse with a pretension to coherence" (Bourdieu 1979, 130). Other scholars, such as Harrison (1995) and Hogan (1997), doubt whether polls do in fact scientifically elicit information from respondents.

   While it may be debatable whether and in what form public opinion actually exists, there is no question that public opinion polling flourishes as an academic, business, journalistic, and political enterprise. Why? One answer may be that polling functions as a symbolic cultural form that sustains, and to some degree fulfills, a deep sense of longing for community and connection. In other words, polling is a highly modernized and technical form of ritual communication, what Carey called the "sacred ceremony that draws persons together in fellowship and commonality" (Carey 1995, 18). Polling reaffirms cultural mythologies about democracy and vox populi—some of the founding original myths of U.S. culture. This symbolic dimension of polling is borne out in the repeated references by politicians and journalists to public opinion, as measured—of course—by polling. Consider, for example, how the incessant polling about welfare was used by politicians during the welfare reform debates of 1994. The following statement was made by Rep. Clyburn (Dem.–S.C.), during the 1994 welfare reform debates: "Many Americans agree that the current system of welfare exacerbates the problems of poverty. A recent poll found that 'many believe the current welfare system encourages dependence and fails to provide sufficient help for people to make the transition to self-reliance'" (U.S. Congress 1994).

In this statement, Rep. Clyburn supports his claim that welfare exacerbates poverty not by citing research on poverty but by citing a recent poll. By doing so, he reaffirms ideologies of both populism and individualism, all the while concealing the dubiousness of the initial claim. He reaffirms populism by using polling data as evidence for a highly polemical claim, and he reaffirms individualism by invoking the dual icons of liberal individualism—self-sufficiency and self-reliance. Similarly, in 1996, Rep. Dan Burton (Rep.–Ind.) attributed the passage of welfare reform legislation to public opinion—as measured by polling:

> They talked about welfare reform, but they never did anything about it. For 40 years we had a welfare state that grew and grew and grew. . . . We changed that. We passed welfare reform. The President has tried to take credit for it, but he vetoed that bill twice. The only reason he signed it the third time we sent it to him was because the American people demanded welfare reform. And he signed it because he saw in the polls that about 78 percent of the people wanted welfare reform because they could not stand that socialistic trend anymore. (U.S. Congress 1996)

Or consider the words of Sen. Olympia Snowe (Rep.–Me.):

> In an August 1993 Yankelovich poll, respondents were asked, "Do you think our current welfare system helps more families than it hurts, or hurts more families than it helps?" Twenty-four percent said that it helps more, while a commanding 62 percent said it hurts more. Many might wonder what it is that we have bought with over $5 trillion in welfare funds over the past 30 years. Many might wonder what the returns have been on an investment we made three generations ago. (U.S. Congress 1995)

In each of these three examples, politicians legitimate their preferred policies and agendas by citing public opinion polls. By doing so, they not only justify their political agendas but also harness the symbolic capital of vox populi. As a symbolic form, polling is born in part from the needs of a vast democratic nation to create the feeling of a city–state. Polling is a way of celebrating democracy. With its inherent appeals to populism, not to mention its scientific allure, polling therefore becomes irresistible. It seems to offer up, in an instant, a coherent portrait of the collective will and tells us, supposedly, who we are, where we're going, what we want. It begs us, urgently and incessantly, to remember that despite our differences, we are a unity.

Thus, regardless of what public opinion "really" is or what polls "really" measure, public opinion polls play an important symbolic role in the construction of democratic consensus. And although the participants in poll interviews themselves are relatively few in number, the symbolic resonance of poll discourse is amplified in the interpretations of pollsters, policymakers, politicians, newspaper readers, and TV audiences.

POLLING AS DISCOURSE

Despite the proliferation of polls and polling research, public opinion scholars recognize that how poll questions are worded can significantly affect responses. As early as the 1940s, when public opinion polling was still in its infancy, researchers discovered that even seemingly minor changes in wording could produce large differences in answers (Cantril 1940; Hyman and Sheatsley 1950; Kornhauser 1966). Yet in spite of this early research, published studies on question wording and its implications for polling were infrequent until the late 1970s. In 1970, Noelle-Neumann warned that the influence of question wording was being underestimated in opinion research and that far from being a "sturdy measuring instrument," the results of structured questionnaires "are highly dependent on detail of questionnaire construction and wording" (Noelle-Neumann 1970, 191).

In the late 1970s, Schuman and Presser (1981) reinvigorated the study of question effects with their systematic study of question form, wording, and content. Their goal was not so much to explain particular variations in word content but rather to deal with general features of question format. This research sparked a host of other studies dealing with such issues as order and context effects (Schuman, Kalton, and Ludwig 1983; Schuman, Presser, and Ludwig 1981); wording effects (Bishop, Oldendick, and Tuchfarber 1978; Bradburn 1982; Hippler and Schwarz 1986; Krosnick 1989; Lockerbie and Borrelli 1990; Rasinski 1989; Schuman and Presser 1981; Smith 1987a); form effects (Bishop, Oldendick, and Tuchfarber 1982; Petty, Rennier, and Cacioppo 1987); vague quantifier effects (Bradburn and Miles 1979); intensifier effects (O'Muircheartaigh, Gaskell, and Wright 1993); prestige name effects (Smith and Squire 1990); and ambiguous term effects (Fowler 1992).

These studies, like much of the research about polling, tend to view question wording as a methodological problem wherein different responses to similar questions are interpreted as a measurement error that interferes with the researcher's goal of reliably and objectively measuring true opinions. Most of these studies appear to assume that language is a relatively transparent medium that transmits consistent and stable meanings from citizens to pollsters and that, given accurate and objective opinion-measuring instruments, people will answer questions in a self-consistent manner. But as communication scholars know, language is not a transparent medium but the means by which humans construct and negotiate their shared social world. Like all public discourse, the wording of poll questions embeds assumptions about how we come to describe, know, and structure the world. Furthermore, meaning (especially the meaning of poll questions) is inherently contested and ambiguous, and people may hold many opinions that may, to researchers, seem contradictory and ambiguous. Scholars know that people can have multiple opinions on the same topic that vary according to the situation in which they are expressed (Bogart 1972; Schiff 1994; Zaller 1994).

Despite the growing understanding of the importance of language in polling, however, few scholars have investigated polling as a form of discourse. Some have likened public opinion polls to conversation, and some linguists have suggested that interviews are essentially conversational in nature (Frankel 1990; Labov and Fanshel 1977; Coulthardt and Ashby 1975). Sudman and Bradburn, for example, contend that survey respondents are often motivated by the opportunity to "talk about a number of topics with a sympathetic listener" (Sudman and Bradburn 1982, 4). They quote Bingham and Moore's definition of the research interview as a "conversation with a purpose" (Bingham and Moore 1959, 4). Atkin and Chaffee (1972) report that survey respondents tend to alter their responses to questions on the basis of conversational social norms, such as coorientation. Similarly, Johnstone (1991) found both interviewers and poll respondents to be sensitive and responsive to social politeness norms in survey interviews. As a general rule, of course, scholars are not oblivious to the dissimilarities between conversations and surveys. Some have noted that, unlike participants in conversation, interviewers are obliged to keep their respondents' answers confidential and are barred from judging or evaluating their comments (Atkin and Chaffee 1972; Sudman and Bradburn 1982). They also note that unlike actual conversation, interviews make evasions difficult because an interviewer will repeat a question until the respondent answers the question as worded. Finally, Sudman and Bradburn contend that respondents have an obligation to "answer each question truthfully and thoughtfully" (Sudman and Bradburn 1982, 5), a dictum that often fails to apply in everyday conversations.

Other scholars have examined how conversational social interaction in poll interviews influences and often conflicts with the intended goals of survey research (Suchman and Jordan 1990; Schaeffer and Maynard 1996; Houtkoop-Steenstra and Antaki 1997). These scholars argue that the social interaction in interviews works to compromise the validity of survey responses because cognition is a social rather than an individual act and interview discourse will therefore, by necessity, be interactive and collaborative. Aside from concerns with validity, other scholars have explored questions of power and control in institutionalized medical and legal interviews. Frankel (1990), for example, noted that the medical interview is far more constrained and asymmetrical than conversation. This is doubly true for closed-ended polling interviews where the structured adjacency pair sequences permit neither reciprocity nor spontaneity. As Briggs has noted, "the typical interview situation grants the interviewer principal rights to topic selection by virtue of her or his provision of the questions. In sum, interviewers maintain a great deal of control over the interaction" (Briggs 1986, 56). Similarly, unlike everyday conversations, neither speaker in the polling interview is licensed to "author" the discourse she or he speaks. Both the interviewer and the respondent are what Goffman (1981) would call "animators" who produce talk but who do not own it completely. Interviewers read a script written by the polling consultant on behalf of the poll sponsor from which they are instructed not to deviate. Similarly, an appropriate "response" from a respondent consists of a number of scripted options provided to the respondent by the interviewer but actually written (or authored) by the concealed and/or unacknowledged poll sponsor who initiates, funds, and publishes the poll research. And even further unlike conversations, neither the author nor the animator is individually committed to (that is, takes personal, individual responsibility or ownership) that which they say. Instead, the words uttered by poll respondents purportedly belong not only to the respondent himself (or herself) but to a greater abstraction—the public. The act of animating the author's speech does not identify the respondent individually with this speech, but instead identifies the public—as represented by the respondent—with the speech. Unlike persons in conversation, the respondent, one of 2,000 or so randomly selected, anonymous people, is "authorized" to speak on behalf of, or as a representative of, "the public."

INSTITUTIONAL DISCOURSE

Given these differences between polls and conversations, it appears that polling discourse cannot be understood simply or even primarily as a subspecies of conversation. Rather, it belongs to the genre of the interrogative—the species of discourse aimed most specifically at eliciting responses from an interlocutor (Lipari 2000). The interview has long been a staple not only of social science research in fields such as anthropology, communication, psychology, and sociolinguistics but of myriad social interactions ranging from doctor/patient encounters to police interrogations. Labov and Fanshel (1977) define the interview as a speech event in which one person extracts information from another person and is thus a staple component of what has recently been dubbed "institutional discourse." According to Drew and Sorjonen, "The study of institutional dialogue focuses on the ways in which conduct is shaped or constrained by the participants' orientations to social institutions . . . on their use of language to pursue institutional goals" (Drew and

Sorjonen 1997, 93). Of the many varieties of institutional discourse, legal discourse presents perhaps the closest relative to polling discourse because of the considerable constraints placed on speakers in both contexts. Like witnesses on a stand, poll respondents are given very little latitude for responding to questions and their wording is strictly proscribed by institutional discourse—that of the court or that of the political elites who sponsor and interpret poll questions. For example, Conley and O'Barr (1990) outline how in American courts, witnesses cannot repeat others' words, speculate, comment on reactions and feelings, digress, incorporate suppositions, judgments, or opinions. "We were repeatedly told by witnesses that the process of testifying under the constraints imposed by the court environment had been one of the most frustrating aspects of their experience with the legal system. . . . Everything witnesses say is framed by the lawyer's questions" (Conley and O'Barr 1990, 168–169). The degree of control exercised by questioners in the court is comparable to the degree of control exercised by pollsters where the discourse is restricted solely to the interview schedule. Atkinson and Drew (1979) note that statements made in court are perceived by witnesses as being more binding than statements made in ordinary conversations. Similarly, like legal discourse, the opinions decreed through the court of "public opinion" gain a legitimacy not found in feelings espoused in ordinary conversation.

In fact, poll respondents may have more constraints placed on their discourse than do witnesses on the stand. For example, witnesses can attempt to resist or correct implications embedded in an attorney's questions by repairing or substituting alternative words or phrases, but poll respondents cannot. Further, poll respondents may be inadvertently subject to the kind of undermining and distortion that witnesses can face on the stand. In a study of courtroom interrogations of child witnesses, Brennan (1995) documents a number of linguistic strategies that lawyers use to undermine the credibility of the witnesses, such as negative rhetorical questions, the use of passive voice, complex embedding, backward referencing, and nominalization. As discussed below, many of these linguistic forms are also found in polling discourse.

POLLING AND IDEOLOGY

Viewing polls as a form of discourse entails more than looking at what answers polls elicit from respondents. It also involves studying what and how poll questions construct political issues and communicate these constructions to respondents and larger audiences of poll readers. Poll questions not only stipulate the shape, scope, and terms of an individual's response but they also play a role in constructing and constricting discourse in larger arenas of political communication, such as the news media, legislative debates, and policy initiatives.

Like all forms of political discourse, polling is a site of ideological struggle. Poll questions play a significant role in the legitimation of social policy, whether by default or design. Although poll results seem to reflect what the public wants, they do so only within the confines of preselected response options provided to respondents. Public opinion poll questions thus serve, in part, to set the terms of public policy debates. Like the media, poll questions perform a status-conferring function (Lazarsfeld and Merton 1960) in society. They identify and thereby legitimate the political issues and public policy options deemed worthy of consideration. They also limit the range of possible answers and, in so doing, conceal a host of ideologically charged presuppositions. As a form of institutional discourse, many of these presuppositions originate in elite (and media) discourse.

Unfortunately, the issue of how public opinion poll questions emerge is still little understood (Smith 1987b). Interestingly, Smith likens the process of selecting and wording poll questions to the process of selecting and wording news stories. But as media scholars have demonstrated, news media content is inextricably bound up with the policy interests of elites, many of whom serve as the primary sources and subjects of news. Dearing (1989) suggests that the content of public opinion polls is derived from a combination of the policy interests of elites (that is, politicians, political parties, and interest groups), and the policy options and issues being covered in the media (which, in turn, are highly influenced by elites). Dearing (1989) reports that poll questions about AIDS were not conducted until after the media increased coverage of the issue. He also found that how AIDS was portrayed in the mass media influenced how survey questions concerning AIDS were framed.

The next section of this chapter provides a general overview of poll questions about welfare from 1994 and examines how these questions are framed in ways that reproduce long-standing presuppositions and preoccupations of elite policy discourse about welfare and poverty, and thereby offer few opportunities for dissenting public discourse. Through critical analyses of the poll questions themselves, I intend to demonstrate how poll questions embed ideologically charged presuppositions that evoke stereotypes, perpetuate myths, and sustain status quo configurations of symbolic, economic, and political power in the contemporary United States.

GENERAL OVERVIEW OF THE CORPUS

The analysis is based on a corpus of 244 poll questions conducted either by or for media or other recognized polling organizations in 1994 and housed in the Roper POLL archives.[3] For reference, table 8.1 displays the number of questions asked by each polling organization included in the analysis.

Of the 244 questions in the 1994 corpus, about half (n = 124) focused on then-current policy initiatives that proposed to solve "the problem" of welfare. These questions invited respondents to favor or oppose a variety of policy proposals such as orphanages, work requirements, time limits, and denying benefits to a variety of people including legal and illegal immigrants, teen mothers, and mothers who give birth while on welfare. They also asked respondents to evaluate proposals such as time limits on receipt of benefits, additional work requirements for recipients, increasing or decreasing public spending on welfare, the general need for "reform," and so forth. These questions thus focused less on welfare recipients and more on the welfare system by asking respondents to evaluate the quality or quantity of factors such as "Do you think that government spending on job training programs for people on welfare should be increased, decreased, or kept about the same?" (CBS News/*New York Times* 1994).

Another forty-seven questions in the corpus invited respondents to agree, disagree, or otherwise identify with a number of global statements about welfare recipients, poor people, the welfare system, and the government. Many of these statements contained stereotypical and stigmatizing judgments about welfare and welfare recipients, such as "immigrants use more than their fair share of government services" (Harris 1994), "many of the poor are trying to get something for nothing" (Greenburg 1994), and "poor people have become too dependent on government assistance programs" (Princeton 1994). Other questions in this group focused on sweeping generalizations about welfare recipients and the reasons why people use welfare. These questions invited respondents to recapitulate stereotypes and misconceptions about welfare recipients and welfare such as: "most people who

Table 8.1.   Number of Questions on Welfare from Each Polling Organization

Polling Organization	Frequency	Percentage
Gallup	59	24
CBS/*New York Times*	37	15
Princeton (*Times Mirror*)	36	15
Yankelovich	35	15
Hart and Teeter	27	11
NBC/Associated Press	21	10
Los Angeles Times	11	4
ABC	5	2
Washington Post	5	2
Other	8	2
n	244	100

receive money from welfare could get by without it if they really tried" (CBS News/*New York Times* 1994), that welfare recipients are "taking advantage of the system" (Yankelovich 1994), that "poor young women have babies in order to collect welfare" (*Los Angeles Times* 1994), that the welfare system "makes poor people dependent and encourages them to stay poor" (*Los Angeles Times* 1994), and that welfare "discourages poor people from finding work" (Yankelovich 1994).

These questions echo well-publicized sentiments expressed by antiwelfare critics. For example, in congressional debates on welfare reform in 1994, Republicans defended the proposition that "welfare has done more harm than good" by demonizing welfare and referring to it, variously, as a drug, a monster, a disease, and a form of slavery (Delay 1994). These poll questions also found their way into page-one news stories. For example, the *Wall Street Journal* printed the following news brief on page one: "Wall Street Journal/NBC News poll finds that 70% of Americans think babies-for-benefits is a major or moderate reason why people are on welfare" (Jaroslovsky 1994, A1).

A third group of forty-seven questions in the corpus focused on the respondent's experiences, knowledge, and behavior. These questions asked about respondents' personal experiences receiving AFDC or food stamps, about their willingness to do certain actions under certain conditions—such as vote for a candidate or pay more taxes; and about their knowledge about welfare, such as the percentage of the federal budget spent on AFDC, whether Congress has reformed welfare, the race of welfare recipients, and whether a variety of social programs were entitlements.

The fourth and smallest group of twenty-six questions focused primarily on electoral issues, such as whether the "Republican Party or the Democratic Party is more likely to reform the welfare system" (CBS News/*New York Times* 1994). Generally, the 1994 poll questions about welfare tended to focus either on the activities and concerns of government and politicians or on value judgments about welfare and welfare policies. Missing were questions about the activities and concerns of poor families, children and families on welfare, antipoverty activists, welfare rights or welfare rights activists, or welfare caseworkers and their activities and concerns about welfare. These omissions suggest that politicians and pollsters consider such perspectives irrelevant to public policy. The overview of the 1994 corpus reveals other notable absences—some of them surprising. For example, few poll questions mention the population most served by welfare programs—children. Children are referred to in only 17 percent of the questions, although they comprise 68 percent of the beneficiaries (U.S. House of Representatives Committee on Ways and Means 1994).[4] Similarly, in spite of the seemingly key role played by race and racism in the welfare reform debates, questions in the 1994 corpus are surprisingly silent on the topic of race. Remarkably, only three questions in the entire corpus mention the words black, white, or race.

Also notably absent from the 1994 corpus are men and fathers. Although the words *women* and *mother* occur in 15 percent of the questions, the word *father* occurs only once, and the words *men* or *man* not at all despite the fact that an estimated 50 percent of welfare mothers are on the rolls because of the failure of judges to order husbands to pay adequate child support (Pollitt 1995). Lastly, the 1994 corpus is surprisingly silent on the topic of poverty—which is mentioned in only 4 percent of the questions. This is a particularly troublesome omission given that poverty is a significant and growing problem in the United States, affecting roughly one in five children, far more than in most developed nations (Handler 1995).

The following close textual analysis of these poll questions aims to illustrate how ideologically saturated presuppositions are smuggled into closed-ended poll questions that presumably solicit opinions from respondents. Seen from this perspective, polling functions as much as a mechanism of information dissemination as of information retrieval. In other words, polling itself is a form of persuasion. As Fraser and Gordon have observed, "when ideological assumptions are tacitly inscribed in social policy discourse, they are difficult to challenge. Policy discourse then becomes a medium through which political hegemony is reproduced" (Fraser and Gordan 1994, 331). As many persuasion scholars have noted, persuasion is far more effective when the audience is made to participate in some way (Lakoff 1982).

THE "PROBLEM" OF WELFARE

A recurring theme in the 1994 corpus is the repeated construction of welfare as a "problem." Nearly one-third of the poll questions in the corpus are framed in a way that discusses welfare, welfare recipients, or the welfare system as "problems." This is done by explicitly referring to welfare as a "problem" (as occurs in about 10 percent of the questions) and by referring to the need to "reform," "change," or "revise" the welfare system (as occurs in 24 percent of the questions). Consider, for example, the following questions (italics added for emphasis):

> (1) We are faced with *many problems in this country*, none of which can be solved easily or inexpensively. I'm going to name *some of these problems*, and for each one I'd like you to tell me whether you think we're spending too much money on it, too little money, or about the right amount . . . *welfare*. (National Opinion 1994)
>
> (2) As I read you *some problem areas*, please tell me how much you think each is affecting this country today. Do you think *the problem of the way the welfare system is working* is about the same as it has been, that the country is making progress in this area, or that the country is losing ground? (Princeton 1994)

Although each of the above questions names welfare as a problem, neither specifies the nature or scope of that problem. In the first question, welfare is simply identified as one of the many problems "we" have—the "we" presumably excluding the fourteen million Americans who received AFDC or the twenty-seven million who received food stamps in 1994. In the second question, the problem is again unspecified—it is simply "the way the welfare system is working." Regardless of which answer the poll readers or respondents choose, they are led to implicitly accept the premise that welfare is a problem. In other words, whether readers or respondents answer "too little," "too much," or "about right" to the first question, they must nevertheless capitulate to the premise that welfare is a problem. Similarly, whether respondents choose "making progress" or "losing ground" in the second question, they are again acceding to the assumption that "the way the welfare system is working" is a problem.

Not all questions, however, are so vague about the nature and scope of the "welfare problem." Consider the following question (italics added):

> (3) On another topic, let me describe two approaches being considered in Congress to address *the welfare problem in America*. Please tell me which approach you tend to favor. . . . The approach would limit welfare to two years, then people would be *required to work*. This approach would spend more money for job placement and child care, but only to change the system to make sure that recipients have the opportunity to work and get off welfare (or) The approach would limit welfare to two years, provide some job training and child care, then people would be *required to work*. It would not spend new dollars on job training or child care. (Greenburg 1994)

In this third question, the phrase "welfare problem in America" is used to introduce two legislative proposals from which the respondent is invited to choose. Again, as with the first two questions, regardless of which response option the respondent chooses, the premise of the question that "welfare is a problem in America" goes unchallenged. But in this question, unlike the previous questions, the quality and nature of the problem is conveyed in both options. The first option states that "people would be required to work . . . make sure that recipients have the opportunity to work and get off welfare" and the second option states that "people would be required to work." In other words, both response options to the third question stipulate work requirements and thereby implicitly define the "problem" of welfare as the presumed failure of welfare recipients to work in the wage labor market. Thus the "problem" of welfare is constructed as a "problem" of recipients.

Similarly, the phrase *welfare reform* embeds within it a host of presuppositions about welfare. Consider the following question:

> (4) What do you think should be the main goal of any welfare reform plan? Do you think it should be to cut the cost of welfare in the short term, or to

get welfare recipients into the workforce, or cut down on the number of illegitimate children born in poverty or what? (*Los Angeles Times* 1994)

To begin with, question #4 presupposes that welfare should be reformed,
even though this is not a follow-up question to one about *whether* welfare
should be reformed or not. Instead, this *Los Angeles Times* question assumes
that the respondent agrees that welfare should be reformed, or, in other
words, that welfare is a problem. Moreover, the question provides three responses, two of which—getting recipients to work and reducing the number
of illegitimate children born into poverty—explicitly involve the behavior of
recipients.[5] As constructed in this question, reforming welfare is not simply
a matter of changing a government program but, more importantly, of reforming the behavior of recipients.

This fourth question also perpetuates the idea that poor mothers *choose*
welfare over work, rather than welfare over, for example, homelessness,
malnutrition, illness, abusive relationships, and so forth. The question also
fosters the myth that the welfare rolls are overrun with teen mothers and "illegitimate" babies, when in fact this is not the case.[6]

Generally speaking, readers of and respondents to poll questions in the
1994 corpus were given five basic policy options to correct the "problem" of
welfare: cutting or increasing government spending, providing services, cutting or denying benefits, restricting eligibility, and requiring work. Each of
these policy options reflects not just the legislative and policy proposals then
under debate in Congress but, perhaps more importantly, the ideologically
saturated presuppositions of that debate. Indeed, many of these poll questions seem to be drawn directly from policy proposals that reflect long-
standing themes in discourse about poverty. Rarely, if ever, do poll questions
name, identify, or address the specific problems of welfare (that is, how and
why it is a problem) and rarely do poll questions name, identify, or otherwise
address the specifics of welfare (that is, what it is, who and how it serves,
what its purpose and goals are, etc.). The goal of welfare, as constructed in
poll questions, is not, for example, to keep poor families or children from being homeless, sick, hungry, or abused; nor is it to meet the basic human needs
of American citizens; nor is it to ensure economic equity and justice; nor is it
to prevent poverty or crime; nor is it to improve the quality life for America's
future citizens. Instead, the goal of welfare, as constructed in poll questions,
is the already failed task of getting people off welfare and into the workforce.
The fact that things like job availability, adequate wages, health insurance,
day care, transportation, job training, education, and the economy play a crucial role in whether or not people work is never addressed in poll questions.
Further, the fact that these factors are far beyond the function, funding, or
grasp of AFDC and food stamps is never mentioned. When the demand for
welfare spending increases (because the need for the programs increases),

the blame is placed on the welfare system and on poor people for failing to eradicate poverty. As many scholars recognize, the problems of poverty are far more closely connected to problems of work than of welfare.

WORK AND WELFARE

The current preoccupation with reforming what we now call "the welfare system" is as old, if not older, than welfare itself. Even the very terms of reform—work at any wage—have remained unchanged for more than 600 years. Handler (1995) traces welfare legislation to 1349, when the Statute of Laborers was enacted during Edward III's reign in England. Written during a labor shortage caused by famine and the Black Death of 1348–1349, this statute not only compels "beggars" (including large numbers of women and children) to work for their livelihood but promises to imprison anyone who aids the poor. Following the thesis first described by Piven and Cloward in their 1971 ground-breaking analysis of how welfare functions to regulate the poor and their labor, Handler observes how this first welfare statute was not about poverty but about the labor market—specifically, about employers losing control over laborers and wages. The statute, Handler writes, "was an attempt to force beggars to seek work by preventing the giving of alms—in other words, by cutting off welfare" (Handler 1995, 10).

The historical relationship of work and welfare can be seen in the 1994 corpus where nearly a third of the poll questions mention either jobs, work requirements, or job training, but no poll questions mention that full-time work at the 1994 federal minimum wage earned a worker only $8,500 (minus $650 in social security taxes), amounting to about two-thirds of the poverty line for a family of three *not including* medical benefits. In fact, it takes working forty hours a week, fifty-two weeks a year (with no sick days or vacations) at $5.75 an hour ($1.50 more per hour than minimum wage) to meet the poverty line for a family of three, and that, as pointed out above, is far from sufficient to raise a family. It does not, for instance, even begin to pay for day care or medical care—indispensable requirements for working single parents. But the underlying assumption of many 1994 poll questions seems to be that the poor should take any job offered, regardless of pay. The following questions exemplify this assumption:

(5) (Here is a list of changes many people would like to make in the current welfare system. For each idea I read, please tell me whether you favor or oppose that change.) . . . Require women to find a job and get off welfare within two years and if they can't take care of their children at that time, give them to an orphanage. (Yankelovich 1994)
(6) I would like to read you two statements about the welfare system. Please tell me which of these statements about this issue comes closer to your point of

view. Statement A: The welfare system does more good than harm, because it provides assistance and training for those who are without jobs and live in poverty. Statement B: The welfare system does more harm than good, because it encourages the breakup of the family and discourages the work ethic. (Hart and Teeter 1994)

Both of these questions focus on work from the perspective of the individual. That is, both questions presuppose that jobs are available to welfare recipients *if they would only find them*, and further, that jobs would bring the recipient/worker out of poverty. However, both presuppositions are highly problematic. In question #5, for example, the *changes in the current welfare system* refer entirely to *women* and their ability *to take care of their children*. The question equates finding a job with taking care of children and portrays working at a job as a way to take care of children, rather than taking care of children as a form of work. Again, reform, or in this case *changes in the system*, refers to the behavior of women (finding jobs, taking care of children) not to the structure or operation of the welfare system itself.

The emphasis on work requirements in question #5 also occludes the economic, racial, and gender inequity in the work world—such as the fact that women, especially women of color, earn significantly less than men, and that low-wage jobs in the United States simply fail to pay a living salary. This emphasis further prevents us from seeing the double standard of expecting single mothers to both raise and financially support their children without the help of either the fathers or the society at large.[7]

Question #6 not only perpetuates stereotypes and misunderstandings about welfare, it also forces respondents to choose between two nonmutually exclusive options. Respondents might feel, for example, that *the welfare system does more harm than good* not for the reasons stated, but because it forces poor families to live in highly stigmatized and deprived conditions. Or, to name another possibility, the respondent might feel that *the welfare system does more good than harm* because, if nothing else, it at least prevents severe malnutrition, illness, and homelessness among some of the poor. Further, this first response option suggests that welfare recipients are on welfare because they do not have jobs—not, as discussed above, because available jobs do not pay enough to live on. This response option also wrongly implies that welfare provides training to welfare recipients, whereas only a small percentage of AFDC recipients receive any job training (Handler 1995). Lastly, the second response option wrongly states that the welfare system *encourages the breakup of the family* when, in fact, since 1990, "all states are required to provide AFDC to two-parent families who are needy because of unemployment of the principal wage earner" (U.S. House 1994, 332).[8] Thus both response options of this question convey misleading and/or erroneous information to respondents.

Many of the questions in the 1994 corpus propose work as a solution to the welfare "problem" and, in so doing, tend to neglect other central problems of welfare such as poverty, child care, low wages, unemployment, and so forth. Further, the way in which poll questions emphasize work tends to turn welfare into a moral issue by implying that welfare recipients don't work and don't want to work. Thus, like all ideological constructs, the concept of *work* becomes distracting. It distracts us from examining the conditions of work itself and conceals a host of assumptions, such as: 1) that work in the marketplace is the only work that counts as work (that is, that raising children is not work); 2) that women on welfare don't have jobs in the marketplace; 3) that jobs in the marketplace are readily available to all who seek them; and 4) that jobs in the marketplace pay a living wage. As Edin and Jencks observed from their in-depth study of single mothers on welfare: "Single mothers do not turn to welfare because they are pathologically dependent on hand-outs or unusually reluctant to work—they do so because they cannot get jobs that pay better than welfare" (Edin and Jencks 1992, 204).

The focus on the work ethic in the 1994 corpus was repeated both in political debates about welfare reform and in news coverage of these debates. For example, the following news brief appeared on the front page of the *Wall Street Journal* in 1994: "Wall Street Journal/NBC News poll finds that Americans list welfare reform as the top priority for the new Congress; 82% say they favor a plan requiring recipients to work and limiting benefits to two years" (Seib 1994, A1).

Thus, while the participants in poll interviews are relatively few in number, poll discourse resonates with pollsters, policymakers, newspaper readers, TV audiences, and other interpreters of political discourse. What makes the tacit assumptions embedded in poll questions all the more powerful is the symbolic invocation of the public in the dissemination and discussion of polling data. The persuasive power of polling discourse thus lies not only with the actual activity of the participants but with the incessant and repeated interpretation, dissemination, and reiteration of poll results in speeches, policy debates, news reports, and other forms of political discourse.

CONCLUSION

This chapter has examined polling from symbolic, discursive, and ideological perspectives in order to argue against the supposition that polling is an objective and reflective instrumentality. Rather than masquerading as a neutral medium, polling can and should be, like other forms of political discourse, a site of struggle over interpretations. As documented in a wealth of scholarship, the illusion of reflective objectivity enables elite perspectives to dominate the mass communication media. Handling public opinion polls as a medium of communication and social interaction means that we can begin to ask the kinds of questions and make the kinds of demands of polling that we ask and make of journalism, political rhetoric, and other forms of policy discourse. It lets us hold polling and pollsters accountable for the kinds of arguments advanced, the voices and perspectives included or marginalized, and the symbols conveyed in and about public opinion polls. It may even open the possibility of using polling to foster truly democratic public discourse.

Thus this chapter calls for a new agenda in political communication that inquires more deeply into how polling narrows and confines political discourse, public agendas, and policy options—how polls are used by candidates to tailor and package political platforms, to marginalize perspectives, and to justify status quo policies. We need to continue to examine the implications of polling to democracy and public life, for as Kenneth Burke observed, "All questions are leading questions" (Burke 1973, 67). The next question is "Where do they lead?"

In the future, research should be done on the construction of poll discourse—how poll questions are formed and understood by the pollsters and journalists who conduct them. How closely is polling tied to official policy discourse? Is there room for more voices and perspectives? Does the diversity of perspectives and presuppositions embedded in poll discourse vary depending on the policy issue? Is there, for example, more diversity of voices and perspectives in poll questions about issues with less political consensus among elites? In other words, are some political issues more susceptible to these hegemonic polling processes than others? What makes the difference? What efforts can be made to frame policy questions using alternative perspectives?

Further, as workplace ethnographies and other research into the practices of journalistic inquiry have demonstrated, the production of news is profoundly shaped by both professional and institutional norms and practices. How do pollsters, journalists, and news organizations tie their poll questions to news stories? Under what conditions are these news media poll questions written? We have yet to begin theorizing about polling as an institutional practice and, moreover, as a site for the production of cultural knowledge. Such studies could be extremely useful to understanding more about polling and its role in public discourse.

From a more historical perspective, questions remain about the long-term impact of polling on cultural, social, and political memory. Given the considerable interest (and increasing investment) of media institutions in conducting and reporting poll results, and given the fact that many consider news to be the "first draft of history," polling appears to be playing an increasingly central role in shaping and defining what is known and what is remembered. The scope and magnitude of that role, however, is as yet relatively unexplored.

NOTES

1. For example, a 1984 editorial claimed that "welfare chiselers nowadays seem to be even more blatant than they were when Ronald Reagan was exposing and denouncing them during his days as governor of California. A candidate for the all-time welfare queen surfaced the other day in Los Angeles when she was indicted on a number of federal pornography charges." Richard Kelly, "Rolls Royce Chiselers," *The San Diego Union-Tribune,* 22 February 1984, B-6.

2. The arguments in this section are fully developed in Lisbeth Lipari, "Polling as Ritual," *Journal of Communication* 49 (1999).

3. Because the POLL archive may update its records over time, it should be noted that the questions were retrieved from the archive in June 1995. The 1994 archive may now include more questions than were retrieved for this study.

4. This excludes the word "children" when used in the program name AFDC.

5. The open-ended response option "or what" was not coded (that is, reported) and the response rate to this question was 1 percent. Another 73 percent responded with the option "get people into the workforce."

6. Contrary to stereotypes, the majority of welfare recipients are neither teenaged, black, inner-city dwellers, nor do they stay on welfare for decades and have dozens of children. See Mary Jo Bane and David Ellwood, *Welfare Realities.* (Cambridge, Mass.: Harvard University Press, 1994), or Steven Schram, *Words of Welfare* (Minneapolis: University of Minnesota Press, 1995).

7. A compelling contrast can be seen in French and German law. For example, Article 6 of the West German Basic Law, passed in 1949 states: "Every mother shall be entitled to the protection and care of the community." The 1946 French Constitution states that "the nation shall ensure to the individual and the family the conditions necessary for their development" (quoted in Glendon 1991).

8. However, man-in-the-house rules for nonspouses, to which this question is indirectly referring, were still enforced in some states (Sidel 1992).

9

Deliberation in Practice: Connecting Theory to the Lives of Citizens

Paul Waldman

> In most circles it is hard work to sustain conversation on a political theme; and once initiated, it is quickly dismissed with a yawn. Let there be introduced the topic of the mechanism and accomplishment of various makes of motor cars or the respective merits of actresses, and the dialogue goes on at a lively pace.
>
> —John Dewey, *The Public and Its Problems* (1927, 138)

Although Dewey was writing in 1927, his statement seems a strikingly accurate description of patterns of discussion in the United States today. Politics, it seems, is not something to be discussed in polite company. Nonetheless, in recent years a growing body of theory has advocated "deliberative democracy," a system in which decisions are made not by coercion or bargaining among interests but through a discursive process in which citizens collectively consider and debate alternatives. This impressive body of literature forces the question, to what extent does true deliberation exist among the citizenry today?

It should be noted that theories of deliberative democracy are "not simply about ensuring a public culture of reasoned discussion on public affairs" (Cohen 1998, 186), but are concerned more broadly with issues of state legitimacy and the exercise of governmental authority. For the present discussion, however, we will leave those issues aside and focus on public culture. In order to assess deliberation in practice we must abandon, at least temporarily, the conception of deliberation as a set of absolute procedures with a single, inviolate set of properties. A better conceptualization is to conceive of a continuum of conversation running from the least to the most deliberative. Where the citizens of a polity find themselves on that continuum provides one measure of the health of a democracy.

Political discussion is often ignored as a form of participation because it appears not to have systematic effects on electoral or policy outcomes (Huckfeldt 1999), but for most people, discussion is the primary arena in which they engage the political world. Voting occurs only occasionally, and other forms of participation, such as political protest or writing letters to representatives, are undertaken by relatively few people. In order to understand the political world in which citizens reside, we must address the most common form of political activity—the conversations about political issues that occur every day in our homes, offices, and public spaces.

Following a review of the deliberation literature and its relationship to everyday conversation, I focus on two areas in which contemporary American democracy fails to be deliberative: (1) the frequency and distribution of political conversation, and (2) the place of political disagreement. I then locate other ways in which the conversation that occurs more closely conforms to the norms of deliberative democracy. Finally, I suggest some avenues further research in this area might follow.

WHAT IS DELIBERATION?

This question has been answered in a variety of ways, but a number of common elements emerge from the body of literature on deliberation. To begin, let us define deliberation as *reasoned discussion* among *equals* about *public issues* with the goal of ascertaining the best *course of action* so as to optimize the *common good*.

The idea of reasoned discourse amounts to a first principle of deliberation. As Cohen (1989, 22) put it, "Deliberation is *reasoned* in that the parties to it are required to state their reasons for advancing proposals, supporting or criticizing them. They give reasons with the expectation that those reasons (and not, for example, power) will settle the fate of the proposal." Each argument must be supported by some evidence or justification; the presentation and critique of these reasons will constitute the bulk of the discussion. The second principle is that all participants in the discussion will be equal. No member, by virtue of social position or any other criterion, will be afforded more opportunity to speak than any other. Nor will any member be exempt from any of the other requirements. While there may be inequalities among people that have consequences for the discussion (for instance, differences in knowledge or eloquence), all will have identical privileges and responsibilities within the deliberation. Next, the discussion will concern public issues, and the best course of action to be pursued. Only those issues in which the state, or citizens acting collectively, have some role will be at issue. Furthermore, the discussion should take place with the understanding that some action will be taken (or not taken). The ultimate purpose of the discussion is to arrive at a decision, whether that decision results in action by the participants themselves or their representatives. Finally, the discussion concerns the common good. The quality of potential outcomes is judged by their effects not on the participants but on the larger collectivity.

WHY DELIBERATE?

There are three general benefits of public deliberation, none of which is beyond question, but each of which offers a compelling argument in favor of deliberative democracy. Citizen deliberation, as opposed to the formal deliberative procedures operating within an institution such as a legislature, presents a unique but related set of problems. In the abstract, the benefits of deliberation are common to both, although their prospects for realization may differ.

The first benefit of deliberation as a core element of democratic practice is that it incorporates fundamental democratic ideals and thus makes good on the democratic promise. Among these ideals are citizen participation (if the people are to rule, they must be involved in the decision-making process in some way) and equality (just as each citizen has an equal vote, each has an equal opportunity to participate in debate). The degree to which citizen deliberation actually displays these ideals is perhaps the thorniest question confronting the advocate of deliberative democracy.

The second benefit is that the process of deliberation engenders a transformation among the participants. In the simplest terms, a citizen should be (1) reasonably well informed, (2) able and willing to participate in the democratic discussion, and (3) motivated at least in part by a desire to advance the common good. The process of deliberation has the potential to transform individuals into citizens on each count. First, all political conversation, even that which is not deliberative, has the potential to enhance political knowledge as facts and arguments are shared. Second, like any participatory process, each positive episode of participation enables and encourages the one succeeding it. Third, participation in a discussion about the common good exposes one to facts and arguments about the interests of others and the larger community to which one might not have had access previously, and forces one to frame one's own arguments in common terms (Bohman 1996). Thus, the citizen must find public reasons for his private views. In the process, those views may change, or at the very least expand to include the interests of others. As a consequence, deliberation not only produces (as opposed to merely articulating) the common will (Warren 1992), but it cultivates a will based on the common good within each citizen.

Like other forms of participation, deliberation builds political efficacy, "the belief that one can be self-governing, and confidence in one's ability to participate responsibly and effectively" (Pateman 1970, 45). The process here is, of course, circular: efficacy encourages participation, which in turn strengthens efficacy (Almond and Verba 1965). Ultimately, deliberation enables one to achieve autonomy, the necessary characteristic of the self-governing citizen. As Warren (1992, 11) describes it, "individuals are autonomous if their preferences, goals, and life plans are not the result of manipulation, brainwashing, unthinking obedience, or reflexive acceptance of ascribed roles but, rather, a result of their examining and evaluating wants, needs, desires, values, roles, and commitments." While we may sometimes leave to others the gathering of information and arguments, we can develop autonomy only through our own participation (Barber 1984). Further, the advocate of expansive democracy argues that autonomy is itself social, and only through the process of deliberating with others can we identify the myriad ways in which our well-being is entwined with that of our fellow citizens.

A final, transformative justification for deliberation is that citizenship (that is, engagement with the other members of the polity in determining and bringing about the progress and improvement of society) is not merely a way of safeguarding our interests or of contributing to the betterment of society but an essential element of the good life. Politics, and one's engagement in it, is not only a means to an end but an end in itself. According to Hannah Arendt (1959, 151), we do not merely pursue our private goals when entering the public realm, but take on an entirely different set of goals. John Stuart Mill also argued that citizenship forces one to consider the welfare of others, which makes one learn and grow. As Rousseau wrote in *The Social Contract*, when a man becomes a citizen, "his faculties are exercised and developed, his ideas are broadened, his feelings are ennobled, his entire soul is elevated."

The final potential benefit of deliberation is that it produces better results than the policy making that occurs in its absence. The "quality" of results is, of course, difficult to assess. Many theorists have argued that good results are simply those that arise from a good process (for example, Christiano 1997; Fishkin 1991). If the process incorporates democratic principles, then the outcome is morally justifiable and legitimate in the sense that the participants will abide by the results even if their favored proposal is not adopted. No external means of evaluating outcomes is necessary.

The requirements of deliberation do not necessarily guarantee that citizens will choose wisely, but they do insist that certain specific distortions and biases will be absent. Arguments based on prejudice or the will of the powerful, for instance, will be insufficient to carry the day. Nonetheless, there is always the possibility that none of the deliberators has the key piece of information central to a particular decision; too, the information they do have could be deceptive and thus it would lead to suboptimal outcomes. The question is less whether deliberation will produce the best answer to a given question than whether deliberation will ultimately produce outcomes that enhance the common good. While it may be impossible to answer this question empirically, what works in favor of deliberation is that democratic goals are incorporated into the deliberative process. Other processes—say, relying on the wisdom of the philosopher-king—certainly may result in beneficial outcomes, but they might not preclude antidemocratic outcomes.

This is not to say, of course, that formally deliberative bodies are perfect. If they do err, however, they fail for human reasons, not systematic reasons. In fact, in American politics it is often the case that officials' tendencies to ignore the common interest vary inversely with the amount of public discussion surrounding a particular decision (Schattschneider 1960). For example, according to Greider (1992), polluting industries are able to receive far better treatment during the regulatory process, which takes place largely outside public view, than they do during the legislative process. And we are all familiar with the narrowly beneficial tax break secretly inserted into a large bill at the eleventh hour. Influence buying is more likely to occur when public deliberation is absent; votes are far less likely to be bought by a contributor on the subject of a heated debate (such as partial-birth abortion) than on relatively obscure banking legislation, for instance.

Other theorists have added additional items to the list of deliberation's benefits. For example, Barber (1984) contends that democratic talk has the ability not simply to mediate conflict but to transform it into agreement. This perspective may be too optimistic; when we extend deliberation to an entire society, true consensus appears impossible and may not even be desirable. There are always dissenters to any policy, after all, whether among the public or in a legislature, and their presence gives some assurance that any proposal will be critiqued and its weaknesses exposed. It is far more important that all participants feel bound by the decision whether their side carries the day or not (Bohman 1996). While deliberation encourages agreement, it by no means guarantees it; ultimately, questions will need to be put to a vote (Knight and Johnson 1994).

OBJECTIONS TO DELIBERATION

While the volume of scholarly writing advocating some form of deliberative democracy is substantial and growing, there have been a number of objections raised to deliberation, particularly when we seek to apply it to society at large. Sanders (1997) contends that one of the core premises of deliberation, that of equality and its corollary of equal respect, is extremely difficult to achieve. Citizens arrive at a discussion with unequal faculties, resources, and rhetorical skills; debate is likely to favor those who can frame their arguments in accord with the deliberative model. Thus, "taking deliberation as a signal of democratic practice paradoxically works undemocratically, discrediting on seemingly democratic grounds the views of those who are less likely to present their arguments in ways that we recognize as characteristically deliberative" (349). One imagines a debate between two people, both of whom are actually seeking to advance their own interests, in which one cleverly cloaks his argument in the language of the common good, while the other is unable to do so and thus loses out. Sanders concludes that those who are already underrepresented—women, racial minorities, and the poor—are most likely to be silenced by deliberative requirements. Nonetheless, inequalities in rhetorical skill are far more easily overcome than inequalities of power; it is the latter and not the former that marginalizes certain groups (Guttman and Thompson 1996).

It is true that societal inequality may be manifested in deliberation just as it is in other political processes and institutions. In order to address that inequality, those who suffer from it must occasionally make special claims to the majority. If the deliberative process is strict in its insistence that all arguments must revolve around the common good, such claims may be ruled out of bounds, or at the very least require substantial logical and rhetorical acrobatics in order to be presented "properly." Thus, the "common good" works best when it becomes the guide and end of deliberation, and not when it is imposed on every utterance within the process. An open deliberation allows an individual claim to be presented, but treats it as a datum to be compared with others in determining the nature of the common good. Personal testimony (Sanders 1997) should not only be permissible but also encouraged. Participants may assume one of a number of roles when speaking: witness, expert, advocate, etc. When one *listens*, however, one's role shifts (Bickford 1996b). It is in this role that consideration of the common good must become paramount. I would also argue that this conception more closely approximates the substance of actual political conversation. People understand intuitively that statements such as "I'm voting for candidate X because he'll cut *my* taxes" will carry little weight in a discussion. Statements of personal interest can be made only if they are placed within the context of a larger good or a fundamental principle (for example, fairness or justice).

The second response to the inequality objection is that ongoing deliberation is itself the cure for the ill of communicative inequality. The more one participates in debate, the greater one's ability to make persuasive arguments and win support for one's positions. While the advantaged may already be well informed and possess autonomy before debate begins, the deliberative process enhances these qualities among the disadvantaged who engage in it.

Sanders also observes that often there is no "common good" at issue. She offers as an example the claims of Japanese Americans for compensation for internment during World War II, a case where "democratic assemblies should do nothing like pursue the common good but instead should just listen and respond to particular complaints" (1997, 361). I agree, but I argue further that such cases are not rare but in fact comprise a great portion, perhaps even the majority, of questions normally placed before the public. True, the allocations of funds in this case had a negligible effect on the federal budget or the economy, whereas, for instance, increases in student loans would extend a greater web of economic effects. In both cases the task of the deliberator is to determine what is best for a finite number of others. It will be exceedingly difficult for her to locate any self-interest in the question at hand. As a consequence, it will not be necessary to insist that she put aside her self-interest; she will have little choice.

Some have raised the possibility that deliberation will, by bringing multiple arguments and information to light, actually increase conflict. Deliberators could discover that the grounds for disagreement are deeper than they had originally imagined. "A participant may conclude that 'if *this* is what is at stake, then I really disagree!'" (Knight and Johnson 1994, 286). This scenario is only problematic, however, if we believe that agreement itself is the end of deliberation, regardless of whether it is based on truth. An agreement brought about by incomplete knowledge or deception is no more preferable than one resulting from coercion. The advantage of deliberation is not simply that it is more likely to result in agreement but that that agreement will be based on shared values and understandings.

Another objection to deliberation is that it imposes too many obligations on the citizenry. People should be able to ignore politics if they so choose, say some observers. They have too many other concerns—their jobs, their families, their hobbies—to take on politics as an ongoing task. In addition, speaking publicly about politics is something many find downright unpleasant (Schudson 1997). However, whether or not the individual chooses to act as a citizen, political decisions will continue to be made. The fact that a citizen ignores them does not mean they will cease to affect him. While a representative system theoretically accounts for the interests of all whether they participate or not, a deliberative conception of democracy focuses on each individual's development as a citizen; while someone may represent my interests, no one can be a citizen in my place. As Barber (1984, 174) observes, "It is far easier for representatives to speak for us than to listen for us."

Because deliberation helps to create citizens, it may be considered an end in itself apart from the results that emerge from it, as Hannah Arendt (1959) argued. Others hold that democratic discussion is not about who we are but about what to do (Elster 1997). One can, however, conceive of discussion that results in no decision as, if nothing else, an investment in subsequent decisions. If the transformative effects of deliberation occur, those who benefit will be more likely to render wise judgments in the future. Deliberation may thus be defended both as a decision-making procedure and as a form of civic engagement from which policies flow only indirectly.

The development of deliberative theory is in part a response to the elitist model of democracy espoused by Schumpeter (Schumpeter 1950) and to Downs's economic model (Downs 1957; Bohman and Rehg 1997). While the elitist model is primarily concerned with system-level outcomes and the economic model with maximization of individual interest, both reject substantial participation either because it exceeds the citizen's capacity in the former case or because it is irrational in the latter case. In either case, representative democracy operates efficiently precisely because it demands so little of people. In a similar vein, Berelson and his colleagues (Berelson, Lazarsfeld, and McPhee 1954) held that universal participation was undesirable and that widespread indifference to politics allowed for a smoothly operating government.[1]

In contrast, contemporary deliberative theory shares with Rousseau and John Stuart Mill an emphasis on individual participation not simply as a mechanism to ensure the proper functioning of institutions but as a core purpose of politics. As Mill argued, political arrangements serve not only to conduct a nation's business but also to educate its citizenry, imbuing them with desirable traits of character. It is here, and not because of efficiency or the protection of private interests, that the strongest argument for democracy can be found.

DELIBERATION IN THE REAL WORLD

When we move from discussions of ideal deliberation to an examination of actual citizen deliberation, two sets of questions present themselves. The first concerns how citizen deliberation stands in relation to the ideal. Are people discussing public affairs? If so, when such conversations occur, do they incorporate deliberative norms? The second and most ignored question is this: exactly how will citizen deliberation affect public policy formation? If we take representative democracy as a given and the current institutions of government as at least semipermanent, how would an engaged, deliberative citizenry make a difference?

One is tempted by some deliberative theories to describe "ideal" political discourse and then to cast all other political talk aside as irrelevant to the operation of deliberation. However, to do so is to ignore the bulk of citizens' political lives. Political talk takes place in diverse settings where norms and patterns of discourse vary. In order to build a theory of deliberation based on actual conversation, we must understand each of these and its relation to deliberative goals.

In real life, things are untidy and uncertain. While formal procedures may be necessary and proper in the context of a small institution like a legislature, there is little purpose in prescribing procedures the public will be required to follow in their political discussions. In ordinary conversation, rules will necessarily be informal and sporadically enforced. Even if we were to imagine that an "ideal speech situation" (Habermas 1989) could be created, it would necessarily comprise only a part of the citizenry's political life. Imagine two coworkers eating their lunch together. One says, "Did you see the State of the Union speech last night?" and the other replies, "I would be happy to discuss it, but we should wait until we go to the salon where the rules of deliberation may be enforced." Democratic discussion takes place in too many and too varied settings where such rules have little applicability.

Furthermore, most theorizing is silent on the question of how, specifically, public deliberation translates into policy. One possibility is that public deliberation could be incorporated into local political institutions with decision-making power, as in the town meeting (Mansbridge 1980). The knowledge and commitment acquired by citizens would then hopefully translate into engagement on larger issues. Currently, this form of government exists only in a few places. A second possibility, which also involves the citizenry in direct policy making is statewide referenda, where deliberation hopefully, but not necessarily, precedes the moment of decision. A third possibility would be the institutionalization of something like Fishkin's (1991) deliberative poll, in which a representative group of citizens engages in formal deliberation, the results of which become binding in some way on a government body, be it local or national. Similar endeavors using "citizen juries" are becoming common in Europe (Smith and Wales 2000). A fourth option would be a nonbinding deliberative poll system, where the results were held to be a true measure of "public opinion," thus exposing legislatures to public sanction if they were ignored. A final possibility is maintenance of current institutional structures, but with improved opportunities for public deliberation that makes the formation of public opinion more considered and less capricious.

ARE PEOPLE TALKING?

If we are to assess the operation of deliberation in practice, the first question to ask is this: Are people talking about politics? In 1996, a multiwave cross-sectional survey of the American electorate was conducted at the Annenberg School for Communication of the University of Pennsylvania.[2] Respondents (n = 3,669) were asked how often they talked about politics. As figure 9.1 shows, about half of the electorate is comprised of infrequent talkers—either never talking about politics or talking less often than once a week. Another quarter talk once or twice a week, and the remaining quarter are frequent talkers, discussing politics at least three times a week. There is reason to believe that these numbers are overstated to some extent, first because this survey interviewed only those who claimed to be registered voters, and second

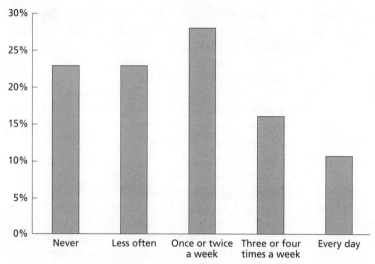

Figure 9.1.　How Often Do You Talk about Politics? (1996 national survey)

because many people claim in surveys to have voted when in fact they have not (Presser and Traugott 1992); in the context of a survey about political affairs, it seems probable that some people will exaggerate the frequency with which they discuss politics. An analysis of National Election Study data from recent years indicates that the level of conversation varies only slightly from year to year; generally, the mean response is between one and two days per week.

What can we conclude about political conversation from this distribution? There is no precise normative standard by which we can measure whether a particular individual has engaged in "enough" talk to be considered an active democratic participant. We can say that political conversation is the exception rather than the rule for the majority of Americans. The next question we must ask is, who's talking?

One of the justifications commonly offered for a deliberative conception of democracy is that it is democratic. While other forms of decision making may operate equally well regardless of any individual's participation or non-participation, deliberative democracy demands that all citizens participate; indeed, the transformative effect of deliberation on individuals is one of its foundations.

In the real world, we would of course not expect that every single citizen in a large society would spend a substantial amount of his or her time discussing politics. There will always be some people for whom the political world holds little interest. However, if those who don't participate are drawn disproportionately from certain groups and not others, then a distortion of democracy occurs. A system may tolerate partial participation and remain truly democratic only if the participants and nonparticipants are essentially the same people. If they are not, the inputs to the system are no longer representative. In fact, this is precisely the case. Political conversation is part of a nexus of activities—including voting, contributing money to political causes, and use of public affairs programming in media—which are highly correlated with those variables we associate with membership in the socioeconomic elite.

Table 9.1 shows that distortions are present in political conversation just as they are in other forms of participation. Men talk about politics more than women, both men and women talk mostly to those of the same gender (Huckfeldt and Sprague 1995), whites talk more than blacks and Hispanics, the wealthy talk more than the poor, and the more educated talk more than the less educated. The table also shows the percentage of respondents who gave answers at the ends of the conversational spectrum. We see, for instance, that nearly half of those with less than a high school education never talk about politics, as compared to only 10 percent of those with a postgraduate degree. Over a third of those earning less than $20,000 a year never talk about politics, while less than 12 percent of those in the highest income category give the same response.

One could argue that the often-observed correlation between political sophistication and participation is actually functional for democracy. Since those who participate are those who know more, their voices are properly being heard more. This argument assumes that sophistication is distributed among the population evenly. If those who participate were merely a representative sample of the larger populace, then the outcomes they produce would be the same as if all were participating. In actuality, of course, participants are not representative of the larger population; they are more wealthy, more white, and more male (Verba et al. 1993).

In the early part of the twentieth century, Walter Lippmann (1922) argued that, given the complexity of the modern world and the varied activities of the state, the ideal of the omnicompetent citizen, who was informed about all issues, was an impossibility. Instead, society should rely on a class of impartial experts who would provide policymakers with the information needed to make decisions. John Dewey (1927, 208) responded that "no government by experts in which the masses do not have the chance to inform the experts as to their needs can be anything but an oligarchy managed in the interests of the few." To those such as Dewey, who advocated expanding democracy to rely more on the input and participation of the citizenry, Lippmann (1927) responded that doing so would only exacerbate democracy's ills by giving more power to a populace ill equipped to make decisions.

Is there a way to reconcile Dewey's optimism and Lippmann's pessimism? One answer to Lippmann would be that greater engagement would enhance knowledge, creating competent if not omnicompetent citizens. Even if the

Table 9.1. Frequency of Conversation by Demographics (Registered Voters, 1996)

	How often do you talk about politics?		
	Mean days per week	Never	Every day
Gender			
Men	2.00	19.7%	11.9%
Women	1.70	28.5	9.3
Age			
18–29	1.56	27.3	6.4
30–44	1.85	20.9	9.5
45–59	2.04	20.8	12.4
60+	1.82	29.5	12.7
Race			
White	1.92	22.8	11.2
Black	1.43	29.8	6.5
Hispanic	1.13	38.6	3.0
Education			
Less than high school	1.14	43.6	4.8
High school graduate	1.52	30.7	9.0
Some college	1.98	22.3	12.1
College graduate	2.00	18.0	10.2
Post-graduate	2.67	10.4	17.5
Income			
Less than $20,000	1.41	35.8	7.8
$20,000–$30,000	1.69	30.7	10.9
$30,000–$50,000	1.88	21.5	10.9
$50,000–$75,000	1.94	17.9	8.8
$75,000+	2.54	11.7	16.3
Party identification			
Republicans	2.16	19.5	15.4
Democrats	1.68	27.5	8.0
Independents	1.73	24.7	8.2
Ideology			
Strong ideologues	2.59	19.2	19.8
Weak ideologues	1.91	23.3	11.5
Moderates	1.62	25.7	7.6

public's abilities to analyze policy are necessarily imperfect, they need not be perfect to arrive at good decisions. The question is not whether the masses have as much information at their disposal as the experts, but whether they have sufficient information to render judgment, and the capacity and ability to do so. Given the time and permission to decide, they may indeed prove wise (Yankelovich 1991), arriving at decisions that benefit not only themselves but the polity as a whole. Page and Shapiro (1992) argue that the question is not how much each individual citizen knows, but whether the citizenry holds enough information collectively. If it does, a collective deliberation may take place without any particular citizen necessarily deliberating (Page 1996). The notion that the public can show sound judgment without any of its members necessarily knowing very much can actually be traced back to Aristotle (Bickford 1996a). But what happens when some are systematically shut out of deliberation? It would be one matter if half the public deliberated on a particular issue and if membership in that half was randomly determined or at least varied from issue to issue. But if certain people usually deliberate and others never do, then a systematic distortion exists.

Although Dewey (1927, 126) conceded that "there are too many publics and too much of public concern for our existing resources to cope with," he also hoped that evolving communication technology could mitigate the atomizing effects of mass society and establish, if not a substitute for face-to-face contact, some basis on which to bond remote citizens to one another. This view is shared by others as well (Abramson 1992; Barber 1984; see Simonson 1996 for a review). Dewey (1927, 155) advocated "the perfecting of the means and ways of communication of meanings so that genuinely shared interest in the consequences of interdependent activities may inform desire and effort and thereby direct action." Unfortunately, it appears that despite advances in communication technology, political engagement still occurs disproportionately among the elite.

DISAGREEMENT AND CONVERSATION

One of the most important characteristics of everyday political conversation is that much of it takes place in the home (Huckfeldt and Sprague 1995). Critically, spouses overwhelmingly share the same general political outlook, so political disagreement in the home is less likely to occur than it might in other contexts. Outside the home, a number of variables will help determine the amount of political disagreement to which an individual is exposed: the range of opinions in her social and work contacts, the range of opinions in her community, her choice of conversation partners, and the extent to which she and those partners avoid disagreement when discussing politics (Huckfeldt et al. 1998). While opportunities to encounter disagreement may be greater outside the home, research going back to Lazarsfeld, Berelson, and Gaudet (1944) has found that people tend to associate with those with whom they agree. Marsden (1987, 126) notes that social networks in which respondents discuss important matters are "small, centered on kin, comparatively dense, and homogeneous." Beck (1991, 378–379) also found that "personal networks of political discussants provide protective cocoons for an individual's political preferences," but noted that "this cocoon is more likely to be penetrated, however, as one's network expands beyond the walls of home and family into the broader world."

Disagreement may have a number of positive effects. Leighly (1990) found that the presence of conflict in one's social network (measured by whether a discussion partner had tried to convince the respondent to change his/her vote) heightened participatory activity, including voting, contacting government officials, and volunteering for a campaign. This finding is in some ways an extension of Granovetter's (1973) work on "the strength of weak ties." Granovetter showed that since the family and friends with whom we are closest usually share our perspectives, experiences, and knowledge, it is our acquaintances who are more critical in bringing new information to our attention. In homogeneous networks, inaccurate information is more likely to go uncorrected (Chaffee 1986). Similarly, those with whom we disagree politically are more likely to bring to our attention uncomfortable facts and novel arguments. In addition, by requiring us to construct arguments to defend our positions, they force clear and logical articulation of our beliefs. These findings accord with one of the principal theoretical justifications for deliberation—that engaging with others in debate not only builds knowledge and political judgment but enhances feelings of citizenship.

Of course, when we encounter someone with differing political views, both parties must be open about their beliefs and be willing to advocate for them, or the benefits of disagreement will not be realized. Huckfeldt et al. (1998) showed that among nonspouse discussion pairs, a full 40.5 percent of respondents misperceived their discussant's presidential preference. In most cases, respondents assumed that their partners either agreed with them or agreed with the prevailing opinion in the local environment. If these data are representative, in two of every five cases one individual in a discussion dyad is vague enough for her partner to misperceive her opinions, a rather striking figure. Such conversations obviously do not include forceful advocacy for the positions of at least one person. In that case, they necessarily fail to be deliberative.

Since conversation between citizens is voluntary, primarily expressive (as opposed to goal-oriented), and undertaken by those with personal relationships existing outside of the political world, norms of friendly engagement must necessarily be in force. The occasions of everyday political discussion are "not perceived as political; therefore, the scripts that apply to them are embedded not in politics but in the routines of friendship, recreation, and parenting" (Merelman 1998, 519). As a consequence, disagreement is seen not as a necessary and useful element of political discussion but an unpleasantness to be avoided.

Many people choose simply to avoid political discussion altogether if disagreement is a possibility. Lane (1962, 375) found that "more than a third of the men say there isn't much point to having political discussion with one's friends." Graber (1984b, 35) reported that "both men and women tended to limit discussions to consensual remarks and to avoid political discussions that were likely to be controversial. In fact, several panelists expressed strong reluctance to discuss politics at all. Some said that politics and religion were topics they avoided because they considered them potentially divisive." Similarly, Eliasoph (1998, 45) was told by one of her subjects, "You don't talk about politics with your friends. Not if you want to keep them." Political disagreement is thus considered so powerful that it can destroy friendships.

The place where people are most likely to encounter disagreement is the workplace, and it is there that political conversation is seen as most risky, precisely because of the possibility of disagreement. Wyatt et al.'s (1995) American subjects cited the workplace as the environment in which they would be least likely to state their political views. On a list of thirty-three possible reasons for keeping quiet, the highest scores were given to "Saying what's on your mind may harm or damage other people," "Speaking your mind may hurt the feelings of those you care for," "You want to be polite," and "You like for everything to go smoothly." All of these justifications assume that the reasons for avoiding political conversation lie in the potential for disagreement. Political disagreement is seen as a threat to friendly relationships that in many cases are built on fragile foundations. Since people seldom choose their coworkers, the possibility of significantly differing political views is a real one. They seem to believe that political disagreement can have negative consequences both personally and professionally (Jensen 1990). Precious opportunities for exposure to new information and arguments are squandered daily in workplaces everywhere.

Thus, if political conversation occurs less often than one might expect in an actively engaged democracy, political disagreement is rarer still. Results from a number of surveys conducted in recent years point to the conclusion that only a sliver of the population is exposed to a substantial amount of disagreement in their political conversations. Figure 9.2 shows data from a survey of California voters taken in 1998. Almost 60 percent of respondents reported encountering political disagreement less than once a month or never at all. Only 12 percent disagreed with their discussion partners regularly.[3]

Can conversation without disagreement be considered deliberative? Most theorists would answer that persuading others and being persuaded is an essential element of the deliberative process. Because persuasion requires arguments to be framed in terms that others will accept, common interest argumentation, or at least argumentation that goes beyond the speaker's preferences, becomes inevitable. But does persuasion require a reversal of opinion? Might we consider affirmation—a process by which uncertainty is reduced and opinions given shape and firmness—a species of persuasion? Even if we answer yes, the question of whether a concordant conversation is truly deliberative remains. One can certainly imagine conversations in which the arguments of the other side are raised, assessed fairly, and rejected

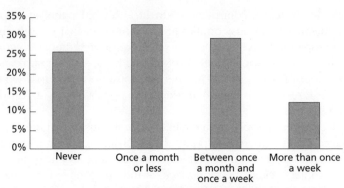

Figure 9.2.   Exposure to Disagreement (1998 California survey)

even if no one is present to advocate for them. Such conversations are theoretically possible but probably unlikely in most cases.

Bruce Ackerman (1989) points out that in cases when conversants reach a point where two fundamental principles suggest opposite positions and no common principle may be invoked, the proper solution is to simply stop talking in the hope that friendly conversation on other matters may continue. In fact, this is what has happened on the subject of abortion: despite its continued presence as a national policy issue, ordinary people have come to understand that opinions on the subject are largely fixed, and attempts at persuasion are likely to fail. Therefore, we have collectively "agreed to disagree," and hence conversations about abortion among those who disagree have become exceedingly rare. Unfortunately, many people have come to a similar conclusion about politics generally: that it is best discussed only in "safe" contexts when we know that disagreement will not occur.

CONVERSATION, DELIBERATION, AND PARTICIPATION

Half a century ago, Lazarsfeld and Merton (1948) suggested that by delivering a seemingly endless supply of political information, modern media make keeping up with politics feel like action. The citizen, they wrote, "comes to mistake *knowing* about problems of the day for *doing* something about them" (106). Discussing the political effects of television, Hart (1997, 9) has argued that "for many citizens, watching governance has become equivalent to engaging governance." If one advocates political conversation as an essential element of democratic life, the question of whether discussion is more like watching or more like participating presents itself.

Discussion resembles participation because it engages other citizens, passing influence in a potentially wide circle. If public opinion itself has a role to play in policy formation, then to participate in the formation of that opinion is to participate in the policy process. If one believes further (and some do not) that public opinion is not merely an aggregation of individual attitudes but something that emerges from the process by which citizens engage one another, then political discussion—sharing information and arguments, attempting to persuade others—qualifies as participation in a way that solitary opinion formation, however considered, does not. It creates a ripple of effects that drifts outward from individuals' immediate circles to their acquaintances and ultimately, to those they have never met. Discussion, therefore, is more than simply practice for "real" participation (Merelman 1998); it *is* participation just as surely as is writing a letter to a member of Congress or marching in a protest.

To understand why this is the case, let us accept that policy proceeds in accordance with public opinion—not public opinion as it might be, or should be, but strictly as it is.[4] The areas in which the public is inattentive, indifferent, or lacks the requisite knowledge to assess options are those in which policymakers have the widest latitude (Page and Shapiro 1992). Public opinion affects policy in these cases by creating a vacuum into which other forces—the preferences of policymakers or the influence of special interests, for instance—may flow. If we further accept the idea that something like "true" public opinion—opinions fashioned under optimal circumstances—does in fact exist, then the amount of deliberation in which the populace engages might well become a good measure of the "quality" of opinion. Higher quality opinion is, in turn, more likely to be reflected in policy. On those questions where there is substantial deliberation, the resulting public opinion will be understood by policymakers and, thus, the sanctions for contradicting it will be more substantial. Where deliberation is minimal, opinions will be more easily manipulated. Where deliberation is completely absent, policymakers will be free to do as they wish without fear of consequence. Of course, in many cases policy will correspond to "true" opinion regardless of its distance from current opinion, but without deliberation it need not necessarily do so. Although the degree of consensus that exists within "true" opinion will be a complicating variable in this process, we may nonetheless assume that, in general terms, deliberation will correlate with responsiveness.

One could argue that in a representative system we delegate both authority *and the obligation to deliberate* to our representatives; as long as they deliberate, the citizenry need not do so. In practice, however, we expect public officials to arrive at decisions through a balance of personal judgment and responsiveness to public opinion. Moreover, to satisfy even the minimum responsibility of assessing whether they have performed their duties well and should thus be returned to office, we must have some understanding of the issues our representatives have confronted. In the absence of deliberation, that understanding will be incomplete. A public opinion that incorporates only certain views, furthermore, is less than truly public. Decision-making bodies acknowledge, through the requirement of a quorum, that some threshold of participation is necessary for a decision to be meaningful. A similar threshold of participation is necessary for a representative public opinion to form.

Does deliberation occur among ordinary Americans? For some people, some of the time, it does. Nonetheless, it appears that deliberation is not as common as we might hope. Some argue that "what happens when American citizens talk to each other is often neither truly deliberative nor really democratic" (Sanders 1997, 349). Political talk occurs more often among the politically interested, strong partisans, and those who are higher in socioeconomic status. Because of variations in personality and knowledge, all parties involved in political conversation don't necessarily have the same opportunity to speak. In addition, political disagreement, an essential element of deliberative conversation, is extremely rare.

There are, however, other ways in which the political talk that does take place resembles deliberation. For instance, basing one's arguments on something other than self-interest (a central tenet in deliberative theory) may well be quite common in everyday conversations. Also, while most policy questions affect many people, very few affect all of us. The result is that—for most people on most issues—there simply is no self-interest to be located. It has been amply demonstrated that self-interest plays a minimal role in the formation of political opinions (Sears and Funk 1991).

Even in concordant conversations, people need to support their positions with reasons acceptable to others to carry the discussion forward. One can say "I prefer Candidate X," but unless we can provide reasons why Candidate X is the better candidate, we will have nothing to talk about (Stoker 1992). This is not to say, of course, that people who are sufficiently similar could not discuss political matters in plainly self-interested terms. Two restaurant owners, for instance, might discuss a proposed increase in the minimum wage without expanding their discussion beyond the effects such an increase would have on their payrolls. But these cases will be relatively less frequent; more often, political discussion will need to expand beyond the interests of the participants simply because of the nature of political issues. In this way, everyday conversation largely adheres to the deliberative standard.

Another area in which everyday conversation resembles deliberation is in the building of political knowledge. One of the key justifications for deliberation is that without having all arguments and information presented to him, the citizen will be unable to render a good judgment. After deliberation, however, he will not only have learned more about the positions of the other side but will also have a deeper understanding of his own position, gained through the formulation of arguments. In practice, political knowledge and frequency of conversation are closely correlated. There is likely a reciprocal process at work: through conversation we learn facts and arguments; armed with more knowledge, we are less reluctant to talk about politics. Obviously, there will be great variation in how much different people learn from their conversations, depending in large part on those with whom they are talking. For some, conversation will be deliberative in this way, while for others it will not.

We may thus conclude that the reasons our democracy largely fails to be deliberative lie less in the substance of political discussion and more in its participants—who discusses politics, and with whom.

FURTHER RESEARCH

The survey data presented here are suggestive, but they go only so far in painting a picture of the degree to which everyday political conversation is deliberative. One obvious task for researchers focusing on political conversation is to spend more time listening to actual citizens talking to one another. While there have been a few excellent works doing so—for example, Gamson's (1992) focus group study and Eliasoph's (1998) ethnography—there is much more to be learned by allowing citizens to not only respond to survey questions but to speak about politics in their own words.

We also need a better understanding of why people choose not to talk about politics. In recent years, a few events have generated a truly national conversation; the Clarence Thomas–Anita Hill hearings and the Monica Lewinsky matter are two examples. In both cases, objective evidence was minimal, questions of fact became less important than the conclusion to be drawn if the allegations were true, and citizens found themselves no less equipped than journalists or pundits to speculate about the proper course of action. If these are the characteristics necessary to push an issue into the realm of widespread discussion, then complex policy questions are unlikely to do so.

We also need to learn more precisely the effects of conversation. The transformative justifications offered for deliberation sound good in theory, but do they operate in practice? Do people find their community spirit enhanced by talking through political questions with one another? Do they gain efficacy and autonomy? Are their opinions of higher quality in some identifiable way? At the moment, we cannot say.

The relationship of the news media to political conversation also requires exploration beyond the simple correlations already identified. For instance, Elihu Katz suggested, using the experience of recent developments in Israel as a case study, that political conversation may depend in part on the perception that one's conversation partners have been exposed to the same news as one's self (Katz 1996). With an ever-increasing number of sources of political information, the possibility that people will become fragmented in their knowledge of political events presents itself. One may no longer be able to speak of an overarching variable called "media exposure"; instead, there are now many kinds of exposure, each of which may influence conversation in unique ways. In addition, some news content may actually discourage people from talking about politics. The observation made by Gabriel Tarde a century ago—that "A pen suffices to set off a thousand tongues" (Tarde 1969, 304)—needs to be explored in today's media context.

Finally, improved measures of political discussion should be developed. Previous surveys on the matter of political conversation have had two things in common: they were conducted in the weeks before or after an election (usually a presidential election), and they asked people how much they talked about "politics." It seems likely that different people consider different issues to fall under the category of politics. For instance, when two people talk about an election they are certainly talking about politics. But what about crime in their city or the actions of the local school board? These topics are political but many people do not conceive of them as such. It may also be the case that, most of the time, people understand many topics to be political but that, when a campaign is underway, respondents hear the word politics and think only of "the campaign." This could be particularly true when they have just been asked a series of questions about the candidates, and have thus been primed to consider the campaign as the sole source of political activity.

People discuss politics for any number of reasons: to express themselves, to impress others, to learn, or merely to pass the time. When doing so, they enter the political world by engaging their fellow citizens. Making this engagement more closely resemble true deliberation—and doing so for more of the citizenry—presents a difficult challenge. But it is a challenge that must be faced, for when deliberation is absent, what remains is a democracy without a public.

NOTES

1. Nonetheless, Berelson et al. (1954, 307) argued that "if there is one characteristic for a democratic system (besides the ballot itself) that is theoretically required, it is the capacity for and the practice of discussion."

2. The surveys discussed in this paper were conducted by the Annenberg Public Policy Center of the University of Pennsylvania.

3. These data were obtained by the combination of two variables. Respondents were asked how often their political conversations included some difference of opinion. Each response to this question was assigned a percentage (never = 0, rarely = .1,

sometimes = .25, often = .5), then this percentage was multiplied by the respondent's frequency of general political conversation to obtain a frequency of disagreement.

4. The extent to which this is the case has been the subject of extensive research, complicated by the issue of causal direction. Whatever the degree to which policy-makers influence public opinion, however, few would argue that public opinion exerts no influence on policy.

10

Presidential Communication as Cultural Form: The Town Hall Meeting

David Michael Ryfe

When President Carter stepped to the podium in the town hall of Clinton, Massachusetts, on March 16, 1977, to conduct his first presidential town meeting, he innovated a new form of presidential communication.[1] Dwight Eisenhower used a quasi–town hall format during the 1956 presidential campaign, but no sitting president had ever engaged in a televised forum so spontaneous, informal, and intimate.[2] During his four-year term, Carter held seventeen of these events. Presidents Reagan and Bush chose to ignore Carter's innovation, but President Clinton resurrected the form to conduct ten town meetings during his first term in office (see appendix). Use of the form by presidential candidates has increased dramatically in the last two election cycles. Thus, though the term has its roots in seventeenth-century Puritan America, the town meeting has become a newly discovered adjunct to American democracy. However, despite its novelty and its persistence across three decades, scholars have devoted little attention to this genre. Indeed, I found no studies of President Carter's town meetings, and only one examination of President Clinton's (Denton and Holloway 1996).

Why this lack of attention? Particular research agendas are difficult to explain or predict. However, the agenda of the field as a whole has largely been shaped by the theoretical lens of the bargaining model of presidential power advanced by Neustadt (1990; see also Ceasar, Thurow, Tulis, and Bessette 1981; Cohen 1997; Kernell 1997; Medhurst 1996; Stuckey and Antczak 1998; Tulis 1987; Windt 1987). This tradition suggests that presidents strategically speak to the public to leverage their bargaining power with other political actors. From this vantage point, the town meetings are wholly uninteresting. President Carter's town meetings were purposefully low-key affairs; they attracted little media attention and consequently did little to help the president mobilize public opinion behind his agenda. President Clinton used the town meeting format more aggressively—particularly in support of his 1993 health care reform proposal—but when that proposal failed, and when the president's extracurricular activities became a focus of attention, interest quickly dissipated.

In this chapter, I show that the town meetings are more interesting than scholars have allowed heretofore; they are interesting not as instruments of political bargaining but as cultural forms. Chaney (1993, 83) writes that a cultural form has three qualities: it is socially organized and produced; it generates narratives (complete with typical plots, characters, and scenery) that provide its meaning; and it establishes a set of roles and behaviors for participants that mark it as a distinctive social activity. As a cultural form, presidential town meetings are structured, meaningful activities. They borrow from long-standing meanings associated with town meetings that stretch back to Puritan America, and they appeal to more recent meanings attached to the form that emanate from new social movements. Within the narrative space of these meanings, presidents and audiences are invited to assume particular roles and to behave in specific ways. In this sense, they register what Stuckey and Antczak (1998, 411) call the "constitutive" dimension of presidential representation: how presidents and publics are produced as particular kinds of social actors within a form of communication.

In the following, I examine these presidential town meetings as the new cultural model of presidential re-presentation. This model has its roots, of course, in political meanings typically associated with the generic town meeting format, but it has particular resonance with the populist and personalist sensibilities of the new social movements as well (Cohen 1985; Melucci 1989, 1996; Touraine 1988). These movements stress a political style that is informal and authentic, rooted in an intimate, interactive sharing of personal experience among participants (rather than the projection of personality). As such, the town hall violates the heavily scripted, televisual forms of re-presentation typically employed by presidents. Presidential town meetings highlight the contours of this new model of re-presentation. More precisely, they illuminate a *conflict* between this model and more traditional varieties of presidential re-presentation associated with the post–World War II presidency.

To make this argument, I assume that presidents do not control the meaning of their speech activities but that this meaning is at least in part structured into the forms of communication they use. This is precisely the kind of assumption made by neoinstitutional theory (Powell and Dimaggio 1991; March and Olsen 1984, 1989; Orren and Skowronek 1994; Skowronek 1982, 1997, 1998). Neoinstitutionalism has elaborated a theory of cultural rules, what Sewell (1992, 8) calls "cultural schemas," that are taken to structure political action by defining appropriate roles and behaviors available in a given context. According to neoinstitutionalists, such schemas construct the range of identities (who it is possible to be) and behaviors (what it is possible to do) available in political interaction by establishing specific senses of appropriateness and legitimacy (see also Zucker 1977, 1983, 1987, 1988).

Drawing on the vocabulary of neoinstitutionalism, I show that the town meetings of Presidents Carter and Clinton indicate a conflict between models of presidential re-presentation. In the process, I build upon recent efforts to incorporate neoinstitutionalist insights into the field of political communication (Cook 1998; Sparrow 1999). The result is an agenda for presidential communication that moves beyond a strategic, bargaining framework to pay greater attention to the cultural meaning of the communicative forms employed by presidents.

THEORIES OF PRESIDENTIAL COMMUNICATION

Modern theories of presidential communication have their roots in the work of Neustadt (1990). Neustadt argued that the primary source of presidential power lay in the president's personal capacity to bargain with Washington elites rather than in the formal institutional mechanisms of the office. Good presidential bargainers carefully manage their reputation among elites and use their public popularity to help them in these relationships. By leveraging his Washington reputation and his public popularity, a president convinces political elites that what he wants them to do is what they ought to do, and he tells the public that what he wants done is what ought to be done.

More recent scholarship has extended this basic model. Kernell (1997) has shown that, due to changes in the institutional environment of Washington politics, "going public" has become a much more prominent presidential strategy. Increasingly, to achieve their political goals, presidents have gone over the heads of Washington elites to mobilize public opinion behind their policies. Scholars of the "rhetorical presidency" (Ceasar et al. 1981; Tulis 1987) share Kernell's insight. Though they trace its source to the Wilsonian theory of presidential leadership (and not to institutional changes), these analysts present empirical data similar to that of Kernell, which suggest that modern (post nineteenth-century) presidents use rhetoric much more often than premodern presidents. They situate this insight within Neustadt's theory of presidential bargaining. According to Tulis (1987, 11–12), the "rhetorical presidency" ought to be "integrated into [the] bargaining perspective [by ascertaining] the conditions under which such appeals strengthen, weaken, or substitute for traditional exchange relations."

The literature spawned by Kernell's metaphor of "going public" and Tulis's "rhetorical presidency" is enormous. Scholars have examined everything from presidential speech to presidential travel (for a review of this literature, see Stuckey and Antczak 1998). Within this diversity, however, the field generally has maintained a strategic view of presidential communication.[3] For instance, a great deal of attention has been paid to strategies of presidential image construction (see also Maltese 1994; Winfield 1990), and to how presidents use instruments like polls, speeches, and travel to increase their popularity (see also Darcy and Richman 1988; Gilboa 1990; Ragsdale 1984; Simon and Ostrom 1989; Sudman 1982). Scholars have examined presidential responses to public opinion (see also Mannheim and Lammers 1981) and have dissected the personal characteristics of individual presidents in search of keys to their rhetorical strategies (see also Glass 1985; Keeter 1987; McCann 1990; Thomas and Siegelman 1984). Perhaps the most work has been done on negotiations between presidents and the press over the mediation of presidential speech (see also Cook 1998; Grossman and Kumar 1981; Smoller 1990; Sparrow 1999; Tebbel and Watts 1985).

Within this literature one can glean several operating assumptions. For instance, it is assumed that presidents are in command of their speech: what they say is what they intend to say. A corollary to this assumption is that presidential personality is a primary determinant of how a president performs his rhetorical duties (Barber 1977). If presidents determine how and what they speak, then it follows that they must personally be disposed to speaking in this manner rather than another. Thus, we have arguments suggesting that President Roosevelt was "good" at using radio in large part because of qualities inherent to his personality (Ryan 1988; Winfield 1990), just as Presidents Kennedy and Reagan were "good" at using television for the same reason (Denton 1988; Henggeler 1995; Watson 1990).

This literature also assumes that the meaning of presidential speech is wholly contained within a president's political goals. When do presidents hold press conferences and to what end (Lammers 1981; Mannheim and Lammers 1981)? When do presidents speak to which groups and why (Kernell 1997; O'Loughlin and Grant 1990)? When do presidents make speeches and to what political end (Ragsdale 1984)? These kinds of questions stress the instrumental character of presidential speech—its use as a strategic weapon in negotiations over policies and issues.

Finally, this literature tends to reduce the mass media in one of two directions. Either the mass media are reduced to the news media, or they are reduced to inherent, technical qualities of the medium. It is telling that, when addressing the mediation of presidential speech, both Kernell (1997, chap. 3) and Tulis (1987, 186–189) confine themselves to discussions of the press. This focus makes sense if one assumes that presidential speech is located within the narrow political universe of Washington, D.C. In this setting, the news media play a substantial role in mediating the influence of the president's words on both the public and on Washington elites. However, in making this assumption, the literature virtually ignores other forms of mass media, such as the movies, fictional television genres, and radio.

Other scholars reduce the mass media, particularly television, to their technical characteristics. For example, Ceasar et al. (1981, 164) suggest that "the mass media . . . must be understood first from the perspective of their technical abilities" (also see Meyrowitz 1985 on this point). This form of technological determinism has led Jamieson (1988, 13), among others, to worry about the influence of television on political communication. "Because television is a visual medium," she writes, it allows politicians to "use [it] to short-circuit the audience's demand that . . . claims . . . be dignified with evidence." In a similar vein, Gronbeck (1996, 39) argues that certain inherent characteristics of broadcast media have destroyed "the veil of mystery, the foundation of political wisdom, and perhaps the presidency itself." Here, media are viewed as containing technical properties that shape the nature and influence of any message broadcast through them.

Each of these assumptions can be challenged drawing on arguments made by neoinstitutional theorists. Take, for instance, the assumption that presidents are in control of their speech. Neoinstitutionalists argue that all social actors are only partially in control of their activities. Presidents, like everyone else, are "socially constructed" (Berger and Luckmann 1967); or, put more poetically by Geertz (1973, 5), they live within "webs of significance" which society itself has spun. If this is so, then presidential communication is less a product of individual, strategic choice than of, what? On a neoinstitutionalist view, they are a product of institutionalized rules.

The exact definition of a rule has been difficult to pinpoint. For instance, March and Olsen (1989, 17) define rules as the "routines, procedures, conventions, roles, strategies, organizational forms, and technologies around which political activity is constructed. We also mean the beliefs, paradigms, codes, cultures, and knowledge that surround, support, elaborate, and contradict these roles and routines." Sewell (1992, 8) has helpfully suggested that this myriad of metaphors can be subsumed within the notion of "cultural schema." Schemas imply that within any given social context individuals are presented with informal "procedures," "aesthetic norms," "recipes for action," "norms of etiquette," and "sets of [symbolic] equivalences." Cultural schemas guide action; they tell individuals how to go on in a given situation and how to assess the actions of others. As such, cultural schemas constrain *and* enable action.

Schemas are embedded in cultural forms. For instance, in cultural forms like the press conference, the nationwide broadcast, or the town meeting, presidents are confronted with "recipes for action" that guide their behavior. These recipes are experienced as expectations as to how they ought to behave in these contexts. Of course, they do not have to use these recipes. They retain a right to resist expectations, but in so doing they must in fact resist—that is, they must strain against expectations that seek to regulate their behavior. In the very act of resistance they illuminate the cultural schemas embedded in these contexts. Moreover, presidents are not always free to choose the cultural forms within which they interact with others. For example, since the presidency of Woodrow Wilson, presidents have been expected to meet with reporters on a routine basis. Similarly, presidents are expected to issue a yearly State of the Union address before Congress and to speak to the nation periodically via television. Again, they might attempt to adapt these communicative forms to their personal strengths and weaknesses, but they cannot fully dictate the expectations—the "recipes for action"—that are embedded within them. In this sense, not only are presidents not fully in control of their speech, neither are they in charge of how they will say what they say.

But let us be more specific. How exactly do presidents lose control of their speech? This general question has given rise to a vibrant debate among neoinstitutionalists (for discussions of this debate, see Powell and Dimaggio 1991; Rockman 1994; Soltan, Uslaner, and Haufler 1998; Zucker 1987). One strand of neoinstitutional theory, particularly popular among economists and political scientists, takes a fairly strong structuralist position (Hall and Taylor 1998). That is, as North (1981, 201) has argued, institutions in this literature simply "constrain people's choice sets." The language of "choice sets" implies that individuals are "rational," that is, strategically oriented, but that they exist in a world of uncertain knowledge and so, to increase decision-making efficiency, they abide by routine, institutionalized rules of conduct. In this manner, cultural schemas might be taken to exercise a regulative constraint on presidential behavior.

An alternative strand of neoinstitutionalism, found more in sociology and history (see also Zucker 1977, 1983, 1987, 1988; March and Olsen 1995), argues that institutions are constitutive as much as regulative. That is, institutions are taken to engender particular identities. Even such bedrock notions as self-interest and rationality are socially constructed, argue some scholars (Dimaggio 1988). Individuals do not enter these environments with pre-formed identities and interests but rather discover these elements in interaction with others. As March and Olsen (1984, 741) put it, "Politics is . . . education . . . a place for discovering, elaborating, and expressing meaning . . . shared (or opposing) conceptions of experience, values and the nature of existence." Rather than a structure imposed on participants, institutions are the "stuff" which makes action possible. On this view, when presidents participate in a forum like the press conference, they experience a set of expectations as to how they ought to behave. To live up to these expectations, they must adopt the recipes for action" the roles and behaviors considered appropriate to that context. In this manner, presidents are not regulated by schemas so much as invited to embody a role that satisfies social expectations. To this extent, their identity as president is in part constituted by the cultural forms in which they find themselves.

This distinction between institutions as regulative and as constitutive is crucial because these approaches orient analysts in two distinctive directions. Viewed as a regulative mechanism, analysts might simply read off the rules of a given social context from its structural features without ever analyzing how actual individuals interact in that environment. As Sparrow (1999, 15) argues, since "structure determines culture," the meaning of a situation is given by its institutional arrangement.

In contrast, the cultural understanding of institutions argues that structure itself is produced and reproduced in interaction. This notion is close to Garfinkel's (1967, 20) suggestion that "social order . . . does not derive automatically from shared patterns of evaluation and social roles, but is constituted in practical activity, in the course of everyday interaction." Geertz (1973, 17) puts the matter in a similar way: "Behavior must be attended to, and with some exactness, because it is through the flow of behavior, or more precisely, social action—that cultural forms find articulation . . . whatever or wherever symbol systems 'in their own terms' may be, we gain empirical access to them by inspecting events." This is to say that cultural schemas are not merely given but are produced in social action, in the *interaction* between individuals who devote resources—cognitive, emotional, material— to the enactment of one schema rather than another.

This point brings us to the second assumption of the bargaining model: that the meaning of presidential speech is wholly contained within a president's strategic goals. That presidents employ strategic thinking to determine their speech activities is undeniable. However, since they are not in complete control of these activities, it is at least as important, perhaps more important, to know something about how those activities are shaped behind the backs of presidents as it is to know of these local strategies. This notion is very close to Foucault's (1990) discussion of discursive power. It is clear, Foucault writes, that power is exercised within a "series of [individual] aims and objectives. But this does not mean that it results from the choice or decision of an individual subject." Rather, the power of discourse lies in the "logic" of the "comprehensive systems" that give shape and meaning to local tactics (95). In terms of presidential communication, much of the power in shaping presidential speech lies not in individual intentionality but in the logic of the cultural forms within which this speech is routinely given expression.

Part of that logic concerns the media through which presidential speech is communicated. From a neoinstitutionalist perspective, it is inappropriate to reduce those media to either the news media or technology. This is so because media themselves are properly understood as cultural forms, that is, as sets of schemas or "logics" (on media "logic," see Altheide and Snow 1979). Chaney's definition of a cultural form is pertinent here. As cultural forms, mass media are defined by how they are socially organized and produced, the narratives that give meaning to this productive process, and the roles and behaviors that

David Michael Ryfe

mark each medium as a distinctive kind of social activity. Television, for instance, may be visually oriented (though see Cavell 1979 on television as talk-oriented), but what this visual orientation means—how it is socially organized, how it is made sense of, how it produces particular roles and behaviors—these things compose the social tissue surrounding the technology. The power of mass media does not inhere in their technical characteristics but in the meanings produced and reproduced in their production and reception.

Cook (1998) and Sparrow (1999) develop this insight with respect to the news media, but they do not extend it to its logical conclusion: that as cultural forms, all mass media, not only the news media, may play a role in shaping political communication. Neoinstitutionalists use the term "isomorphism" to describe the process by which schemas from one cultural form, say the movies, migrate to other cultural forms, like a president's televised speech to the nation (Strang and Meyer 1993). In principle, any given form of presidential communication might be constructed by the system of production, the narratives, and the roles and behaviors of mass-mediated cultural forms that have gravitated from any of the culture industries into national political discourse. The news media is only one of these industries, and to focus attention strictly on them unduly ignores the potential influence of other media. Thus, one must not reduce mass media in either direction: to their technical qualities or to the news media.

Taken together, these insights compose a very different perspective on presidential speech than that suggested by the traditional bargaining model. According to neoinstitutionalism, presidential speech is shaped by cultural form as much as individual intention or personality. Cultural forms are defined by processes of production, narratives developed to lend meaning to these processes, and typical roles and behaviors that distinguish the form as a particular type of social activity. These aspects of cultural forms are not imposed top-down onto presidents, but rather are available to social actors as cultural resources in context-specific interactions. Presidents turn to such resources because they are rewarded for doing so—that is, these resources are associated with prevailing expectations and hold the promise of showing presidents to be legitimate and successful leaders of public opinion. This process may not be easy or uncomplicated. Presidents may resist expectations, expectations may change, or cultural forms may contain competing recipes for action that pull them in different directions. Such breaches only make the analysis of presidential communication more informative about the culture of political discourse.

PRESIDENTIAL TOWN MEETINGS

In the post–World War II period, presidents typically spoke to mass publics through one of two forms: nationwide addresses or televised press conferences. There was the occasional televised interview, and of course presidents traveled across the country to meet with small groups, but they engaged mass publics primarily by holding televised press conferences and giving nationwide addresses. These forms contributed to a presidential image unique to the twentieth century, one that was familiar and intimate, yet magisterial and larger than life. In the past two decades, it has inspired analysts to write of the personal president (Lowi 1985) and the prime-time presidency (Denton 1988); electronic eloquence (Jamieson 1988) and statecraft as stagecraft (Schmuhl 1990); video-game politics (Schram 1987) and leadership as spectacle (Miroff 1998). Such metaphors are meant to convey the sense of presidents crafting images that at once distanced them from the public and yet allowed them to speak to them in intimate and sincere terms. Another way of putting this observation is that these communicative forms were infused with the cultural schema of movie stardom.

Stardom is a distinctive recipe for action designed to solve economic dilemmas encountered by the early Hollywood movie industry (King 1986). Like any cultural form, it involved a distinctive system of production: media professionals used routine procedures to turn ordinary actors into intimate, yet larger-than-life personalities (see also deCordova 1990; Fowles 1992; Gamson 1994). Stars and their publics came to occupy particular roles—they were expected to be both larger than life and ordinary persons—and particular meanings about the status of stardom were circulated through the culture (Cavell 1979; Dyer 1986).

By mid-century, forms of presidential address like the nationwide broadcast and the televised press conference were infused with the schema of stardom (Ryfe 1997, 1999); that is, these forms were organized in the same manner, and by the same media professionals, as that of movie stardom (Ryfe 1997; Winfield 1990). Not surprisingly, American society began to associate qualities of intimacy and mysteriousness with the role of the presidency (Lowi 1985). Even traditional scholars of the presidency, including Binkley (1962), Ranney (1962), Koenig (1996) and Rossiter (1987), shared in the general feeling that the best modern presidents were like movie stars—mysterious in their ways, powerful in their influence. Theodore White (quoted in Reichard 1982, 364) summarizes this conventional wisdom when he writes that "about the President there must be an air of remoteness and distance to make majestic American power." After the presidency of Franklin Roosevelt, the set of expectations, beliefs, norms, and practices associated with political stardom became a kind of recipe for presidential communication with mass publics (Leuchtenburg 1983).

Presidential town meetings represent a conflict between this traditional model and that of a new schema of presidential re-presentation. This latter schema is more populist, participatory, and personalist than the star model. Its roots lay not in the media industries but in the new social movements of the postwar period, particularly in the civil rights movement (Franklin and

Moss 1994; Chalmers 1996; Weisbrot 1990). In practices like sit-ins and study groups, the civil rights movement innovated a new form of political leadership that stressed grassroots participation and authentic interaction between leaders and followers. Inspired by this vision of participatory democracy, the student movement of the 1960s popularized notions of authenticity and personal experience as proper foundations of politics (Clecak 1983). As women participated in these new techniques of protest and grassroots organizing, they turned this brand of personal politics into a new form of political practice (Evans 1980). Within this political current, good politics was considered local, not mass mediated, experiential rather than strategic, personal rather than professional, democratic, not elitist, and rooted in individual identity and personal conviction, not in impersonal, rational procedures.

This schema encouraged presidents to stress their authentic connection to real people—an expectation that fit naturally the form and structure of the town meeting. However, when President Carter adopted the town meeting form, it raised an inherent conflict with the more traditional model of presidential re-presentation.[4] For instance, the first of these gatherings took place in Clinton, Mass., population 13,000. Subsequent meetings took place in Yazoo City, Miss., population 12,000; Nashua, N.H.; Aliquippa, Pa.; Portsmouth, N.H.; Bardstown, Ky., population 7,000; Burlington, Iowa, population 7,000; Tampa, Fla.; Dolton, Ill.; and Merced, Calif. Purposely "off the beaten track," as one aide involved in selecting the sites put it, these towns evoked images of a "real" America outside the Washington beltway (quoted in Walsh 1977, A1). The town's population often turned out to greet the president in parade style along the town's main street. At the town meeting in Merced, the walls of the gymnasium were lined with placards that read "A Big Howdy from a Small Town" (Weisman 1980). As if to accentuate the intimate atmosphere, Carter often took off his jacket and rolled up his shirtsleeves when answering audience questions. To emphasize his intention to get close to real Americans, Carter made it a point to stay overnight in the homes of townspeople like Catherine Thompson of Clinton, Mass., even going so far as to write a note explaining why her children were late for school.

Yet, although the meetings evoked notions of intimacy and authenticity, each was held in a kind of rally format that put a great deal of distance between the president and his audience. Given that the average attendance at these events was nearly 1,500, the audience resembled a crowd of fans more than a small gathering of "real" people, and the meetings took on the feel of a campaign event more than an intimate discussion with the president. Often, the gymnasiums were so full that people in the back took to holding placards or signs for the president to read. There is a curious contradiction then, between the expectation that the event would be intimate and its actual design.

There are other contradictions. For example, since the meetings evoked a sense of "realness" and "informality," the mass media played a limited role in their production. Most of the town meetings were held in high school gymnasiums, and one (in Burlington, Iowa) was held outside, on a grassy hill overlooking a bluff. Poorly lit, and unable to carry sound very well, these venues were not ideal environments for broadcasting a televisual event. Given where they were held, it is not surprising that only three of the town meetings in my sample (in Clinton, Yazoo, and Aliquippa) were broadcast live. The first was broadcast nationwide, while the other two were broadcast regionally; all three were aired on the public broadcasting system (PBS), not on the major television networks.

The absence of television freed the audience to be spontaneous, asking any question they desired. In Yazoo (July 21, 1977, 1321–1323), the president was asked successively about Public Law 93-641, and about "how it feels to be president." Questioners asked about the Middle East peace process and about local redevelopment programs. They spoke on behalf of the homeless, the children of America, taxpayers, and small businesspeople, among others. One woman (Dolton, October 16, 1979, 1947) told of the personal dilemma of paying for her children's college education. Another (Bardstown, July 31, 1979, 1343) wanted to know how she could get direct-dial telephone service in her county. Audience members (Portsmouth, April 25, 1979, 708) joked with the president: "Mr. President, excuse me if I'm nervous, but the last time I won anything in a government raffle, I was drafted"; and on two occasions (in Portsmouth and Tampa) audience members held up protest banners, heckled the president and other audience members, and held town meetings of their own outside the gymnasium. In this way, interactions between the president and citizens approximated the expectation that these events would allow informal and authentic interaction.

At the same time, the meetings contained elements that contradicted this expectation. For instance, President Carter rarely moved from behind a lectern located in the middle of a raised stage. The lectern came complete with the presidential seal, a representation of the president's unique position. Spatially, the meetings resembled a press conference. The effect of this arrangement was to accentuate the position of the president, who stood before the audience as a singular, stationary performer, while diminishing the individuality of the audience members, who remained faceless within an audience of over a thousand people. Rather than being a "real" person speaking to average Americans, this arrangement constructed Carter as "the president," a star performing in front of a mass audience.

The hold of this more traditional representation of the president/public relationship is also apparent in the verbal interactions between the president and his audiences. Though allowed to address the president in any way they saw fit, audience members chose to approach him most often in terms that emphasized their roles as part of a mass public. A questioner during the Clinton town meeting (March 16, 1977, 394) began this way: "Bill Clinley, 26 Cotchelay

Street. Mr. President . . . *we* ask that despite many pressures which are exerted upon you to mold your programs to conform to special interests. . . . *We* have faith that you will always place *our* interests above all of these." Another questioner (Aliquippa, September 3, 1978, 1606), after Carter's Camp David summit with Menachem Begin and Anwar Sadat, took the time to "commend [Carter] on [his] splendid efforts . . . I think I can speak for the majority of Americans in saying that we are extremely proud. . . ." Still another (Tampa, August 10, 1979, 1577) asked the president about natural gas: "Do you think *you* and *we*, the *people*, can get the Congress to listen to *you* and to *us* and help *us* get an energy program that will keep *us* the richest and the greatest and the freest nation on Earth?"

Despite his intention to get closer to the people, President Carter also felt more comfortable assuming the traditional role of "the president." For instance, in his first town meeting (Clinton, March 16, 1977, 386), the president was asked what he "personally fe[lt]" must be done to secure peace in the Middle East. Here, Carter is presented with an opportunity to speak in personal tones about an issue of some political importance. Instead of doing so, he offered a diplomatic lecture on the "prerequisites for peace," ending with an appeal to Israeli and Palestinian leaders: "we offer our good offices . . . [to] get all of the parties to agree to come together to Geneva." The president not only instructed (rather than conversed) with the audience member, he used the question—much as he might in a press conference—as a platform for issuing a message to political actors outside the forum. At other times Carter relied upon the sense of power rooted in his office to lend his answers force and drama. To a question about inflation (Portsmouth, April 25 1979, 704), the president began his response by saying: "The first thing we can do, I as President, is to set an example. . . ." Carter also often portrayed himself as a model whom the American public might emulate. For example, to a question about how Americans might conserve energy (Burlington, August 22, 1979, 1500), he asserted that "I try to run four or five miles every day," the implication being that if he could do it, others should try as well. Finally, at the end of nearly every town meeting, President Carter sought to rally Americans behind a grand image of the nation. "We're the strongest nation on Earth," he told his audience in Dolton, Illinois (October 16, 1979, 1953). "Militarily, we're the strongest; economically, we're the strongest . . . let's don't ever forget that the United States of America is the best place on Earth to live. It's the greatest nation on Earth."

Thus, these events register a conflict of expectations. One the one hand, they implied that presidents ought to present themselves as real people, not as a kind of political star; they suggested that it was legitimate for "average Americans" to interact with rather than to simply applaud their president; and they indicated that presidential leadership might be done not by mobilizing and organizing mass publics through the mass media, but by speaking to Americans face to face, in intimate, informal settings. This is to say that these events modeled a populist form of re-presentation.

One the other hand, the president routinely engaged in a kind of moral cheerleading. In a forum advertised as a "town hall meeting," a face-to-face meeting of ordinary folks with their political leader, President Carter stood behind a lectern as if he were at a press conference; he regularly assumed the identity of "the president," an individual with grave and serious responsibilities, a star for the public to adore. For their part, audience members were presented with an opportunity to speak to the president in any manner they saw fit, but most often they strode to the microphones to speak in the voice of "the people," "average Americans" calling on their president for information and inspiration.

What one sees in these events, then, is a clash between conflicting recipes for action. Ought the president construct himself as a "real" person or as a larger-than-life figure? Should he engage in a spontaneous conversation with real Americans or conduct himself as a more formal instructor on world events? Should audience members speak to the president in their own voices or in the voice of the "average American"? These kinds of issues arose only because it was no longer taken for granted that presidents ought to use the machinery of the mass media to construct themselves as political stars. This confusion is registered in both the form and the content of these meetings.

Though it was displayed in new ways, this confusion was also apparent in President Clinton's town meetings.[5] Differences between the Clinton and Carter town meetings are clear in the arrangement and mood of the events. Unlike President Carter's version, President Clinton's meetings were highly mediated events. Broadcast from local television stations, these meetings were linked via satellite to three or four audiences located in other local stations in the region. Where Carter targeted small towns for his meetings, Clinton focused on regional television markets. Television studios in Atlanta, San Diego, and Kansas City replaced the high school gymnasiums of Clinton, Dolton, and Aliquippa.

This use of media created a different feeling of openness from Carter's forums. In particular, Clinton's meetings borrowed the feeling of the daytime television talk show that had become so popular in the early 1990s. An audience of no more than a few hundred sat in seats low and near to the stage. Only a few feet separated the president from audience members. Wide-screen monitors beamed audiences linked by satellite into the forum. Clinton had nothing more than a stool on stage with him; instead of standing behind a lectern, he carried a microphone, walking around the stage to get closer to questioners. Audience members were not forced to move down an aisle to a fixed microphone to address the president. Instead, local news journalists walked down the aisles, approaching individuals much like Phil Donahue on his television talk show. The effect was to reconfigure the symbolic power relationship between the president and the audience. Audience members did not remain part of a faceless crowd watching the president perform. They held as much of the stage as the president, participating in the discussion far more than Carter's audiences were allowed.

The intimacy engendered by this format is clear in the kinds of questions asked of the president. Recall that most questions asked of President Carter were policy-oriented, tending toward the voice of the mass citizen. In contrast, many of the questions put to President Clinton were explicitly framed in terms of the audience member's personal experience. A woman's question during the San Diego town meeting (May 17, 1993, 623) is typical:

> I'm really frustrated with the welfare system. Right now, I'm a single parent, and I just moved into the apartment. Since I moved into the apartment, my benefits have been cut, and I figured I'd try to make a better life for my child and myself, so I started to go to school. Since I've been going to school, I can't get any child care benefits. . . . What changes are you willing to make within that welfare system so that people such as myself can make a better life for their child and themselves?

Here, the warrant for this woman's question stems from her personal experience rather than, as in Carter's town meetings, from a claim to speak for the mass public.

President Clinton also contributed to this intimate atmosphere. Much more than Carter, Clinton used the informal language of personal pronouns, breezily talking in the form of "I," "you," and "we."[6] Often, the president linked the many stories of personal experience expressed by audience members. For example, after several persons discussed the issue of drugs at one town meeting (Sacramento, October 3, 1993, 1661), the president responded: "If you think what he said, plus what the young man said here who wanted the job for his friends, plus what the young man said whose brother got shot in school—it goes back to the bigger point." Where Carter embodied the role of "the president," distant from the public, Clinton brought the presidency down to the level of ordinary personal experience.

One sees this clearly in the many occasions when Clinton tried to draw audience members into his perspective as president. To a question about why he had not sought more middle-class tax cuts as he had promised during the campaign (Charlotte, April 5, 1994, 595), the president began this way: "After the election, the deficit by the previous administration was revised upward. So here's what I had to do. Do I go through with a whole middle-class tax cut and let the deficit balloon . . . or do I tell the American people the truth?" Here, instead of assuming the identity of "the president" (in which case, he might have responded, "As president, I think it is best that . . ."), Clinton tries to put the audience member into his shoes: here is the situation with which I was faced; here were my options; can you (audience member) now see why I have not asked for more tax cuts? This framing is subtle, but important. Rather than constructing an image of strength and vision, this frame deconstructs Clinton's role as president, making it available to others. If the frame is successful, audience members will come to agree with Clinton in this matter not because they trust his character or are awed by his power, but because they themselves have understood his situation and perspective. It is a frame that fits perfectly with the new personalist sensibility.

At the same time, Clinton's meetings were just as fractured as those of Carter, only they were fractured along different fault lines. Unlike Carter, who clearly did not intend to use his town meetings as a method of mobilizing the mass public behind a particular policy agenda, Clinton sought to use these events much as he might a press conference of a nationwide address. For example, although audience members spoke from their own experience, they were intended to represent the experience of a larger group. This is apparent in the method by which they were selected. Unlike in the Carter town meetings, where audience members were chosen at random or by raffle, when the Clinton White House agreed to do a town meeting, it asked local stations, as one report put it (Condon 1993, A8), to "assemble a representative audience." News directors (Freeman 1993, E6) took this cue to mean that the president wanted to face "real people" doing "real things." Therefore, instead of raffling off tickets, or handing them out on a first-come, first-served basis, news directors naturally turned to the tool with which they were most familiar: demographic marketing analysis. That is, audience members were selected according to how well they represented a particular social type.

It is clear in the moderators' introductions of audience members that it was this representativeness, rather than the questioner's individual experience, which local stations wanted to stress. For instance, during the meeting in Minneapolis, Minnesota, the moderator introduced a man as "providing the perspective of tonight's program of the small businessperson in small-town America." On another occasion (May 17, 1993, 685), the moderator gave this introduction: "Mr. President, you mentioned laid-off defense workers. Well, coincidentally, we just happen to have a couple, both of whom are laid-off defense workers." Doug Casey, WJAR Channel 10 anchor in Rhode Island, introduced a questioner during the May 9, 1994, town meeting as "a woman from Providence [who] has an artificial leg that has always been paid for under her medical plan" (880).

Personal experience, then, is translated in the Clinton town meetings into demographic representativeness. Individuals and families were trotted out to symbolize particular dilemmas: HIV-positive men and the health care system, children with preexisting medical conditions, mothers and fathers whose children had been shot to death at school. This tendency went so far that during the town meeting in Minneapolis, Minnesota (April 8,1994, 645–658), several video segments dramatized the predicaments of individuals in the audience before these individuals asked their questions so that those watching in the studio and at home could make the connection between personal problems and group dilemmas.

Clinton's own actions also violated the expectations of intimacy and authenticity engendered by the format. For instance, although he worked with the personal experiences of others, Clinton rarely shared his own personal experiences. Instead, he outlined a policy or plan. In fact, many of his responses were fashioned as policy lists. Some of these lists were fairly simple. The president's answer to a question on illegal immigration and health care, for example (San Diego, May 17, 1993, 682), consisted of only two points. Another list, addressed to a question about how his health care reform proposal would handle the issue of malpractice, consisted of three things: "We propose to do three things: number one, develop more alternative-dispute-resolution mechanisms; number two, limit the amount of contingency fees [for lawyers]; and number three . . . develop . . . a set of medical practice guidelines." But sometimes Clinton's answers became very complex. A four-part answer to a question concerning the issue of handguns in public schools (Cranston 1994) was so complex that the moderator felt compelled to break in: "Do you think you [audience member] can remember all that?" After the audience laughter died down, Clinton summarized his position: "Sure you can. Get the assault weapons off, take the handguns away from the kids, metal detectors and other security devices at schools, teach kids nonviolent ways to resolve their differences, and organize every school" (881).

This last example illustrates particularly well that, for every type of question, Clinton simply memorized a list of pertinent policies or proposals. This preparation is easily apparent in his contributions to the events. For instance, during the *Nightline* town meeting (September 1993, 1571), an audience member who was introduced as a retired educator with AIDS rambled on about how difficult it was to receive treatment under Medicare. As Koppel moved to cut him off, the president interjected: "I know what you're—can I get to the—I know the question. First of all . . ." It was not difficult to predetermine the kinds of questions that demographically selected audiences would ask. In this case, all Clinton needed were the key words "AIDS" and "Medicare" to produce an appropriate answer—even without a question being asked. At the end of the San Diego town meeting (May 17, 1993, 691), the president said he "thought you [the audience] were going to ask me about the problems with the sewage treatment in Tijuana." Without waiting for a direct question, he went ahead and listed a series of proposals for solving this problem. On another occasion (Minneapolis, April 8, 1994, 653), after an audience member was introduced as a self-employed farmer, but asked a question about organ donation, the president briefly answered his question and then said: "Now, let me also say to you since you were introduced in a slightly different way—as a farmer who's self-employed, who already had a medical problem, who has folks working for you on the farm. Farmers, in my opinion . . . ."

Combined with the representativeness of audience members, Clinton's scripted performance indicates that these events were in part structured by traditional notions of presidential re-presentation. In a televised forum such as this, Clinton abided by the conventional notion that presidents ought not to be excessively spontaneous or informal. Moreover, he employed the meetings to "sell" his policies to the public. The implicit rhetorical form was this: these individuals represent social groups with real problems; my (Clinton's) proposals address these problems; you (audience member) either are a member of these groups (and hence you ought to agree with me) or you see that these policies help large numbers of people (and hence ought to agree with me). These meanings are implicit in the interactions of the meetings—in how audience members were framed, in the role President Clinton assumed, and in the meanings attached to the event.[7]

This ought not to detract from the extraordinary nature of these events. In place of a mass public, the president constructed the audience as a fragmented set of social groups. Audience members at home and in the studio were invited to adopt the perspective of the social groups to which they belonged and to see the benefit of Clinton's proposals from these points of view. At times—especially on difficult issues—they even were invited to assume the perspective of the president himself. This expectation was reinforced by the similarity of the events to the daytime talk show. Thus, instead of constructing an image of power and awe to which a mass public might bond, Clinton sought to persuade by juggling a diverse set of perspectives. His own perspective was only one among the many viewpoints represented at these events. Clinton's perspective was privileged, to be sure, and he tried to sell his programs to the public. But Clinton's re-presentation of himself was much more permeable, and more transferable, than had been permitted his twentieth-century predecessors.

Together, the Carter and Clinton town meetings illuminate a conflict between competing expectations concerning the proper roles and behaviors of presidents and publics. At the heart of this conflict lay a struggle over re-presentation: how should the president re-present himself to a mass public? How should the public be represented in national politics? As a form of communication, the town meeting is an effort to satisfy these competing expectations. One sees in the Carter and Clinton town meetings, then, an attempt to innovate a new cultural form of presidential re-presentation. The contradictions and ambiguities produced by this effort—and the fact that the two formats look and feel so different from one another—reveal their highly experimental nature. The fact that presidential candidates continue to play with the form, looking for a way to balance the complex social and political expectations, indicates that the conflict between them has not abated.

CONCLUSION

Many objections might be made about the agenda I am proposing for future study. One might argue that Presidents Carter and Clinton were personally disposed to being more informal and authentic in their public self-presentation and, hence, that their forums were too unique to tell a larger story. Since both presidents were populist and personalist, their re-presentations may be due less to the form itself than to their idiosyncracies. One might also point out that the town hall form has utterly failed as a tool for "going public." After his health care reform proposal died in 1994, for example, Clinton did only one more town meeting, and in his second administration he attempted none. Finally, one might claim that within the case studies presented here, there is more evidence of presidents controlling their speech than being constituted by the format of the events.

To my mind, these criticisms may be correct and still not detract from the importance of the agenda I endorse here. Indeed, neoinstitutionalist theory does not suggest that individuals do not matter or that they do not have strategic goals or the ability to make discursive choices. Clearly, these two presidents chose to employ town meetings, just as Presidents Reagan and Bush did not. The question, however, is two-fold: is something larger, something cultural, going on here more than mere strategic choice? And if so, are wider meanings embedded within these events?

I would answer yes to both questions. I have shown that there are interesting contradictions and ambiguities in these presidential town meetings. Within each version, one sees presidents and audiences acting according to contradictory expectations: to be formal yet informal; to be intimate yet impersonal; to speak for oneself or to speak for a larger role (of the "presidency" or the "mass citizen"); to use the meetings to share knowledge and experiences or to move public opinion polls. These kinds of ambiguities hint at a cultural struggle between competing understandings of what it means to re-present oneself before the public as president, and to engage with the president as a citizen. This struggle is not confined to presidents with a populist bent. During the 1996 Republican National Convention, candidate Bob Dole found himself upstaged by his wife precisely because she established an intimacy with the public that Dole could not muster. Similarly, during the 2000 presidential campaign, Vice President Al Gore reinvented his public self-presentation so as to appear "more authentic," just as George W. Bush sought to appear less "real" and more "presidential." This struggle over expectations lies not only at the level of personality and individual choice but also, and most profoundly, at the level of culture. Communicative forms like town meetings register this struggle. Analyzing them requires different assumptions and tools than the standard bargaining model of politics has embraced. It requires a new agenda for the study of presidential communication, an agenda sensitive to the cultural fabric of the nation and not just to the personalities and situations that come and go in politics.

NOTES

1. To give one a sense of the rarity of this development, only three other new forms of presidential communication were created in the twentieth century: the press conference (under Theodore Roosevelt and Woodrow Wilson); the nationwide broadcast (under Calvin Coolidge, Herbert Hoover, and Franklin D. Roosevelt); and the televised press conference (under Dwight Eisenhower and John F. Kennedy).

2. President Eisenhower's quasi–town hall meetings took place in October 1956 and were televised live. They were organized by the Republican National Committee (RNC) and the advertising agency Batten, Barton, Durstine & Osborne (BBD&O). Individuals were hand picked by the RNC. These individuals were given questions to ask and they rehearsed their delivery before the live program with a stand-in for President Eisenhower. Thus, not only were they campaign events rather than tools of governance, Eisenhower's formats were also not nearly as informal and spontaneous as President Carter's renditions. It should also be noted that a few presidential candidates, such as Hubert Humphrey during the 1960 presidential campaign and Richard Nixon during the 1968 presidential campaign, have used a similar type of format as Eisenhower.

3. I should point out that there is a small literature on the symbolic dimensions of the presidency (see also Denton 1982; Hart 1987; Hinckley 1990). This work is largely inspired by the writings of Murray Edelman (1964, 1971). I do not consider this literature in more detail because it does not represent the mainstream of presidential communication research and because it is generally interested in how presidents use symbols strategically, a focus which I wish to avoid.

4. The following analysis is based upon a randomly selected sample of ten of the seventeen town meetings President Carter conducted during his term of office. A list of these meetings can be found in the appendix. Transcripts of these events were obtained from the Jimmy Carter *Public Papers of the Presidents* series. Quotes from the transcripts are referred to by place, year, and page number.

5. The following is based upon an analysis of the ten town hall meetings that President Clinton conducted during his first term in office. A list of these meetings can be found in the appendix. Transcripts of these meetings were obtained from the William Jefferson Clinton *Public Papers of the Presidents* series. References to these transcripts are given according to place, date, and page number in this series.

6. The exact numbers of pronouns used are the following: President Carter employed 2,997 "I's" "you's" and "we's" in ten events. In comparison, President Clinton used these terms 3,898 times in the same number of meetings.

7. In this regard, it is telling that of seven newspapers I examined (the *New York Times*, the *Washington Post*, the *Washington Star*, the *Kansas City Star*, the *Chicago*

Tribune, the *Los Angeles Times,* and the *San Diego Union-Tribune*) every headline for President Clinton's first town meeting suggested that it was an occasion for the president to "sell" himself and his policies to the public.

APPENDIX: DATA SET FOR CARTER AND CLINTON TOWN MEETINGS

President Carter

The following ten town meetings were selected from the seventeen that Carter conducted during his term in office.

March 16, 1977	Clinton, Mass.
July 21, 1977	Yazoo City, Miss.
February 18, 1978	Nashua, N.H.
September 23, 1978	Aliquippa, Pa.
April 25, 1979	Portsmouth, N.H.
July 31, 1979	Bardstown, Ky.
August 22, 1979	Burlington, Iowa.
August 10, 1979	Tampa, Fla.
October 16, 1979	Dolton, Ill.
July 4, 1980	Merced, Calif.

President Clinton

The following ten town meetings were conducted by President Clinton during his first term in office. He conducted ten total during this period.

February 10, 1993	Detroit, Mich.
May 17, 1993	San Diego, Calif.
September 23, 1993	Tampa, Fla.
October 3, 1993	Sacramento, Calif.
March 15, 1994	Nashua, N.H.
April 5, 1994	Charlotte, N.C.
April 7, 1994	Kansas City, Mo.
April 8, 1994	Minneapolis, Minn.
May 9, 1994	Cranston, R.I.
June 1, 1995	Billings, Mont.

11

Forums for Citizenship in Popular Culture

Jeffrey P. Jones

Four men walk into a bar: Jesse Ventura, Ross Perot, Donald Trump, and Warren Beatty, each dressed as a political candidate. The five regulars at the bar offer their opinions: The *New York Times* reporter summarily dismisses them; Larry King wildly celebrates them; Jay Leno jokingly exploits them; Joe Public is somewhat intrigued by them; and the research scholar at the end of the bar ignores them.

What sounds like a bad joke is actually a somewhat accurate representation of how recent commentators have reacted to the increasingly blurred boundaries between popular culture and politics. Although we have witnessed a profound change in how formal politics appears in popular culture—including its appearance at times *as* popular culture—the academic community has generally turned a blind eye to how such changes are shaping political culture in the United States.

To speak of separate realms for the "serious" business of politics on the one hand and "entertainment" culture on the other is simply no longer possible, at least in the public's eye. Witness the following: politicians acting like celebrities (appearances on David Letterman and Arsenio Hall); politicians' personal lives scrutinized as if they were celebrities (Bill Clinton's impeachment and Bob Livingston's dethronement); news media acting like tabloids (circulating Clinton's supposed illegitimate child rumor); tabloids acting like news media (the Gennifer Flowers story in *The Star*); entertainment programs featuring politics (Comedy Central's *Indecision 2000* and *Politically Incorrect with Bill Maher*); political news as soap opera (the Clinton impeachment and the Clarence Thomas hearings); former politicians becoming talk show hosts (Mario Cuomo and Jesse Jackson); talk show hosts becoming politicians (Jesse Ventura and Pat Buchanan); new forms of political talk programming that include the voices of laity in place of or alongside "experts" (CNN's *TalkBack Live*); and young adults receiving more of their political news from Jay Leno than from Dan Rather. Although one might argue that many of these occurrences are not unprecedented, never has there been such a confluence of these improbable events.

Of special concern is the overall lack of attention these phenomena have received by scholars. While the expansion and institutionalization of cultural studies in the last twenty years has resulted in important examinations of "the political" in society, those studies rarely examine the impact of culture on "official," institutional politics. Similarly, traditional political communication research has far too rarely employed the theoretical insights gained from cultural studies, retaining its primary focus on traditional institutional political players and processes (elite–elite interactions or elite–lay interactions) with little recognition of how these agents are (or are not) incorporated into the everyday lives of citizens. These two academic camps have kept their respective campfires bright, although with seemingly little interest in appropriating the illuminating light coming from nearby campers.

An important new agenda for political communication research is this: scholars must study how popular culture is trying to shape political culture and vice versa. That includes the recognition of how popular culture affects political meaning in a consumer-driven society. As the mass media increasingly encode "the political" as entertainment offerings, these encodings become popular sites for the formation of common knowledge about politics. As such, we should no longer dismiss the late-night comedian/talk show host's characterizations of our politicians. Nor should we dismiss the seriousness of public reaction to celebrity entrants into formal politics as political candidates. No longer can we dismiss the politician's sense that popular cultural venues are good ways of reaching his or her constituency. And no longer should we dismiss new forms of radio and television talk shows as duping, distracting, and diverting citizens from the "real" business of politics. As culture industries continue to search for new means of profit making through diversified programming—including new encodings of politics as entertainment—we must recognize that the viewing audience may not find these offerings any less legitimate (or farcical) than the newscasters and pundits who traditionally shape and reflect political meaning through the media. Alan Wolfe, in a book review article in the early 1990's, made the argument with special effect.

> Americans are increasingly oblivious to politics, but they are exceptionally sensitive to culture. . . . Politics in the classic sense of who gets what, when and how is carried out by a tiny elite watched over by a somewhat larger, but still infinitesimally small, audience of news followers. The attitude of the great majority of Americans to such traditional political subjects is an unstable combination

of boredom, resentment, and sporadic attention. . . . Culture, on the other hand, grabs everyone's attention all the time. . . . Because they practice politics in cultural terms, Americans cannot be understood with the tool kits developed by political scientists. (Wolfe 1991, quoted in Grossberg 1992)

As Wolfe suggests, we must examine how citizens practice politics in cultural terms. One example offered here could easily be dismissed as "farcical entertainment"—the talk show *Politically Incorrect with Bill Maher*. Although produced as competition to other entertainment shows, political discussion programs (such as *P.I.*) that feature the voice of the laity offer *alternative* political interpretations of political events not found in traditional forums. As such, those "meanings" may be more *meaningful* to the average citizen/ television viewer than those developed by political elites whose legitimacy has been severely challenged in the last two decades. Because most political communication research on media focuses on elite–elite interactions (that is, the dance between politicians and the press) or elite–lay interactions (that is, public opinion polling, voter reactions to campaign advertising, etc.), we have a special opportunity to step outside the bounds of the traditional to take seriously the interactions *among laity* within the mass media.

I situate this new agenda in recent writings that have begun to explore the notion of "cultural citizenship." Next, I examine two types of television talk show texts, both centered on the Clinton–Lewinsky scandal, to exemplify how popular cultural texts can produce very different meanings from those produced by the elite-based media. Next, an entertainment-based program featuring lay political discussion, *Politically Incorrect with Bill Maher*, will be compared to the discourse found on *This Week with Sam Donaldson and Cokie Roberts*, with a special focus on the sense-making strategies employed by each show's discussants/participants. Finally, the chapter offers suggestions for ways in which this new agenda might be pursued to produce new insights into the maintenance of citizenship in popular culture.

NOTIONS OF "CULTURAL CITIZENSHIP"

Some scholars are beginning to grapple with the importance of popular culture as a primary site for the maintenance of public interest in, and development of common knowledge of, politics. While focused more on citizenship than on popular culture, Michael Schudson's recent writings examine how citizens contend with the political information they encounter daily, regardless of whether that information could be categorized as "serious" (for example, news) or "entertainment." Schudson contends that modern citizens "monitor" politics and political information in a crowded media landscape, as opposed to an earlier model of "informed" citizenship in which the ideal citizen was expected to gather and process political information in a rational-critical manner. Because the monitorial citizen is bombarded with loads of information, he or she "engages in environmental surveillance more than information-gathering. . . . Monitorial citizens scan (rather than read) the information environment in a way so that they may be alerted on a very wide variety of issues for a very wide variety of ends and may be mobilized around those issues in a large variety of ways" (Schudson 1998a, 311, 310).

Schudson's new model of citizenship is bolstered by research that explores the use of media in everyday life. This research suggests that consumers attend to media (and the information content they employ) in haphazard, partial, distracted, and combinatory ways (Bausinger 1984; Lull 1988; Silverstone and Hirsch 1992). If Schudson is correct, citizens may read about issues or events in the newspaper, watch *Nightline* to see what policymakers are saying, and then tune in to *Politically Incorrect* to see what "common sense" other public personalities offer on the matter. Or they may only pay scant attention to all three if nothing "significant" is occurring. The entertainment packaging of political discourse, then, does not necessarily diminish public interest and awareness, but provides another venue through which sense is made of public affairs.

In the field of television studies, several authors have begun to explore the interrelationships between television entertainment and political citizenship, although none has advanced anything approximating a full theory of "cultural citizenship." John Hartley, for instance, refers to media content as *democratainment*, "the means by which popular participation in public issues is conducted in the mediasphere" (Hartley 1999, 209). The audiences for this fusion, according to Hartley, are "citizens of media," a concept to "connect political participation with media-readership" (206–207). Hartley's exploration of these concepts is part of a larger project to understand changes occurring in the transformation of a public-service model of broadcasting in an age dominated by private media ownership, resulting in what he calls "do-it-yourself" citizenship, or semiotic self-determination. That is, Hartley is interested in how citizens use television as a "transcultural teacher" to educate themselves about what it means to be a citizen of Britain, Australia, etc. In his usual style as provocateur, though, Hartley's concepts are quite short on specifics, data, or further theorization.

Toby Miller (1998) extends the analysis of cultural citizenship through his writings on film. Miller is interested in the moments in which "the popular and the civic brush up against one another," and his work examines the "intersection of textual, social, and economic forms of knowledge with the popular under the sign of government" (Miller 1998, 4, 12). His attention is directed to what he calls "technologies of truth," in essence, the "popular logics for establishing fact." Miller recognizes that it is through citizen interaction with these technologies (media) that meaningful development and maintenance of citizenship occurs. As he notes, "when these technologies congeal to forge loyalty to the sovereign state through custom or art, they do so through the cultural citizen, who steps, sits, and shits outside the formalities of the Constitution, a citizen in need of daily maintenance through lore as much as its homonym." More than simply an alternate version of hegemony theory, Miller applies Foucault's theories of governmentality to examine the "consumer–citizen couplet" and the ways in which "the population knows itself and its duties" (17–18).

In sum, there is a growing recognition among scholars of the increased importance of popular culture for the day-to-day relationship between citizens and their government. As I have noted here, however, this relationship needs considerably more examination. After providing an illustration of the type of research this new agenda might produce, I offer some thoughts on the types of questions further research in this area might address.

Before moving forward, however, it is necessary to define what is meant by the terms "political culture" and "popular culture." I define *political culture* as the beliefs and behaviors citizens hold toward what is permissible and expected from their system of governance (Berger 1989). I use the term *popular culture* to refer to the mass-produced, usually commodified, offerings of culture industries for consumption by viewers, audiences, subscribers, and consumers, often through the mass media. Although it is possible to argue with both of these definitions, they are offered simply to locate more precisely the characteristics and arenas of operation being dealt with here.

MAKING SENSE OF POLITICS: THE CASE OF TWO TALK SHOWS

As a means of illustrating what is at stake for audiences who attend to differing presentations of politics on television, I have chosen two different forms of political talk shows—one incorporating discussions by Washington insiders and journalists, the other centered around discussions by celebrities and other nonexperts on politics. Specifically, I examine four weeks of programming on *Politically Incorrect with Bill Maher* (*P.I.*) from January 26 through February 3, 1998, and August 10 through 21, 1998. The first two weeks encompass the period when revelations of President Clinton's affair with White House intern Monica Lewinsky (and his subsequent denial of any wrongdoing) went public. The second two weeks surrounded the president's admission of the affair to the American people and his testimony before a grand jury. Both of these dates were high-water marks in the scandal, especially with regard to public interest in the matter. The first was the "gossip" period, when revelations and rumors were swirling about what the president did or might have done. The second covers the period in which the president finally admitted and apologized for his transgressions.

The pundit show examined is *This Week with Sam Donaldson and Cokie Roberts* aired during the same time frame.[1] *This Week* is hosted by two senior broadcast journalists, and the roundtable discussion includes a former top White House official and advisor to President Clinton (George Stephanopoulos), an editor of a conservative weekly journal of political opinion (Bill Kristol), and a conservative syndicated columnist (George Will). All three guests are active in Republican and Democratic policy circles, though none is an officeholder.

Politically Incorrect with Bill Maher is also a roundtable discussion show specifically dedicated to the discussion of politics and contemporary social issues. Hosted by the comedian Maher, guests typically include comedians, actors/actresses, authors/journalists, activists, musicians, athletes, pundits, lawyers, entrepreneurs, the occasional politician, and "citizen panelist." Most of the participants are "public persons," but they are often not celebrities in the formal sense of the word. Foremost, though, is their general lack of "expertise" about politics. They tend to bring to the discussion the same understanding and sense of politics (however weak or strong that might be) as that held by the program's viewers. Indeed, the expertise of the show's guests is not what gains them admission to the program. Instead, the show tries to assemble a diverse mix of people from various sections of public culture, hoping that their differences in viewpoints will create an interesting discussion, a televised cocktail party with an odd mixture of guests, if you will.

THIS WEEK WITH SAM DONALDSON AND COKIE ROBERTS

One of the distinguishing features of the discourse on *This Week* is the high level of agreement among the participants. For an issue like the Clinton scandal that was so discordant in American society, there was relatively little disagreement over what the scandal "meant" at any given time on the show. The participants' fundamental concern was for the political system, or the "constitutional order" as they referred to it. The issue that drove that concern was the threat to the system resulting from Clinton's lying. The explanation offered for this threat was the weak moral character of Bill Clinton, or "this man" as George Will often referred to the president.[2] And, finally, the discussants based their conclusion on the fundamental faith, despite continued evidence to the contrary, that the American people would do the "right" thing (that is, stop supporting Clinton) once they realized the "truth."

From the time the scandal broke as a story until the president's confession some seven months later, the primary issue these pundits discussed was "did Clinton lie?" If he did, they contended, his presidency was through.

January 25
   Sam Donaldson: If he's not telling the truth, I think his presidency is numbered in days. This isn't going to drag out. We're not going to be here three months from now talking about this. Mr. Clinton, if he's not telling the truth and the evidence shows that, will resign, perhaps this week.

August 16
   George Stephanopoulos: It all depends on what he does tomorrow. I think if he tells the truth and comes forward to the American people, he can at least go on with his presidency.
   George Will: The presidency is over.

There was relatively little interest in *what* the president lied about or *why* he lied, questions that were of utmost importance on *Politically Incorrect*. Instead, lying itself was deemed unacceptable. The act of lying was considered so serious that its occurrence alone meant the president would have to leave office; hence, the unanimous predictions for his early departure. Lying, their arguments suggested, was harmful in two ways. First, it damages the president's ability to lead as a politician, to advance a political agenda, and the necessary moral leadership of the office.

August 23
   Cokie Roberts: There is the question of can he govern if he stays in office? Can he go up and twist an arm and get a bill?
   George Stephanopoulos: He can govern, but he can't advance his agenda.

Second was the threat Clinton's supposed lying presents to the political system:

January 25
   George Will: This man's condition is known. His moral authority is gone. He will resign when he acquires the moral sense to understand. . . .

August 23
   Bill Kristol: To let him stay now, I think, is fundamentally corrupting.
   George Will: The metastasizing corruption spread by this man is apparent now, and the corruption of the very idea of what it means to be a representative.
   Bill Kristol: The president is at the center of the constitutional order. Credibility in him matters.

February 1
   George Will: This is a great uncontrolled experiment now under way about having vulgarians in the most conspicuous offices in the republic. And it can't be good.

The explanation given for why Clinton lied was simple—he had no moral character; he was a "vulgarian," a "lout." As George Will argued, "he can't tell the truth. . . . I mean, that's the reasonable assumption on the evidence informed by the context in which it occurs, which is six years of evidence of his deceit."

The pundits continued to exhibit a fundamental faith that the American public would ultimately agree with them about what was right and wrong. With "lying" as the centerpiece premise, the pundits maintained the hope that eventually the public would realize the wrongs that had been committed and rise up to punish the president. Ultimately, their conception of "the people" was quite paternalistic, although not condescending. For instance, George Will seemed to suggest that the people would recognize the right thing to do (what the political class already knew) once the Starr report was made public: The public, he argued, "will not be able to change their mind. . . . Once that report [by Kenneth Starr] is written and published, Congress will be dragged along in the wake of the public" (August 23). They saw a good and virtuous public, although one that was a bit naïve and unsophisticated. As Bill Kristol stated, "I think it is that the American people are nice people. They're too nice, in fact, too trusting" (February 1). This was a public fashioned in their own image, with little connection to what ordinary Americans were actually saying about the scandal.

August 23
   George Will: But beneath the argument there's a visceral process. And it has to do with the peculiar intimacy of the modern presidency. Because of television, the president is in our living rooms night after night after night. And once the dress comes in and once some of the details come in from the Ken Starr report, people—there's going to come a critical mass, the yuck factor—where people say, "I don't want him in my living room anymore."

In summary, the pundits on *This Week* reduced the scandal to one fundamental question—did the president lie? If he did—which they all assumed was true because of Clinton's supposed pattern of deceit—then it would be necessary for him to depart the office, either willingly or unwillingly. The foundation of legitimacy in American democracy, they suggested, was based on the president's telling the truth; should the president violate that cornerstone principle, then the system would remove him. It was also assumed that the public shared the same understanding of how the system works, and that they would ultimately respond in a fitting manner.

What led to such formulations is that these pundits used "political sense" for assessing political matters. By political sense I mean a learned understanding of how politics works, what actions and behaviors are admissible, correct, justifiable, and workable; an acquired sense of what matters and what does not. Political sense is like any other intellectualized system—legal sense, scientific sense, artistic sense—a philosophy or an intellectual world-view. "Philosophy," Gramsci argues, is "official conceptions of the world" that are "elaborated, systematic, and politically organized and centralized" (Gramsci 1988, 360). Practitioners of politics are trained (through schooling and professional experiences) to think in certain ways about how the system works.[3] Political sense is different from common sense in that it is a conscious creation of an abstracted mode of thinking. As John Dewey notes,

> science is the example, par excellence, of the liberative effect of abstraction. . . . The liberative outcome of the abstraction that is supremely manifested in scientific activity is the transformation of the affairs of common sense concern which has come about through the vast return wave of the methods and conclusions of scientific concern into the uses and enjoyments (and sufferings) of everyday affairs; together with an accompanying transformation of judgment and of the emotional affections, preferences, and aversions of everyday human beings. (Dewey and Bentley 1949, 282)

The political sense used by the pundits of the "political class" (to use George Will's term) is the product of just such a transformation, an alteration of the "emotional affections, preferences, and aversions of everyday human beings" into an abstraction with its own set of rules and understandings about what is valid, right, just, and legitimate. According to political sense, politics in a representative democracy is centered around the contract between the polity and the trust they bestow on their elected officials to conduct the affairs of state in an honest and open fashion, operating in the people's best interest. Political legitimacy in such a system is based on public trust. A politician caught in a lie has naturally betrayed that trust. The pundits argued that the president was at the center of the constitutional order; for him to violate that order threatens the whole system and everyone in it. The pundits recognized that the political system was fragile but they had faith that the constitutional system would purge individuals who betrayed that trust.

Those who employ political sense maintain a systematic logic—a structured understanding of the workings of a complex political system that guarantees the functioning of democracy. Within that system, though, the public is only one of several factors. Executive leadership, legislative agendas, and political parties are also crucial to the system's functioning. But the public was also key. The political sense employed by these pundits led to a paternalistic view of the public—a public that is good and decent, but one that would need to overcome its naiveté to understand the seriousness of Clinton's violations. The pundits' faith was therefore not in the people per se but in the system itself. The public's role in the scandal was simply to acquiesce to what the system needed to do—to purge itself of sin. This type of systematic logic was so strong that the pundits were almost incapable of recognizing those who felt differently; that is, an overwhelming majority of the public was not interested in having the system purge itself. Indeed, "the public" was a pure abstraction for the pundits, whereas the political "players" (whom they all knew) and the functioning of the arenas in which they operated (with which they were already thoroughly familiar) were much more real.

What the pundits could not entertain was the idea that citizens might employ a different logic of politics altogether. The fact that many citizens considered Clinton's lying about sex to be a private matter and not a public concern should lead us to examine more fully the "common sense structures" of the people themselves. If the pundits had tuned into *Politically Incorrect*, they would have seen a quite different public than the one the pundits themselves had constructed. The citizens on *P.I.* knew quite well that the president was lying. For them, however, the issue was not "did he lie?" but "what did he lie about?" Because they featured the second question, the public did not respond in ways the pundits had imagined.

POLITICALLY INCORRECT WITH BILL MAHER

If there was a high level of agreement among the pundits on *This Week*, the discussions on *Politically Incorrect* were much more fractious, with no unified conclusions to the debates offered. Despite the great variety of guests, the arguments made by the panelists tended to coalesce around several issues, with quite similar arguments appearing time and again. The primary focus for most panelists was not on the political system, but on how Clinton as president should be judged. That is, most discussions focused on assessing Clinton as a legitimate or illegitimate president in light of his "wrongdoing"— were his activities a threat to leadership itself or were his activities innocuous? The fundamental issue in the scandal was Clinton's sexual affair and his lying about it. Most panelists assumed he lied, but the focus of his lying was not when or where he lied, or even that he lied, but what he lied *about*.

Because the lying was about sex, the arguments split over how to assess Clinton—as a human being (which made the actions normal, comprehensible, fathomable, and ultimately benign) or as a moral leader (which made the actions unacceptable, unfathomable, and therefore a threat). At a broader level, those assessments were based on whether the lying was seen as a public or private matter, and ultimately hinged on concerns over the politicization of private life.

January 29

Joley Fisher (actress): We don't have to know about it. I don't want to hear about other people's orgasms unless I'm involved [laughter, applause, cheers].

August 17

Michael Moore (director): He didn't have to tell the truth in January. You don't have to answer a question nobody has a right to ask. [applause] It's nobody's business.

Another defense of Clinton was based on conceptions of human nature. Although Clinton may be guilty of lying, some panelists suggested, he couldn't help it because the need for sex—and lots of it—was part of the male nature. Clinton did this, they argued, because he is a man, and it is a simple fact that men, in their efforts to fulfill these human needs, have extramarital sex and lie about it. Furthermore, that behavior is understandable, if not justified, because men need sex more than women. Behavior and agency are explained in essentialist terms:

August 18

Star Parker (author): We are a land of law. And if man starts to do whatever he wants to, then so is everybody else. And when you do it from the highest office so are the lowest.

Donzaleigh Abernathy (actress): They have been doing it already. They have been doing it since the beginning of time. . . . It's the nature of men. They need to cast their seed everywhere they can.

Panelists who did not embrace essentialist arguments sometimes resorted to claims that *all* humans are fallible and therefore deserving of mercy:

August 17

Michael Moore (director): We are human beings. Have you ever made a mistake? Have you ever made a mistake?

Jackie Collins (author): Yeah, but I'm not president, Michael.

Michael Moore: Well, but you're a public figure. You're a public figure. You're in the press.

Jackie Collins: I am not the president. The president we expect something more of.

Other panelists advanced the argument that Clinton was just a regular guy, an average American like everyone else. Instead of exalting Clinton as a distant leader, these panelists embraced the notion that their leader was just like them. It was not his higher moral stature that garnered their respect (or the lack thereof in both instances), but rather his position as both a political leader *and* a regular guy that inspired them. Many citizens, that is, fashioned the president in their own image.

January 29

Coolio (rapper): What it really is, is that he's human, and that's why people like Clinton because he's showing that 'I'm human. O.K., I had an affair, whether I admit it or not, or whether I did it or not, I'm human.'

Dennis Prager (talk radio host): Exactly! A guy called my show and said, 'Dennis, Clinton is the sort of guy I can see drinking beers with and chasing women with.'

But arguments also ensued over Clinton's position as leader and role model, and the relationship of lying to leadership.

January 29
Bill Maher: Over and over again, the polls say [the people] think he had an affair, and they don't care. So what they're saying is, let him live, we don't need him as a role model. We'll look to ourselves for our own moral guidance. [applause]
Brad Keena (political analyst): But it's important that we don't normalize this kind of behavior and that's what we're allowing to happen. . . . I think it is time to have a president, to elect a president who is a role model, someone who has good moral values.

Some panelists extended the conception of Clinton-as-leader a step further, invoking the metaphor of the country as a family. In this metaphor, Clinton was the "father" of the country, the people were his "children," and the White House (the site of the indiscretions) the family's "home."

January 26
Eartha Kitt (singer/actress): The president is head of the family. He sets an example for the rest of us. If he can't live by moral standards, then what does he expect of us?

August 13
Jeffrey Tambor (actor): Any household can look within their own selves and their families and say, "There have been transgressions in my family." There are transgressions here. And the smart thing to do is separate the presidency from the man.

The arguments on *Politically Incorrect* form a central dialectic—the tension that exists between the desire to separate Clinton-the-man from Clinton-the-leader. When viewed as a *leader*, a split occurred between those who argued that:

A. *Leaders and the people have different rules.* These discussants invoked history (all presidents have done this), explained power (men in power have affairs the world over), and made his job performance more important than his off-the-job activities (he can do whatever he wants if he's doing a good job).
B. *Leaders are not exempt from the rules guiding the people.* Presidents get no special treatment when it comes to moral behavior.

When viewed as a *human*, a split occurred between those who argued that:

C. *Clinton should represent the people by being better than them as a moral person.* He should be a model for how the people should behave.

D. *Clinton is no different from the people he represents.* He has the same flaws, he does the same foolish things that all humans do.

It seems that panelists wanted it both ways—Clinton was like the average person and unlike the average person, with special rules and with the same rules. Despite their contradictory positioning, both liberal and conservative guests tended to adopt these dual stances. The more liberal voices tended to use both arguments A and D (different rules as a leader, but Clinton the man is no different than the rest of us), while conservatives tended to use both arguments B and C (leaders have the same rules as the people, yet as a man he has different rules; he should be better than us). From the perspective of political culture in the 1990s, these positions seem grounded in populist premises (for instance, the suspicion of political elites disconnected from the people; a desire to have politicians behave like the people) and the culture wars (elites who don't lead, who have no morals). These positions also represent the contradictory and disjointed dimensions of common sense thinking that Gramsci (1988), Geertz (1975), and other theorists of common sense have described so well.

MAKING SENSE OF COMPETING SENSE

The panelists on *P.I.* utilized common sense to understand politics—elements derived from everyday experiences, other belief systems, and intellectualized philosophical concepts. Citizens on *P.I.* often employed arguments which included claims to universality, claims based on personal or group experience which defined the situation in universalistic terms: "*Everyone* does this," "*All* politicians lie," "*Never* trust a liar," "*All* families have problems," "*All* men are this way." These claims to universality render the common sense reliable, constantly reassuring citizens that "this is the way of the world." Clinton is not exceptional, such persons argued; the case is not exceptional either. Its universality was the key to understanding it.

The most prominent themes in citizens' arguments over the scandal were conflicts over whether the Clinton affair was a public or a private matter. For those who argued the latter, the liberal notions of freedom and individuality were embedded in their arguments. Similarly, for those who argued the former, republican notions of responsibility and community came to bear. Rarely were these concepts enunciated as theoretical postulates, but rather as beliefs about how the world works. As Billig et al. note, "within the ideology of liberalism is a dialectic, which contains negative counter-themes and which gives rise to debates. These debates are not confined to the level of intellectual analysis; both themes and counter-themes have arisen from, and passed into, everyday consciousness. And, of course, this everyday consciousness provides the material for further intellectual debate" (Billig et al. 1988, 27). American liberalism battles republicanism here, yet these ideological formulations appeared simply as common sense: "This is none of your business"; "This is between him and his wife"; "If his wife is O.K. with it, what concern is it of yours?" "He did this in our house, the people's house"; "What type of example does this set for the people/the children?" "Lying is lying, so how can we trust a liar?"

Panelists did not argue on the basis of political sense—the chief law enforcement officer lying, the implications for systems of justice, the precedent this sets for future presidents, etc. Instead, they used accessible terms that not only made sense but that made the scandal interesting to discuss. In other words, the terms and conditions of the Clinton scandal (for example, sex, lying, adultery, cigars, dresses, semen, fellatio) favored the application of common sense (certainly in ways that the Savings & Loan scandal did not). People could *relate* to this kind of politics, for it had resonance with their own lives. As one guest on *P.I.* intimated, "You know, I've been following this [scandal] 'cause I haven't seen *All My Children* in a long time."

This latter remark is telling in that it exemplifies how politics is becoming fused with entertainment and consumer culture. As a result, the sense making found in those realms will increasingly be used when it comes to formal politics. Politics in American society, that is, has come to center around the activities of politicians as celebrities. David Marshall argues that "the celebrity offers a discursive focus for the discussion of realms that are considered outside the bounds of public debate in the most public fashion. The celebrity system is a way in which the sphere of the irrational, emotional, personal, and affective is contained and negotiated in contemporary culture" (Marshall 1998, 72–73). He goes on to argue that "celebrities . . . are intense sites for determining the meaning and significance of the private sphere and its implications for the public sphere. . . . The private sphere is constructed to be revelatory, the ultimate site of truth and meaning for any representation in the public sphere. . . . Celebrities . . . are sites for the dispersal of power and meaning into the personal and therefore universal" (247).

By making politics personal and universal, the invitation is made to treat all politics on these same terms. *Formal* political sense about how politics functions therefore comes to be seen as nonsense, and publics revert to the sorts of thinking used in other realms of their everyday existence. Defenders of Clinton appealed to the common sense "truth" of the private realm, including essentialist claims about a man's needs or human biology, or personal identification with Clinton because of his human frailties. For some guests, Clinton-as-celebrity was easier to judge than Clinton-as-leader and politician. Clinton's actions as a celebrity seemed all too familiar when compared with other celebrities. For instance, the foibles of Bill Clinton, and actor Hugh Grant's sexual misconduct, come to be seen in similar ways when such criteria are used for judgment.

But as Joshua Gamson points out, the celebrity sign is composed of oppositional characteristics that allow for different readings, depending on the situation. "Contemporary celebrity," he notes, "is composed of a string of antinomies: public roles opposing private selves, artificial opposing natural, image opposing reality, ideal opposing typical, special opposing ordinary, hierarchy opposing equality" (Gamson 1994, 195). As the analysis above suggests, these are *exactly* the means through which *P.I.* panelists attempted to read Clinton as a political celebrity—Clinton as special or ordinary, equal to the people or better than the people, an ideal leader or a typical American, etc. Pundit discourse based on political sense, a perspective that didn't position Clinton as a celebrity but as a politician required to play the game of politics by certain rules, was much more unified in how to make sense of the scandal.

The means through which talk show guests think through the political matters of the day will greatly affect the realities they create, as will the discursive frames of the two types of television. The political sense of *This Week* tended to stifle debate, efficiently organizing the scandal around a particular set of meanings apart from which other explanations made no sense. This particular ordering framed Clinton as a systemic threat, and the integrity and continuity of the system necessitated his exit from the system. Alternative means of making sense of the scandal, however rare, were not entertained. On *P.I.*, however, the Clinton scandal became an opportunity for citizens to explore a range of interpretations about the changing relationships between leaders and the public. Commonsense thinking led panelists to explore what Clinton as (fallen) archetypal hero meant for America—is this scandal just about him, an amoral and selfish baby boomer, or is the public implicated in some way? It also led citizens to investigate the nature of leadership and political privilege and the normative expectations that should exist given contemporary social realities. Those investigations, in essence, raised fundamental questions affecting citizens' relationships with their government, matters rarely considered on the pundit program.

What this study suggests, then, is that entertainment-based programming can offer alternative forums for citizens to make sense, in their own language, of politics at any given moment. These forums become a site through which common knowledge can be developed, even during the pursuit of entertainment pleasure. They become a site where citizens need not segregate their "private" lives and pleasures from their simultaneous role as "public" beings. They become a site where the values, meanings, and sense used in their private lives can have direct bearing on politics itself.

ADVANCING THE NEW AGENDA

To further the agenda sketched out here, numerous sites within popular culture should be examined. While this chapter has focused on television talk shows as an important genre for cultural citizenship, the analysis should be extended to other sites—stand-up comedians and the monologues of late-night talk show hosts, comedy channels, Internet discussion and parody sites, and magazines such as *George*, which intentionally obfuscate the boundaries between politics and popular culture. Examining the content of these genres can provide important insight into the types of civic knowledge citizens encounter about their government on a daily basis.

But the study of politics in popular culture should not be an end in itself. Indeed, what the study of culture can contribute to our understandings of politics begins by returning to the arena of electoral politics itself. That is to say, these examinations should ultimately lead us to rethink traditional issues in the study of formal politics (questions traditionally entertained by political scientists). Those issues lie primarily in the areas of *political behavior* and *political culture*. In terms of political behavior, we must begin to question how traditional modes of interaction with politics may have changed. For instance, do these new sites of citizenship affect political attitude formation? Do they affect voting behaviors? Do they influence citizens' attitudes, opinions, and behaviors more than news shows and pundit talk shows? Do citizens feel more engaged or involved with politics when attending to political information packaged in a more common vernacular? Do these new sites affect how, when, and where citizens talk about politics among themselves? In short, how do these cultural presentations of politics affect the *practices* of representative democracy?

Questions of political cognition are also important here: do citizens develop different types of "knowingness" in this narrow-casted media environment, and how does this environment affect "common knowledge" about politics? How do factors with great currency in popular culture (for example, celebrity) affect citizen evaluation of politicians (what one critic calls "celebriticians") (Gabler 2000)? In short, if politics is increasingly attended to in the realm of culture, we must ask how political participation and behavior are affected as a result.

The second set of questions this new agenda raises concerns American political culture. Not only should we recognize how politics is played out in popular culture but also the converse: how the language of popular culture can become the language of politics. We have already witnessed events such as Bill Clinton's saxophone on the *Arsenio Hall Show*, his fielding questions on MTV about the types of underwear he wore, the eerie relationship between art and life in films like *Wag the Dog*, the usage of rock music in political campaign events, and the embrace of radio performer Rush Limbaugh by the 104th Congress. These phenomena exemplify ways in which political players use the symbolic material of popular culture in the conduct of political activity. Whether these events are trivial or significant needs to be determined.

One of the most important questions with regard to voters, however, is the ways in which the dominant language of pop culture—the ethos of consumption—may be shaping our political culture. As political party affiliation and loyalty decline and as the number of independent voters increases, as politics becomes not something one does with other people but what one watches on television, how much does the selection of politicians for political office resemble models of consumer choice? With the surprising popularity of populist candidates such as Ross Perot and Jesse Ventura, we should begin to question how the culture of consumption might be leaching into the political mainstream. Are voters now becoming "bored" with politics just as they become bored with long-running sitcoms? Why should a voter's relationship to the politics she watches on television be any different from her relationship to other programming found there? And then there is the practiced question: Does a populist leadership style play better in attracting bored but hopeful voters? We should ask whether these pop culture forums help shape expectations of a more "relational" style of political leadership for voters (for example, Reagan as loveable grandfather, Clinton as drinking buddy, George W. Bush as fraternity brother)?[4] The point to be made here is that the boundary between cultural practices and traditional politics may have eroded entirely by now. Scholars would be wise to examine if this is so.

What is ultimately at stake is a better understanding of how American democracy is manifested, attended to, and maintained through cultural practices in the daily mediascape. We must alter our conceptions of political citizenship as being determined solely through traditional means, and look more carefully at the fluid interchange of politics and culture in everyday life. The forums for citizenship contested in popular culture are a good place to begin that investigation.

NOTES

1. Actual broadcast dates are January 25, February 1, August 16, and August 23, 1998. The analysis was conducted from transcripts of these broadcasts.
2. Will's usage of "this man" is similar to Clinton's usage of "that woman," referring to Monica Lewinsky, in his denial of the affair. Both are semantic moves to distance

themselves from the object of referral. In Will's case, he seeks to distance Clinton from any *legitimate* place in the political system.

3. Of the pundits on *This Week*, for instance, both of Roberts's parents served in Congress. Kristol's father is the conservative intellectual Irving Kristol. Will's wife was a manager in Bob Dole's 1996 presidential campaign. Stephanopoulos was a senior advisor to President Clinton, and Donaldson has been a senior White House reporter for over two decades.

4. Ronald Lee argues that political leaders in this new era of politics are "feeling conduits" for voters; they must embody the voters' interests in a visceral way (Lee 1994).

12

Political Authenticity, Television News, and Hillary Rodham Clinton

Shawn J. Parry-Giles

In the November 15, 1999, issue of *Newsweek* magazine, journalist Howard Fineman quipped, "Bradley and McCain are selling this year's hottest commodity: the aura of authenticity that comes from a life that starts outside politics." Also addressing issues of authenticity, Eric Pooley (1999) of *Time* argued that Bill Bradley's "genteel shabbiness signifies authenticity," while they represented for *Time's* Margaret Carlson (1999) "[t]he Anti-Clinton [who] . . . slicks himself up for no man." This "aura of authenticity," an outgrowth of character-driven politics, represents a notable means by which political candidates of the twenty-first century are being measured.

The search for authenticity—although centuries old—is undoubtedly more acute in an advanced technological context where politics are mediated and where the media are political. Ironically, President Bill Clinton's own contribution to the anxiety surrounding the "authentic" politician exacerbates the obstacles that his wife faced as she sought the U.S. Senate seat from New York in the 2000 election. Concerns over Hillary Rodham Clinton's authenticity are reflected in Andrea Mitchell's question for Mike Daly of the *New York Daily News*, when she asked if Hillary Rodham Clinton's "kick off rally" was "authentic to New Yorkers." In response, Daly replied: "it didn't seem to me to be real authentic in any regards. It seemed pretty scripted" (*Decision 2000*). In even more definitive terms, Maureen Dowd (1999) of the *New York Times* concluded, "We have lost all hope of getting any shred of authenticity from either Bill or Hillary—unless it's the authenticity of the deluded."

The focus of this chapter is on the news media's quest for an authentic utopia. I explore how the television news media contribute to the practice of what I term "political authenticity" and how the intersection of visual and verbal components of television news works to naturalize (that is, enhance the realism of) texts devoted to political authenticity. Political authenticity represents a symbolic, mediated, interactional, and highly contested process by which political candidates attempt to "make real" a vision of self and political character to the electorate. In response, the media evaluate such claims and challenges of authenticity. An interaction between the visual strategies and the media's search for the authentic candidate enhances the omniscient power and authority of journalists. Ultimately, though, the news media further inauthenticate candidates' images because of their visual production practices, exacerbating the hyperreal nature of image making in the postmodern age.[1]

I first ground political authenticity in a review of authenticity theories. After explicating the uniqueness of *political authenticity* associated with electoral politics, I examine television news broadcasts of Hillary Rodham Clinton (HRC), who represents an archetype of how the media deal with the issue of political authenticity. This study covers the first rumors of HRC's candidacy for the New York Senate seat (January 1999) through her official announcement as a U.S. Senate candidate (February 2000).[2]

THEORIES OF AUTHENTICITY

Although political authenticity represents a contemporary and mediated contest among political candidates, their opponents, and the "fourth estate," the quest for authenticity represents a historical and, according to many scholars, a Western-based concern grounded in the ideology of individualism (Taylor 1992). Nehamas (1999, xxxii) contends that issues of authenticity were significant to Plato because he feared that Athenians could not distinguish between "the genuine [the virtuous], represented by Socrates" and the "fake," which epitomized the "jury's conception of what a good human being was" during Socrates' trial.

Although such concerns over authenticity are classically rooted, many scholars of philosophy, psychology, and politics contextualize the study of authenticity in the modern age. Ferrara (1993, 25) explores Rousseau's philosophies of authenticity and the effects of "autonomy upon the identity of the individual." Issues of modernity, morality, and autonomy gave rise to a quest for authenticity in the Industrial Age. As Hardt (1993, 52) maintains, "considerations of authenticity . . . emerge as social and ideological problems from the collective experience of industrialization and urbanization in nineteenth century Western societies." Identifying the tension between "imitation and authenticity" during the post-industrial age, Orvell (1989, xvi, xv) references the gradual and overlapping shift between a nineteenth-century "culture of imitation" and a twentieth-century "culture of authenticity."

Conceptions of authenticity are often grounded in questions of morality, truth, individualism, and culture. Taylor (1992, 25–26) situates authenticity's "starting point in the eighteenth-century notion that human beings are endowed with a moral sense, an intuitive feeling for what is right and wrong . . . it comes to be something we have to attain to be true and full human beings." To be authentic, according to Baruss (1996, 152), is to be "that which is true to its own nature." Isolating the anxiety between morality and self, Ferrara (1993, 136) expresses how "all ethics of authenticity try to respond to the modern tension between morality and self-realization." Although many of the early theories of authenticity were linked to the individual or to "an actor's personality" (Ferrara 1998, 5), changes in the concept began to emerge during the postmodern period. Noting the progression to a more social understanding of authenticity, Ferrara (1998) asserts, "there is no such thing as an authentic identity which does not presuppose a moment of recognition on the part of another" (16). Authenticity thus represents an "intersubjective" activity (54) "inaugurated by the Linguistic Turn" (14).

While assuming a social basis, the individual and the psychological are still foundational to many studying issues of authenticity. The interplay between the cultural and individual understanding of authenticity is born out of the social and political turbulence in the United States during the 1950s and 1960s. Berman (1970, xix) calls "the problem of authenticity" one of "the most politically explosive of human impulses" in contemporary society, relating it to "the social and political structures men live in [that] are keeping the self stifled, chained down, locked up." Rossinow (1998, 4) locates the contemporary search for authenticity in the "heart of the new left" movement, arguing that although the authenticity quest is situated in the immediate post-industrial age, "only after World War II did it become a widespread preoccupation" in U.S. politics.

Even though the activities of the New Left ceased decades ago, the problems the movement addressed are foundational to many existing tensions in U.S. politics. Rossinow (1998, 20) charges that "the new left's agenda ["alienation, powerlessness, racism, war, sexism"] remains regrettably current," and bound up with "identity politics" (1998, 343). Such a search for the authentic is now centered in expressions of "popular culture," making it a "politically promiscuous" activity (Rossinow 1998, 340) that relies upon the media's perpetuating "the art of chatter" (Hardt 1993, 51). Despite its "promiscuousness," though, Hardt (1993, 59) concludes that "questions of authenticity have turned into questions of authority"—the backdrop out of which political authenticity emerges.

POLITICAL AUTHENTICITY

Political authenticity is a concept that is central to contemporary American political campaigns. Although scholars of philosophy, psychology, and politics link authenticity to psychological processes, cultural phenomena (for example, Industrial Age), political agendas (for example, the New Left), or to popular culture, little attention is devoted to the role of authenticity quests during the electoral process. Although political authenticity represents a broad political phenomenon where candidates attempt to articulate a "real" or genuine political image, the media evaluate these authenticity messages through visual and verbal production strategies, which serve as the focus of this chapter.[3]

As stated above, political authenticity is a symbolic, mediated, interactional, and highly contested process by which political candidates attempt to "make real" a vision of their selves and their political characters within the public sphere. In response, political opponents seek to deconstruct the authenticated image. The television news media enter the image fray by actively examining, critiquing, and assessing competing depictions of authenticity on the grounds of truth and realism. The news media thus function as authenticating agents in this image-making exercise. News narratives test the authenticity of a candidate's character constructions to determine the "real" behind the "image"; visuals offer evidence for the media's authenticity conclusions. While the media's motives may be linked to the historical search for truth and morality, other motives associated with commodification issues cannot be ignored nor can the perpetual pursuit of social control by media elites (Hardt 1993).

The anxiety produced by the Vietnam War, Watergate, Iran–Contra, and the Clinton impeachment helped create a political quest for the authentic candidate. The hunt for authenticity has moved from the context of new left politics to the mainstream political environment as journalists search for what they believe is a "truth" masked by the political candidates' image-making activities. Although politics has always been about image making (Sigelman 1992), there is a growing concern with what Mitchell (1994, 423) calls a "nostalgia for a lost authenticity understood as responsible representation."

The struggle over political authenticity emerges from the larger issue of image making, which is alleged to constitute the substance of political reality (Meyrowitz 1985). Central to image making is the issue of character. Political authenticity derives from character concerns as candidates (and their surrogates) attempt to authenticate a candidate's image, as political opponents attempt to inauthenticate that image, and as the news media serve as an arbiter of political authenticity within this image-making struggle. Such a political exercise operates within a public/political sphere, culminating in a socially constructed image. Even though there is a sense that the news media is capturing the real, any conclusions about realism represent journalistic constructions and audience judgments rather than individual essences. Thus, political authenticity represents a cultural and symbolic phenomenon rather than a search for an individual's true self; any conclusions about political authenticity operate in the realm of what Baudrillard (1994, 1) terms the "hyperreal."

Various journalistic assumptions inspire the frenzied news quest to authenticate candidates' personae. One journalistic assumption is that image messages mask a candidate's true character, which increasingly centers on personality traits (Thurow 1996). The media thus assume the responsibility for unmasking that image in order to capture the essence of the candidate's character (Parry-Giles and Parry-Giles 1999); after all, journalists often view themselves as having the access and authority as the "fourth estate" to act as the image-making mediator (Hart 1987, 138). Although the news media may recognize that they can never uncover the truly "authentic" nature of the candidate, they seem determined to showcase the *inauthentic*, which accents their authority as the vanguards of political truth.

Multiple markers serve as criteria by which a candidate's authenticity is tested by the television news media. *Motive* constitutes the first such marker. A candidate's authenticity is often questioned when (s)he lacks what the news media determine to be a compelling rationale for a campaign bid. *Consistency* in the candidate's story is a second criterion by which political authenticity is measured. Certainly, a changing or contradictory story of the self is a primary sign of a candidate's inauthenticity, as are changes in a candidate's political positions over time. *Geography* is a third way by which a candidate's authenticity is evaluated. To be authentic, a candidate's affiliation with a state or locality must reflect a genuine association with that geographical marker over time. Fourth, the authentic candidate assumes *oppositional opinions*, especially ones that counter public opinion. While this list of criteria in no way exhausts the means by which a candidate's political authenticity is measured, these four criteria are commonly operating in contemporary U.S. politics.

In the process of mediating political authenticity, the news media's own authority in the political process, particularly in relation to political authenticity, is further entrenched. Many visual techniques common to television news further reify the media's ontological status in this image-making struggle. Yet, the television news media's practice of decontextualizing and recontextualizing visual images works to inauthenticate the image being authenticated. Thus, as the news media work to inauthenticate a candidate's image, their own mediated practices further the hyperreal nature of image making (Parry-Giles and Parry-Giles 1999).

QUESTIONS OF AUTHENTICITY AND THE POLITICAL IMAGE OF HRC

To illustrate the media's role within political authenticity, I examine how the television news media cover Hillary Rodham Clinton during the early stages of her U.S. Senate bid in New York. Offering a case study from the 2000 campaign

is warranted given the emphasis on issues of political authenticity in the aftermath of the Clinton impeachment. HRC's Senate bid also garnered considerable media attention centering on issues of authenticity, as HRC attempted to
transform her image from that of First Lady to U.S. Senate candidate.

I first evidence the four markers of authenticity detailed above. For HRC, the
question of motive consumed the coverage of her Senate exploratory activities. Peter Jennings, for example, reviewed potential reasons for HRC's Senate
bid: "[some] think it's a practical joke being played on the press, others think
it's her way of no longer being a victim now that the impeachment process is
over . . ." (*ABC World News Tonight* 1999, February 16). Tony Snow of *Fox
News Sunday* (1999, November 28) also wondered if she was in the race "for
redemption" in the aftermath of the Lewinsky scandal. Still others like NBC's
Tim Russert speculated that HRC's Senate bid might be a "brilliant public relations [move] in this post-Monica time period" to get people's "minds off impeachment" (*The Today Show* 1999, February 17). Journalists also speculated
that HRC's Senate run constituted a "stepping stone for personal ambition, an
eventual run for the presidency" (*The Today Show* 1999, June 4). Although
journalists held out the possibility that this political candidate's motives were
genuine and thus driven by a commitment to public service (*Meet the Press*
1999, February 21), the coverage most clearly evidences the propensity of the
television news media to question a candidate's motives.

HRC's consistency in her personal narrative and her position on issues
pervaded the coverage between 1999 and 2000. In a *CBS Evening News*
broadcast, journalist Diana Olick reported that HRC was accused of changing her position on the Palestinian homeland question. Even though HRC's
campaign declared she was not "flip-flopping on this issue," Olick stressed
that Jewish leaders "seemed pleased but cautious" about her alleged support
for the Israeli position (1999, July 8). In response to a *Talk Magazine* interview where HRC implied that her husband was a victim of an abusive grand-
mother, John McLaughlin of the *McLaughlin Group* raised other inconsistencies: "Which Hillary are we to believe? The Hillary of 1992 which extols
grandma's virtues or the Hillary of 1999 who blames grandma's abuse for her
husband's shortcomings" (1999, August 8). Emphasizing changes in HRC's
image during an MSNBC program, *USA Today* journalist Tom Squitieri alleged "she changed her look, changed her appearance, not just her physical
appearance, but sort of the aura she puts out when meeting with people.
She's a canny politician and she knows how to get the job done" (*Today in
America* 1999, February 20). Such statements raise questions about authenticity in relation to alleged policy and image inconsistencies.

HRC's geographical lineage constitutes another means by which her character is evaluated. Because HRC never lived or worked in New York before the
campaign, many questioned her credibility as a Senate candidate from that
state. During an interview with HRC's one-time campaign opponent, Rudy

Giuliani, George Will of ABC's *This Week* asked: "Do you think that she is sufficiently New York to run in your state" (1999, February 21)? Reflecting a similar sentiment, Tim Russert of *Meet the Press* asked the following of Representative Charles Rangel (D–N.Y.): "She's never lived there, she's never worked there, she's never gone to school there. Why would you want a carpetbagger representing your party?" (1999, July 4). In a later *Meet the Press* broadcast concerning HRC's New York connection, *New York Times* reporter Bob Herbert (2000) asserted: "She's got to get away from these issues that make her look like a phony. . . . Nobody in the state of New York thinks she's a basic Westchester housewife, so just give that up and focus on the issues." The issue of geography, while an understandable issue for HRC, transcends this more obvious case of so-called carpetbagging. It also, for example, affected candidates like President George Herbert Walker Bush, whose Texas allegiances were questioned in light of his Eastern roots. For political campaigns, a geographical essentialism acts as a key test of one's political authenticity.

The fourth marker of political authenticity is linked to the practice of assuming oppositional stances, especially ones that might counter public opinion. Working to authenticate HRC's image while simultaneously critiquing her, news host Gregg Jarrett of MSNBC's *Hotwire* asserted: "The fact is, she's on the edge, she's sometimes abrasive, caustic, she speaks her mind. New Yorkers love that, so isn't she perfect for New York?" (1999, July 6). Whenever a candidate like HRC articulates statements that deviate from the political norm, such statements are assumed to represent the authentic character of the candidate. As MSNBC's Brian Williams proclaimed: "When the going has gotten tough in the past, she [HRC] has said things about 'staying home and baking cookies' and 'standing by your man.' Those have been two blow-ups when it's been tough" (*The News* 1999, July 8). Although implied, such an oppositional stance on behalf of HRC seemingly offers insight into her "true" character, more so than when she articulates contradictory policy positions on the Palestinian homeland controversy. Yet there is another dimension to this issue of oppositional behavior. Journalists frequently critique candidates like the Clintons for being too poll-driven on controversial issues and thus not oppositional enough, evidencing another dimension to this authenticity marker (*Larry King Live* 2000, January 6). In examining such television news broadcasts, there seem to be multiple ways to inauthenticate a candidate's political image. The news media's authority on such issues, though, is further "authenticated" by visual strategies inherent to television news practices.

NATURALIZING AUTHENTICITY THROUGH VISUAL PRACTICES

In recent decades, scholars have begun to recognize the importance of visuals to the political process and the element of realism that visual discourse is granted (Mitchell 1980). Apart from their entertainment value in news (Robinson and Levy 1986), Arnheim (1969, 88) notes that the epistemological nature of visuals has "no break between what is known and what is seen." Addressing the naturalizing role of visual discourse, Mitchell (1986, 43) asserts that "[t]he image is the sign that pretends not to be a sign, masquerading as . . . natural immediacy and presence." In this section, I analyze typical visual techniques and other production strategies that help authenticate the news media's authority in stories concerning political authenticity. In particular, I assess the concepts of insider access, repetition, editing and motion, close-ups, and the role of the camera.[4] In the end, I evidence how the production practices further inauthenticate candidate images.

One means that helps secure the credibility that journalists rely on to authenticate a candidate's image is insider access, which is linked to field reporting. As Graddol and Boyd-Barrett (1994, 155) contend, "[t]he brief authentication of the reporter's presence 'in the field' helps the viewer calibrate the modality of the report they have just seen." Hartley (1992, 144) reveals how journalists situate themselves as observers of live action, promoting, in turn, an "ideology of eyewitness authenticity."

Stories about HRC's authenticity as a U.S. Senate candidate showcase the journalists-as-authenticators by means of their field reporting or their close proximity to the First Lady. To begin with, most of the experts on HRC are other journalists. As with many television news stories, Andrea Mitchell narrated a visual segment of HRC for *The Today Show*. To authenticate Mitchell's credibility in the story, we see a short clip of the journalist talking to the camera on a New York street during the taped segment; we also hear Mitchell asking HRC a question during a photo opportunity at a New York children's center (1999, March 4). Such visuals and sounds demonstrated Mitchell's participation within the news event, which awards her the expertise to speak on issues related to the candidate's authenticity. The sound qualities, narration, and moving images add what Morse (1986, 63) calls "a crucial element of 'liveness' to events already in the past tense," furthering the realism of the images.

Even greater visual insider access is evidenced during an MSNBC *Time and Again* segment. Like all *Time and Again* broadcasts, this feature spliced together historical interview footage of the subject (for example, HRC) as a means to recycle news stories (Parry-Giles 2000). The focal point of this 1999 story is to rebroadcast a 1993 interview between Katie Couric and HRC. Couric's credibility is established when Jane Pauley, the narrator of *Time and Again*, mentions that this is HRC's "first major television interview as First Lady." Couric also accents the "rare" presence of the camera within the Clinton family living quarters at the White House, reported to be "off-limits to tourists." Such visual insider access awards Couric credibility to comment on issues of HRC's authenticity, especially when coupled with comments like: "She rarely shows this kind of emotion in public. In fact, there are many sides of her that are seldom seen" (1999, February 27). The implication is that Couric has now been granted increased insight to the real HRC through such insider access.[5]

In a separate story, CNN correspondent Christiane Amanpour served as the expert on a story about HRC's trip to Macedonia, Amanpour's journalistic beat. In addition to narrating a visual piece on HRC's travelogue in Macedonia, we also see Amanpour positioned as though she is being interviewed without the visible presence of an accompanying interviewer, testifying to HRC's mood on the Kosovo crisis and the Lewinsky matter. Amanpour thus serves as both narrator and expert; she noted HRC's lack of "irrita[tion]" when responding to questions about the Lewinsky scandal and she commented on how "moved" HRC seemed by the conditions in Macedonia (*Newsstand* 1999, May 15). Such visual insider access evidenced by the camera helps authenticate the journalists' stories of authenticity.

Repetition is a second production strategy that helps authenticate stories about political authenticity. Philo (1990, 172) argues that messages that are "persistently repeated are most likely to be retained by the audience." Linking the issue of repetition to collective memory, Gurevitch and Kavoori (1992, 417) contend that images "resonate and become part of our collective memory through repetition over time." Explaining the process further, Zelizer (1998, 7) asserts that such "collectively held images act as signposts, directing people who remember to preferred meanings by the fastest route."

Repetition acts then as an authenticating force albeit through distinct means. For the NBC news organizations especially, many of these stories and visuals are recycled from NBC to MSNBC or repeatedly broadcast over MSNBC. The *Time and Again* episode referenced above aired on February 27 and July 8, 1999. With the exception of Jane Pauley's narration, all of the stories represented recycled features from *The Today Show* or *NBC Nightly News*. The retelling and reairing of the same image helps authenticate NBC's construction of HRC. Simultaneously, such repetition legitimates the credibility of the journalists relaying the consistent story. As Zelizer (1992, 36) alleges, "telling the story . . . of the story . . . accommodate[s] the inclusion of narrators regardless of the part they had originally played, . . . [giving] journalists a way to legitimate their connection to the story." Journalists thus become "custodians of memory" (Zelizer 1992, 36)—a memory that is naturalized through the repetition of images.

Repetition also functions to naturalize the message in another way. News stations often rely on the same "experts" to substantiate a candidate's character; through such testimony, the messages are rearticulated over time. For NBC, two experts are frequently called upon to testify to HRC's true self: Gail Sheehy of *Vanity Fair*, who wrote a biography of HRC (*Hillary's Choice*), and David Maraniss of the *Washington Post*, who authored a biography of

HRC's husband (*First in His Class*). During a January 3, 1999, appearance on *Meet the Press*, Sheehy argued that HRC served as Bill Clinton's "protector"; "she . . . raise[d] him as a political star." Later that year, Sheehy appeared on another *Meet the Press* broadcast, typecasting HRC in a parental role once again. According to Sheehy, HRC sees Bill Clinton as "an emotional child" who needs "protect[ing]" (1999, August 8). Even though Sheehy acknowledged that HRC's staff failed to substantiate questionable conclusions in her book (*Meet the Press* 1999, December 5), she still was granted credibility to speak about the true nature of HRC. The role of repetition helped naturalize her message of authentication.

David Marannis, even though his biography is about Bill Clinton, served as the authenticating expert in at least three NBC/MSNBC programs (*Hockenberry* 1999, June 7; *Headliners and Legends* 2000, January 27; *Meet the Press* 1999, January 3). During MSNBC's program *Hockenberry—The Bottom Line*, Marannis argued that HRC "doesn't want to be 'the victim'" (1999, June 7). Six months later, Marannis repeated the same message during a different MSNBC feature: "Hillary Clinton her whole life has never wanted to seem a victim" (*Headliners and Legends* 2000, January 27). These retold narratives that derive from the selected experts aid in creating an authenticated collective memory of HRC through their recirculation (Gurevitch and Kavoori 1992). These experts seemingly exhibit enhanced insight because the television news media insinuate that their journalistic peers know the candidates best.

A third means by which messages of authenticity are naturalized is through the fast-paced motion of the visual images and the editing techniques commonly practiced by the television news media. As Schlesinger (1978, 128) asserts, many assume that "moving pictures are . . . a form of actuality, a medium through which reality can be genuinely and authentically captured and presented." The motion inherent in film is further energized by a contemporary trend, where everything moves so as to enhance attention. As Stephens (1998, 92–93) explains, "When someone walks, meets, reaches, removes, places, points, or pulls, it tends to catch the eye. . . . This alone gives moving images an advantage over static images in the effort to express meaning clearly." Increased motion designed to gain the viewers' attention furthers the naturalization process associated with the moving image, which helps reify messages of authenticity.

One common production technique for television news is the sequencing of images in rapid fashion. During a *Headliners and Legends* episode, for example, MSNBC presented ten different images of HRC in campaign mode within a twenty-two-second period—almost one image per two-second interval (2000, January 27). At an even faster rate, MSNBC spliced together sixteen different shots of HRC during a twenty-second interval in a *Time and Again* piece. These rapid-fire images served as visual evidence for Katie

Couric's claim: "She is constantly in motion . . . talking, listening, politicking" (*Time and Again* 1999, February 27). The message communicated is that just as HRC is constantly in motion, so too is NBC, catching her every move. The fast-paced motion combined with the assumed realism of the moving image further authenticates the news media's messages of authenticity.

Another means by which the production practices of television news work to naturalize stories of authentication is through the seamlessness of the editing process coupled with the placement of visuals. Messaris (1994, 35) argues that "[t]wo shots joined together in the context of a broader narrative are 'read' by the viewer as being part of a coherent stream of space, time, and action, even if the shots were in fact taken at widely separate times and places." Although the editing of visuals is apparent, Messaris (1994, 36) asserts that viewers still "succumb to the illusion of false continuity." The interpretation of visuals is thus highly dependent on their placement with other visuals (Messaris 1994), awarding the television news media significant power in defining the referents of the visuals used in the news (Parry-Giles 2000).

One clear example of the seamlessness and the epistemological role of visuals is reflected in the same *Headliners and Legends* episode noted above. Within the MSNBC episode, David Marannis offered a sense of HRC's motives as First Lady: "I think what was going through Hillary's mind when they reached the White House was, 'what can I do in the White House to sort of create an Eleanor Roosevelt legacy?' I don't think it was anything other than that." This image of Marannis talking is followed by images of Eleanor Roosevelt and Lady Bird Johnson as we hear, and then see, HRC talking in an interview style about how "impressed" she is by "the women who have been here before" (2000, January 27). This placement of HRC's images offered support for Marannis' contention. The seamlessness of the shot implied that perhaps David Marannis is the one who interviewed HRC as she made the revealing remarks. HRC's statements, however, originated from Katie Couric's 1993 White House interview for *The Today Show,* which was rebroadcast during the February 27, 1999, *Time and Again.* The placement of the visuals connoted a narrative continuity despite the six-year discrepancy in their origins. Marannis' credibility is substantiated as his argument is supported through the visual placement, which simultaneously works to naturalize the authenticating statements.

An additional production technique that helps authenticate the messages of authenticity is the combined use of close-ups with the role that eye contact plays in relation to camera positioning. As Hart (1994) asserts, "television turns faces into arguments" and politics into an activity of "face watching" (38, 40). Just as close-up images act as visual evidence for journalistic claims, so they serve as visual evidence for assertions of authenticity. Such visual evidence is further naturalized by the lack of eye contact between the subject and the camera, which communicates a sense of unobtrusiveness on the part of the camera. As Snyder (1980, 225) alleges, "The camera is sometimes construed as a substitute for or an extension of the eye." When the subject of the camera does not look back, the assumption is that (s)he is "unaware of the camera's presence," which achieves "an utterly natural, unguarded expression, an authentic bit of life lifted from the stream of everyday social interaction" (Orvell 1989, 238).

A different 1999 *Time and Again* episode evidences most clearly the role that close-ups and eye contact play in authenticating the message of authenticity. During a broadcast focusing on how HRC dealt with the Clinton–Lewinsky crisis of 1998, MSNBC re-aired an August 17, 1998, *NBC Nightly News* broadcast as part of the *Time and Again* feature. Andrea Mitchell voiced the following statement on the day that Bill Clinton admitted publicly to an "inappropriate relationship" with Monica Lewinsky: "She's [HRC] right there at his side, smiling for the cameras despite the biggest crisis of their twenty-three year marriage. Over the weekend of public humiliation and private pain, sources tell NBC News she helped her husband prepare . . . to admit to adultery to Ken Starr" (1999, January 30). As Mitchell talks of HRC "smiling for the cameras," a visual is shown of HRC and her husband leaving church as HRC turns briefly to the camera and smiles. Such a shot connotes her awareness of the camera's presence; a potentially defiant move that, some scholars argue, turns the camera gaze back on itself, "where the visual doubles as a voice" (Hill 1994, 202). As Mitchell then talked of a "weekend of public humiliation and private pain," an extreme close-up of HRC is offered as visual evidence. HRC is not looking toward the camera; rather, it is a profile shot of her appearing quite solemn. In this latter case, the lack of eye contact made it appear as if the camera caught HRC in a private moment of "pain." Given the extreme close-up of the face, no additional contextual clues are offered, which awards NBC the ability to contextualize the image to fit its authenticating message. Although production techniques often work well to naturalize these character-based messages, the next section demonstrates how television news practices can also inauthenticate candidate images, making it even more difficult to discern the real from the simulated.

THE TECHNICAL INAUTHENTICATION OF IMAGE

Although visuals connote a sense of realism for television news, many scholars emphasize the constructed nature of filmed and photographed images. As Zelizer (1998, 201) contends, photographs often lose their "linkage with the events that [they] . . . first depicted." Messaris (1997) explains that little accountability exists for the visual message, awarding the news media considerable power in defining the referents for the visual images. This leads to a process of decontextualization and recontextualization (Parry-Giles 2000), which evidences how the news media act as a creative rather than a detective agent in the image-making process.

In illustrating the process of decontextualization/recontextualization, I return to the visual evidence from MSNBC's *Time and Again* regarding HRC's "private pain" in dealing with her husband's infidelity. Originally, the close-up/ profile image was shot during the August 13, 1998, memorial service of the American embassy bombings in Kenya and Tanzania, an event that occurred four days before Bill Clinton's admission of his relationship with Lewinsky. Prior to the memorial service, both Clintons met with family members of the bombing victims in a closed-door setting. As the coffins were carried from the airplane to the Andrews Air Force Base hanger, somber music played; family members, military personnel, Clinton administration officials, and both Clintons looked on. The ceremony was quite emotional and many, including Bill Clinton, were crying. Hillary Clinton too appeared quite distressed (*Ceremony* 1998, August 13).

NBC, however, decontextualized the visuals from the memorial ceremony and recontextualized them within narratives about HRC's reaction to the Clinton–Lewinsky scandal. This example of visual manipulation is first evidenced during the August 17, 1998, *NBC Nightly News* program. Yet the same close-up of HRC's face repeatedly stands in as authenticating evidence of her state of mind during the days following her husband's apologia speech. When the *Time and Again* episode of January 30, 1999, aired, the memorial ceremony image is so visually entrenched with HRC's emotional state in the aftermath of the Lewinsky matter, that MSNBC used the visual to introduce the segment dealing with the post–August 17th disclosures. The close-up/ profiled image is also superimposed over a shot of the White House as MSNBC went to and returned from a commercial break. In this instance, NBC created the referent for the image that seemingly authenticated HRC's state of mind, evidencing the increasing difficulty in discerning the "real" from the "simulated" in television news.[6] The use of extreme close-ups allows for this decontextualization process to occur with minimal resistance. Thus, even as the television news media gain a measure of authority to assess the authenticity of political candidates, such stories tells us more about the media production practices of U.S. politics than they do about a candidate's political character.

FUTURE RESEARCH IN AUTHENTICITY AND VISUAL DISCOURSE

The media's quest for the authentic candidate certainly transcends the political campaign of Hillary Rodham Clinton and even television news coverage. Within an October 11, 1999, *Newsweek* article, Howard Fineman addressed

Shawn J. Parry-Giles

this authenticity quest, charging that "No plain politician . . . can give America what it seems to want in the post–Clinton era: an authentic leader who isn't merely the sum of the polls he takes." Assessing the complexities of the authenticity claims, *Time*'s Matthew Cooper (1999, December 27) argued that "today's political culture craves authenticity but bristles when it actually gets some" in his story about Governor Jesse Ventura of Minnesota. And in her November 22, 1999, story for *Time*, Margaret Carlson evaluated Bill Bradley's authenticity attempts, arguing that on one level, "the authenticity thing has worked well for Bradley." In the end, though, Carlson questioned Bradley's image, noting that he "sought help for his campaign from Madison Avenue . . . secretly." Carlson concluded that rather than dwelling on his past basketball experiences, Bradley needed to "now tell us who [he is]." Thus, the print news media also expend considerable energy assessing the authentic dimensions of a political candidate's character.

Although this chapter examines the media's role vis-à-vis political authenticity, the approach also involves examining the role of campaigns in their attempts to create authentic images of their candidates and inauthentic images of their opponents. The 2000 election was one where such issues were paramount. Before withdrawing from the U.S. Senate race in May 2000, for example, Rudy Giuliani drew upon Republican presidential candidate John McCain's credibility and thus portrayed himself as the "authentic" candidate in the New York Senate campaign during an April 2000 advertisement. The announcer within the Giuliani ad stated: "Together they [McCain and Giuliani] rode a bus to spread a message of hope and humanity to the people of New York. One an authentic American hero dedicated to integrity and reform. The other an authentic New York leader ready to make a difference for an entire state and the nation" (Rudy Boards . . . , 2000, April 13). Relying on the same theme, the Giuliani campaign also questioned the authenticity of his then-opponent Hillary Rodham Clinton. In a news release from Giuliani's U.S. Senate campaign, his staffers featured the following quotation from New York City Councilman Tom Oginbene: "[HRC] adds up to a candidate [that] values ambition and image over integrity and authenticity" (U.S. Senate 2000).

What such examples indicate is the need for further study of political authenticity in electoral politics. Of particular importance is the role that visual cues play in the process of granting political authenticity. For television news, the production techniques typically used make it virtually impossible for the viewer to discern the simulated from the real. Television news, rather than serving a "mimetic relationship to real events" (Mander 1987, 54), actually serves a creative function in its production of political reality. The news media's authority, though, rests on the realism of its newscasts. As Mander (1987, 54–55) maintains, news "reports pretend to reflect social reality, but in fact offer selected interpretation of discrete events."

Within this creative process, the virtual world sometimes appears more real than real; "images often look better than nature" (Stephens 1998, 126). As the virtual world's dominance becomes more pervasive with computers, Stephens argues that "[w]e are beginning to accept the idea that the world can be distorted, reimagined, that it can be made to collide with alternative visions of itself" (195). The result is hyperreality, where images or the simulated become indistinguishable from the "real" (Baudrillard 1994, 3).

The intersection of computer technology and image creation represents an area of study for scholars interested in contemporary politics. The week following the Super Bowl of 2000, ABC's *World News Tonight* aired a broadcast assessing the "latest technology" in advertising. According to ABC, advertisers superimposed product labels on billboards and sports stadiums for the television viewer even though such logos were not visible to those attending the sporting event. As Ned Potter of *World News Tonight* wondered: "The technology is so powerful, it leaves people wondering how realistic is too realistic. In commercials, you fully expect illusions. . . . But in live television, don't you think you're seeing the real thing" (2000, February 1)? The news profession is now even debating the ethics of computer-generated images as *CBS Evening News* superimposed its own logo over the electronic billboard logo of *NBC Nightly News* during its Times Square New Year's Eve broadcast (*ABC World News Tonight* 2000, February 1). The debate over the "virtual billboard" and other computer creations is one that scholars must enter since, as Jones (1993, 238) asserts, "Virtual reality calls into question our very notions of authenticity." How are such computer enhancements and creations influencing the practice of politics and the dissemination of political news?

More specifically, scholarly pursuits must engage the ethical and educational dimensions of computer enhancement, computer creation, and political and mediated image making. Zelizer (1998, 239) contends that "the media's use of images is inadvertently creating a breach between representation and responsibility"; Gitlin (1980), however, views such strategies as much more deliberate. Such issues of "visual distortion" (Messaris 1997, 142), regardless of their intentionality, are problematic for two reasons. First, visual discourse is subjected less stringently to ethical standards of accuracy than are verbal messages (Messaris 1997). Second, viewers are presumably less aware of the possibility for manipulation. As Arnheim (1969, 102) suggests, "imagery may do its best work below the level of consciousness." The task of political scholars is to continue examining the political images produced by candidates, their campaigns, the opposing campaigns, and the news media to assess the kinds of visual enhancements and distortions present. In doing so, we must deal squarely with the ethics of such practices.

Political scholars should examine further the effects of visual discourse and their distortions on audiences. Currently, there is inconsistent evidence concerning the effects of the visual messages. Robinson and Levy (1986, 15) assert that visuals can "aid . . . understanding" and Gunter (1987, 72) contends that "[p]ictures may enhance memory." Philo (1990, 5), however, offers a different interpretation, arguing that "we cannot assume that . . . [the] audience will . . . accept" the interpretation articulated by the news media. Graber's 1990 study evidences the equivocality of visual encoding's effectiveness. While the data reveal that "visuals allowed [respondents] . . . to form more complete and accurate impressions of people and events," the data also suggest that attending to both pictures and words "may interfere with comprehension" (149, 137). Obviously, further inquiry is needed. The realm of visual enhancement and distortion opens up a new area of study for social scientists attending to the impact that such manipulations may have on political audiences and voter behavior.

Hartley (1992, 3) argues that the political process is now "performed" through "pictures." Given the importance of visuals to the image-making process, much more work is needed in the intersections between politics, visuals, and image making. Scholars often are uninterested in studying the image-making process, arguing that this process debases political practice (Bennett 1992), yet to examine such matters is to understand them. The employment of authenticating messages represents another outgrowth of the image-making, character-building process integral to politics. Scholars must begin to assess the complex intersection of these all-important political issues.

NOTES

1. At times, I use the terms "image," "visuals," and "pictures" interchangeably. In these instances, I am attending to the visual connotations of the concept—what Mitchell (1994, 4n) defines as concrete "visual representations." When I talk though about the "image" aspects of "image making," I am referring to the symbolic (verbal and visual) means of constructing a candidate's political persona for the electorate.

2. While the majority of the texts center on the U.S. Senate race from New York, some of the broadcasts are more biographical and thus address issues prior to 1999. Many of the texts used in this study derive from MSNBC, NBC, and CNN broadcasts. Part of the disproportion is linked to MSNBC's and CNN's 24-hour news cycle, which increases the amount of coverage devoted to political activities. Many of the people cited from these newscasts are journalists from other news sources, which furthers the diversity of thought on issues related to political authenticity.

3. In assessing the relationship between verbal and visual symbols, I agree with Hunter's (1987, 1) contention that because "words and pictures . . . routinely appear together," they both thus "contribute" to the meaning of discourse. Yet I also believe that visual and verbal strategies are read differently and can perform unique functions within discourse. As Snyder (1980, 222) contends, visuals are often treated as "substitutes for the objects they represent" or the "equivalent to looking at what is pic-

tured"; verbal discourse is viewed more often as a construction under the control of the author. Identifying another difference, Mitchell (1980, 3) argues that "language works with arbitrary, conventional signs, while images [work] with natural, universal signs. Language unfolds in temporal succession, images reside in a realm of timeless spatiality and simultaneity." Within political authenticity, the visual discourse often serves as pictorial evidence of the journalists' contentions about a candidate's authenticity.

4. Even though I talk about five media-production strategies that help reify media messages of authenticity (for example, insider access, repetition, editing and motion, close-ups, and the role of the camera), there are undoubtedly additional strategies that substantiate the media's authority within this process. The existence of these strategies is detailed in the scholarship about the production practices of television (news) and film. Here I am attempting to exhibit the relationship between these production strategies and the media's electoral role within political authenticity.

5. To learn more about the negotiations that occur between political candidates and news organizations regarding journalistic insider access, see Cook (1998) and Sparrow (1999).

6. Some might contend that this particular instance of decontextualization and recontextualization represents a fraudulent practice. This chapter, however, is centered on the strategies at work within the texts rather than the motives for such media practices. Regardless of the circumstances upon which a visual is taken out of one context and redefined in relation to another, the practice still evidences the creative role involved with news visuals. For a discussion of the reasons why news organizations engage in such practices, see Cook (1998) and Sparrow (1999).

References

ABC World News Tonight. 1999. ABC: February 16.

———. 2000. ABC: February 1.

Aberbach, J. 1996. The Federal Executive under Clinton. In *The Clinton Presidency: First Appraisals*, edited by Colin Campbell and Bert A. Rockman. Chatham, N.J.: Chatham House.

Abramson, J. 1992. Democratic Designs for Electronic Town Meetings. Paper presented at the Conference on Electronic Town Meetings, Aspen Institute.

Ackerman, B. 1989. Why Dialogue? *Journal of Philosophy* 86:5–22.

Adhikari, G. 2000. From the Press to the Media. *Journal of Democracy* 2 (1): 56–63.

Aks, J., W. Haltom, and M. McCann. 1997. Symbolic Stella—On Media Coverage of Personal Injury Litigation and the Production of Legal Knowledge. *Law and Courts* (summer): 5–7.

Alger, D. E. 1998. *Megamedia: How Giant Corporations Dominate Mass Media, Distort Competition, and Endanger Democracy.* Lanham, Md.: Rowman & Littlefield.

Allen, F. A. 1954. Chief Justice Vinson and the Theory of Constitutional Government: A Tentative Appraisal. *Northwestern University Law Review* 48 (March/April).

Almond, G., and G. B. Powell Jr. 1966. *Comparative Politics: A Developmental Approach.* Boston: Little, Brown.

Almond, G., and S. Verba. 1965. *The Civic Culture.* Boston: Little, Brown.

Altheide, D., and R. Snow. 1979. *Media Logic.* Beverly Hills, Calif.: Sage.

Ambrose, S. E. 1984. *Eisenhower: The President.* New York: Simon & Schuster.

American League of Lobbyists. 2001. Washington, D.C. [www.alldc.org].

Anderson, B. 1991. *Imagined Communities.* London: Verso Press.

Archer, M. 1996. *Culture and Agency.* Cambridge: Cambridge University Press.

Arendt, H. 1959. *The Human Condition.* Garden City, N.Y.: Anchor Books.

Arnheim, R. 1969. *Visual Thinking.* Berkeley: University of California Press.

Association of Electronic Journalists. 2000. [www.rtnda.org] (accessed January 2000).

Atkin, C., and S. Chaffee. 1972. Instrumental Response Strategies in Opinion Interviews. *Public Opinion Quarterly* 36:69–79.

Atkinson, J. M., and P. Drew. 1979. *Order in Court: The Organization of Verbal Interaction in Judicial Settings*. Atlantic Highlands, N.J.: Humanities Press.

Aversa, Jeannine. 1997. Digital TV Will Cost. *Associated Press,* April 4. [www.ap.org].

Bagdikian, B. 1992. *The Media Monopoly.* 4th ed. Boston: Beacon.

Bane, M., and D. Ellwood. 1994. *Welfare Realities.* Cambridge, Mass.: Harvard University Press.

Barber, B. 1984. *Strong Democracy: Participatory Politics for a New Age.* Berkeley: University of California Press.

Barber, J. 1972. *The Presidential Character: Predicting Performance in the White House.* Englewood Cliffs: Prentice Hall.

———. 1977. *The Presidential Character: Predicting Performance in the White House.* 2nd ed. Englewood Cliffs, N.J.: Prentice Hall.

Barnhurst, K. G., and D. Mutz. 1997. American Journalism and the Decline of Event-Centered Reporting. *Journal of Communication* 47(4): 27–53.

Barry, H. 1932. The Early Years. *Virginia Law Review* 18:121–152.

Baruss, I. 1996. *Authentic Knowing: The Convergence of Science and Spiritual Aspiration.* West Lafayette, Ind.: Purdue University Press.

Baudrillard, J. 1994. *Simulacra and Simulation,* translated by. S. F. Glaser. Ann Arbor: University of Michigan Press.

Baughman, J. L. 1985. *Television's Guardians: The FCC and the Politics of Programming 1958–1967.* Knoxville: University of Tennessee Press.

Bauman, S., and S. Herbst. 1994. Managing Perceptions of Public Opinion: Candidates' and Journalists' Reactions to the 1992 Poll. *Political Communication* 11:133–144.

Baumgartner, F., and B. Leech. 1998. *Basic Interests.* Princeton, N.J.: Princeton University Press.

Bausinger, H. 1984. Media, Technology and Daily Life. *Media, Culture, and Society* 6:343–351.

Beck, P. 1991. Voters' Intermediation Environments in the 1988 Presidential Contest. *Public Opinion Quarterly* 55:371–394.

Bennet, J., and R. Pear. 1997. How a Presidency Was Defined by the Thousand Parts of Its Sum. *New York Times,* 8 December.

Bennett, W. L. 1990. Toward a Theory of Press–State Relations. *Journal of Communication* 40(2): 103–125.

———. 1992. *The Governing Crisis: Media, Money, and Marketing in American Elections.* New York: St. Martin's Press.

———. 1993. Constructing Publics and their Opinions. *Political Communication* 10:101–120.

Bennett, W. L., and R. G. Lawrence. 1995. News Icons and the Mainstreaming of Social Change. *Journal of Communication* 45(3): 20–39.

Berelson, B., P. Lazarsfeld, and W. McPhee. 1954. *Voting.* Chicago: University of Chicago Press.

Berger, A., ed. 1989. *Political Culture and Public Opinion.* New Brunswick, N.J.: Transaction Publishers.

Berger, P., and T. Luckmann. 1967. *The Social Construction of Reality.* Garden City, N.J.: Anchor Books.

Berke, R., and J. Broder. 1997. Analysis: A Mellow Clinton at Ease in His Role. *New York Times*, 7 December.

Berlin, I. 1969. Two Concepts of Liberty. In *Four Essays on Liberty*. London: Oxford University Press

Berlin, I., and R. Jahanbegloo. 1991. *Conversations with Isaiah Berlin*. Scribner's.

Berman, M. 1970. *The Politics of Authenticity: Radical Individualism and the Emergence of Modern Society*. New York: Atheneum.

Bessette, J. 1997. *The Mild Voice of Reason*. Chicago: University of Chicago Press.

Bessette, J. M., and J. Tulis, eds. 1981. *The Presidency in the Constitutional Order*. Baton Rouge: Louisiana State University Press.

Best, J. 1999. *Random Violence: How We Think about New Crimes and New Victims*. Berkeley: University of California Press.

Bickford, S. 1996a. Beyond Friendship: Aristotle on Conflict, Deliberation, and Attention. *Journal of Politics* 58:398–421.

———. 1996b. *The Dissonance of Democracy: Listening, Conflict, and Citizenship*. Ithaca, N.Y.: Cornell University Press.

Billig, M., S. Condor, D. Edwards, M. Gane, D. Middleton, and A. Radley. 1988. *Ideological Dilemmas: A Social Psychology of Everyday Thinking*. London: Sage.

Bingham, W., and B. Moore. 1959. *How to Interview*. New York: Harper and Row.

Binkley, W. 1962. *Presidents and Congress*. New York: Vintage.

Birkland, T. 1997. *After Disaster*. Washington, D.C.: Georgetown University Press.

Bishop, G., R. Oldendick, and A. Tuchfarber. 1978. Effects of Question Wording and Format on Political Attitude Consistency. *Public Opinion Quarterly* 42:81–92.

———. 1982. Effects of Presenting One versus Two Sides of an Issue in Survey Questions. *Public Opinion Quarterly* 46:69–85.

Blumer, H. 1960. Public Opinion and Public Opinion Polling. In *Public Opinion and Propaganda*, edited by D. Katz, D. Cartwright, S. Eldersveld, and A. M. Lee. New York: Henry Holt.

Bodnar, J. 1992. *Remaking America: Public Memory, Commemoration and Patriotism in the Twentieth Century*. Princeton, N.J.: Princeton University Press.

Boesche, R. 1987. *The Strange Liberalism of Alexis de Tocqueville*. Ithaca, N.Y.: Cornell University Press.

Bogart, L. 1972. *Silent Politics: Polls and the Awareness of Public Opinion*. New York: Wiley.

Bohman, J. 1996. *Public Deliberation*. Cambridge, Mass.: MIT Press.

Bohman, J., and W. Rehg, eds. 1997. *Deliberative Democracy: Essays on Reason and Politics*. Cambridge, Mass.: MIT Press.

Bommes, M., and P. Wright. 1982. Charms of Residence: The Public and the Past. In *Making Histories: Studies in History-Writing and Politics,* edited by R. Johnson, G. McLennan, B. Schwarz, and D. Sutton. Minneapolis: University of Minnesota Press.

Bourdieu, P. 1979. Public Opinion Does Not Exist. In *Communication and Class Struggle*, edited by A. Mattleart and S. Siegelaub. New York: International General.

Bradburn, N. 1982. Question-Wording Effects in Surveys. In *Question Framing and Response Consistency,* edited by R. M. Hogarth. San Francisco: Jossey-Bass.

Bradburn, N., and C. Miles. 1979. Vague Quantifiers. *Public Opinion Quarterly* 43:92–101.

Brennan, M. 1995. The Discourse of Denial: Cross-Examining Child Victim Witnesses. *Journal of Pragmatics* 23:71–91.

Brennan, W. J. 1965. The Supreme Court and the Meiklejohn Interpretation of the First Amendement. *Harvard Law Review* 79:1–20.

Briggs, C. 1986. *Learning How to Ask*. New York: Cambridge University Press.

Brinkley, J. 1997. *Defining Vision: The Battle for the Future of Television*. New York: Harcourt Brace.

Brint, M. 1991. *A Genealogy of Political Culture*. Boulder, Colo.: Westview Press.

Brownstein, R. 1994. Polarization Politics Seen as Key Obstacle to Welfare Proposal. *Los Angeles Times*, 15 June.

Bureau of Justice Statistics. 1999. *Criminal Victimization 1998: Changes 1997–98 with Trends 1993–98*. Washington, D.C.: U.S. Department of Justice. [http://www.ojp.usdoj.gov/bjs/abstract/cv98.html].

Burke, K. 1973. *The Philosophy of Literary Form*. Berkeley, Calif.: University of California Press.

Burnham, W. D. 1970. *Critical Elections and the Mainsprings of American Politics*. New York: Norton.

———. 1991. Critical Realignment: Dead or Alive? In *The End of Realignment? Interpreting American Electoral Eras*, edited by Byron E. Shafer. Madison: University of Wisconsin Press.

Burns, J. M. 1956. *The Lion and the Fox*. New York: Harcourt Brace.

Campbell, A., P. E. Converse, W. E. Miller, and D. E. Stokes. 1966. *Elections and the Political Order*. New York: Wiley.

Cantril, A. 1940. Experiments in the Wording of Questions. *Public Opinion Quarterly* 4:330–332.

Carey, J. 1995. The Press, Public Opinion, and Public Discourse. In *Public Opinion and the Communication of Consent*, edited by T. Glasser and C. Salmon. New York: Guilford.

Carlson, M. 1999. The Branding of Bill Bradley. *Time*. November 22. [http://www.pathfinder.com/time/magazine/articles/0,3226,34376,00.html].

Carmines, E. G., and J. A. Stimson. 1989. *Issue Evolution: Race and the Transformation of American Politics*. Princeton, N.J.: Princeton University Press.

Carpenter, T. G. 1994. *The Captive Press*. Washington, D.C.: Cato Institute.

Cavell, S. 1979. *The World Viewed: Reflections on the Ontology of Film*. Cambridge, Mass.: Harvard University Press.

CBS Evening News. 1999. Central Broadcasting System: July 8.

CBS News/*New York Times*. 1994. Roper Center POLL Database.

Ceasar, J., G. E. Thurow, J. K. Tulis, and J. M. Bessette. 1981. The Rise of the Rhetorical Presidency. *Presidential Studies Quarterly* 11:158–171.

Ceremony for Embassy Bombing Victims. 1998. C-SPAN: August 13. West Lafayette, Ind.: Purdue Research Foundation.

Chaffee, S. 1986. Mass Media and Interpersonal Channels: Competitive, Convergent, or Complementary? In *Inter/Media*, edited by G. Gumpert and R. Cathcart. New York: Oxford University Press.

Chalmers, D. 1996. *And the Crooked Places Made Straight: The Struggle for Social Change in the 1960s*. 2nd ed. Baltimore: Johns Hopkins University Press.

Chaney, D. 1993. *Fictions of Collective Life: Public Drama in Late Modern Culture*. London: Routledge.

Chang, D. 1991. Discriminatory Impact, Affirmative Action and Innocent Victims: Judicial Conservatism or Conservative Justices. *Columbia Law Review* 91.

Chayes, A. 1976. The Role of the Judge in Public Law Litigation. *Harvard Law Review* 89.

Chermak, S. 1994. Crime in the News Media: A Refined Understanding of How Crimes Become News. In *Media, Process, and the Social Construction of Crime*, edited by Gregg Barak. New York: Garland.

Christiano, T. 1997. The Significance of Public Deliberation. In *Deliberative Democracy: Essays on Reason and Politics*, edited by J. Bohman and W. Rehg. Cambridge, Mass.: MIT Press.

Chubb, J. E., and P. Peterson. 1985. Realignment and Institutionalization. In *The New Direction in American Politics*, edited by J. E. Chubb and P. E. Peterson. Washington, D.C.: Brookings.

Clark, T. 1947. A Federal Prosecutor Looks at the Civil Rights Statutes. *Columbia Law Review* 47.

Clecak, P. 1983. *America's Quest for an Ideal Self: Dissent and Fulfillment in the 60s and 70s*. New York: Oxford University Press.

CNN Late Edition. 2000. CNN: February 6.

Cohen, J. 1985. Strategy or Identity: New Theoretical Paradigms and Contemporary Social Movements. *Social Research* 52:663–716.

———. 1989. Deliberation and Democratic Legitimacy. In *The Good Polity*, edited by A. Hamlin and P. Petit. Oxford: Blackwell.

———. 1997. *Presidential Responsiveness and Public Policy-Making: The Public and the Policies That Presidents Choose*. Ann Arbor: University of Michigan Press.

———. 1998. Democracy and Liberty. In *Deliberative Democracy*, edited by J. Elster. New York: Cambridge University Press.

Commager, H. S. 1965. The Search for a Usable Past. *American Heritage* 16:4–9 (February).

———. 1993. *Commager on Tocqueville*. Columbia: University of Missouri Press.

Condon, G. E. 1993. Clinton Plans a Detroit Sales Pitch. *San Diego Union-Tribune*, 4 February.

Conley, J., and W. O'Barr. 1990. *Rules versus Relationships: The Ethnography of Legal Discourse*. Chicago: University of Chicago Press.

———. 1998. *Just Words*. Chicago: University of Chicago Press.

Converse, P. 1964. The Nature of Belief Systems in Mass Publics. In *Ideology and Discontent*, edited by David Apter. New York: Free Press.

Cook, T. 1998. *Governing with the News: The News Media as a Political Institution*. Chicago: University of Chicago Press.

Cook, T. E. 1994. Domesticating a Crisis: Washington Newsbeats and Network News after the Iraq Invasion of Kuwait. In *Taken by Storm*, edited by W. L. Bennett and D. L. Paletz. Chicago: University of Chicago Press.

———. 1996. Political Values and Production Values. *Political Communication* 13:469–481.

Cook, W. 1907. What Is the Police Power? *Columbia Law Review* 7.

Cooper, M. 1999. Keeping His Eye on the Ball. *Time*, December 27. [http://www.time.com/time/magazine/articles/0,3266,36291,00.html].

Corwin, E. 1948. *The President: Office and Powers*. New York: New York University.

Coulthardt, M., and M. Ashby. 1975. Talking with the Doctor I. *Journal of Communication* 3:140–152.

Cox, A. 1978. Federalism and Individual Rights under the Burger Court. *Northwestern University Law Review* 73:1.

Cronin, T., and M. Genovese. 1998. *The Paradoxes of the American Presidency.* New York: Oxford University Press.

Currie, D. 1986. Positive and Negative Constitutional Rights. *University of Chicago Law Review* 53:864–891.

Dahl, R. 1998. *On Democracy.* New Haven, Conn.: Yale University Press.

Daniels, B. 1998. A Defining Moment. *Broadcasting & Cable,* November 16.

Daniels, S. 1986. Are Caseloads Really Increasing? No. *The Judges Journal* (summer): 24–25.

Darcy, R., and A. Richman. 1988. Presidential Travel and Public Opinion. *Presidential Studies Quarterly* 18:85–90.

Darnton, R. 1975. Writing News and Telling Stories. *Daedalus* 2:175–194.

Dearing, J. 1989. Setting the Polling Agenda for the Issue of Aids. *Public Opinion Quarterly* 53:309–329.

Dearing, J. W., and E. M. Rogers. 1996. *Agenda-Setting.* Thousand Oaks, Calif.: Sage.

Decision 2000. 2000. MSNBC: February 7.

deCordova, R. 1990. *Picture Personalities: The Emergence of the Star System in America.* Urbana: University of Illinois Press.

Delay, T. 1994. Welfare Reform. *Congressional Record,* May 4.

Denton, R. 1982. *The Symbolic Dimensions of the American Presidency: Description and Analysis.* Prospect Heights, Ill.: Waveland Press.

———. 1988. *The Primetime Presidency of Ronald Reagan: The Era of the Television.* New York: Praeger.

Denton, R., and R. Holloway. 1996. Clinton and the Town Hall Meetings: Mediated Conversation and the Risk of Being "in Touch." In *The Clinton Presidency: Images, Issues and Communication Strategies,* edited by R. Denton and R. Holloway. New York: Praeger, 17–42.

Dewey, J. 1927. *The Public and Its Problems.* Denver: Henry Holt.

Dewey, J., and A. F. Bentley. 1949. *Knowing and the Known.* Boston: Beacon.

Dimaggio, P. 1988. Interest and Agency in Institutional Theory. In *Institutional Patterns and Organizations: Culture and Environment,* edited by L. Zucker, 3–21. Cambridge, Mass.: Ballinger.

Divine, R. A. 1985. *Since 1945: Politics and Diplomacy in Recent American History.* 3rd ed. New York: McGraw-Hill.

Donohue, E., V. Schiraldi, and J. Ziedenberg. 1999. *School House Hype.* Justice Policy Institute. [http://www.cjcj.org/jpi/schoolhouse.html].

Donahue, G. A., P. Tichenor, and C. Olien. 1995. A Guard Dog Perspective on the Role of Media. *Journal of Communication* 45(2): 115–132.

Dowd, M. 1999. Liberties: The Boy Can't Help It. *New York Times,* 4 August.

Dowding, K. 1996. *Power.* Minneapolis: University of Minnesota Press.

Downs, A. 1957. *An Economic Theory of Democracy.* New York: HarperCollins.

Drew, E. 1994. *On the Edge: The Clinton Presidency.* New York: Simon & Schuster.

———. 1996. *Showdown: The Struggle between the Gingrich Congress and the Clinton White House.* New York: Simon & Schuster.

———. 1997. *Whatever It Takes: The Real Struggle for Political Power in America.* New York: Viking.

Drew, P., and M-L. Sorjonen. 1997. Institutional Dialogue. In *Discourse as Social Interaction*, vol. 2, edited by Teun Van Dijk. London: Sage.

Dyer, R. 1986. *Heavenly Bodies: Film Stars and Society*. New York: St. Martin's Press.

Edelman, M. 1964. *The Symbolic Uses of Politics*. Urbana: University of Illinois Press.

———. 1971. *Politics as Symbolic Action*. Chicago: Markham Publishing Company.

———. 1977. *Political Language*. New York: Academic.

———. 1988. *Constructing the Political Spectacle*. Chicago: University of Chicago Press.

———. 1993. Contestable Categories and Public Opinion. *Political Communication* 10:231–242.

Edin, K., and C. Jencks, 1992. Welfare. In *Rethinking Social Policy*, edited by C. Jencks. New York: Harper.

Edy, J. A. 1998. *Troubled Pasts: Journalism and the Development of Collective Memory*. Ph.D. diss., Northwestern University.

———. 1999. Journalistic Uses of Collective Memory. *Journal of Communication* 49 (2): 71–85.

Elder, C. B. 1934. Some Constitutional Aspects of the National Industrial Recovery Act. *Illinois Law Review* 28 (January).

Eliasoph, N. 1998. *Avoiding Politics: How Americans Produce Apathy in Everyday Life*. Cambridge: Cambridge University Press.

Ellis, R. J., ed. 1998. *Speaking to the People: The Rhetorical Presidency in Historical Perspective*. Amherst: University of Massachusetts Press.

Elster, J. 1997. The Market and the Forum: Three Varieties of Political Theory. In *Deliberative Democracy: Essays on Reason and Politics*, edited by J. Bohman and W. Rehg. Cambridge, Mass.: MIT Press.

Emerson, T. 1982. The Power of Congress to Change Constitutional Decisions of the Supreme Court: The Human Life Bill. *Northwestern University Law Review* 76.

Entman, R. M. 1989. *Democracy without Citizens: Media and the Decay of American Politics*. New York: Oxford.

———. 1991. Framing U.S. Coverage of International News: Contrasts in Narratives of the KAL and Iran Air Incidents. *Journal of Communication* 41:6–27.

———. 1993. Framing: Toward Clarification of a Fractured Paradigm. *Journal of Communication* 43(4): 51–58.

Entman, R. M., and B. I. Page. 1994. The News before the Storm: The Iraq War Debate and the Limits to Media Independence. In *Taken by Storm: The News Media, Public Opinion, and U.S. Foreign Policy in the Gulf War*, edited by W. L. Bennett and D. L. Paletz. Chicago: University of Chicago Press.

Entman, R. M., and A. Rojecki. 1993. Freezing Out the Public: Elite and Media Framing of the U.S. Anti-Nuclear Movement. *Political Communication* 10:155–173.

Ericson, R. V., P. Baranek, and J. Chan. 1991. *Representing Order: Crime, Law, and Justice in the News Media*. Milton Keynes: Open University Press.

Etelson, J., and F. Smith. 1969. Union Discipline under the Landrum-Griffin Act. *Harvard Law Review* 82.

Ettema, J. S. 1994. A Discourse That Is Closer to Silence than to Talk: The Politics and Possibilities of Reporting on Victims of War. *Critical Studies in Mass Communication* 11:1-21.

Evans, S. M. 1980. *Personal Politics: The Roots of Women's Liberation in the Civil Rights Movement and the New Left*. New York: Vintage.

Fackler, T. 1999. The Dynamics of Valence Issues: A Time-Series Analysis of Public Opinion and Media Accounts of Political Corruption and Economic Performance, 1956–1996. Paper delivered at the annual meeting of the American Political Science Association, Atlanta, Georgia.

Faigman, D. L. 1992. Reconciling Individual Rights and Government Interests: Madisonian Principals versus Supreme Court Practice. *Virginia Law Review* 78.

Farber, D. 1988. *Chicago '68.* Chicago: University of Chicago Press.

FCC Begins Digital TV Channel Allocations. 1996. *Television Digest* 36, 29 July: 2.

Felstiner, W., R. Abel, and A. Sarat. 1980. The Emergence and Transformation of Disputes: Naming, Blaming and Claiming. *Law and Society Review* 15.

Fentress, J., and C. Wickham. 1992. *Social Memory.* Oxford: Blackwell.

Ferrara, A. 1993. *Modernity and Authenticity: A Study of the Social and Ethical Thought of Jean-Jacques Rousseau.* Albany: SUNY Press.

———. 1998. *Reflective Authenticity: Rethinking the Project of Modernity.* London: Routledge.

Fineman, H. 1999a. Look Who's Running. *Newsweek,* 11 October. [http://newsweek.com/nw-srv/issue/15_99b/printed/us/na/na0815_1.html].

———. 1999b. The Outside Shooter . . . and the Fighting Pilot. *Newsweek,* 15 November. [http://newsweek.com/nw-srv/printed/us/na/a26005-1999nov7.html].

Finkelstein, M. 1927. From Munn v. Illinois to Tyson v. Banton: A Study in the Judicial Process. *Columbia Law Review* 27.

Fisher, W. 1980. Rhetorical Fiction and the Presidency. *Quarterly Journal of Speech* 21:116–132.

Fishkin, J. 1991. *Democracy and Deliberation.* New Haven, Conn.: Yale University Press.

———. 1992. *The Dialogue of Justice.* New Haven, Conn.: Yale University Press.

———. 1995. *The Voice of the People: Public Opinion and Democracy.* New Haven, Conn.: Yale University Press.

Fishman, M. 1978. Crime Waves as Ideology. *Social Problems* 25:531–543.

———. 1980. *Manufacturing the News.* Austin: University of Texas Press.

Ford, G. R. 1976. Address before a Joint Session of the Congress Reporting on the State of the Union. *Public Papers of the President* 31, 19 January.

Foucault, M. 1977. *Discipline and Punish: The Birth of the Prison,* translated by A. Sheridan. New York: Random.

———. 1990. *The History of Sexuality,* vol. 1. New York: Vintage.

Fowler, F. 1992. How Unclear Terms Affect Survey Data. *Public Opinion Quarterly* 56:218–231.

Fowles, J. 1992. *Starstruck: Celebrity Performers and the American Public.* Washington, D.C.: Smithsonian Institution Press.

Fox News Sunday. 1999. Fox: 28 November.

Frankel, R. 1990. Talking in Interviews: A Dispreference for Patient-Questions in Physician-Patient Encounters. In *Interaction Competence,* edited by G. Psathas. Washington, D.C.: International Institute for Ethnomethodology and Conversation Analysis and University Press of America, 1990.

Frankfurter, F., 1939. Mr. Justice Cardozo and Public Law. *Columbia Law Review* 80.

Franklin, J. H., and A. Moss Jr. 1994. *From Slavery to Freedom: A History of African-Americans.* 7th ed. New York: Knopf.

Fraser, N. 1994. Rethinking the Public Sphere: A Contribution to the Critique of Actually Existing Democracy. In *Habermas and the Public Sphere*, edited by C. Calhoun. Cambridge, Mass.: MIT Press.

Fraser, N., and L. Gordon. 1994. A Genealogy of Dependency. *Signs* 19:309–336.

Freeman, J. 1993. Town Hall Meeting with Clinton Will Be Local TV First. S*an Diego Union-Tribune*, 17 May.

Friedman, L. M. 1971. The Idea of Right as a Social and Legal Concept. *Journal of Social Issues* 27.

———. 1980. The Six Million Dollar Man: Litigation and Rights Consciousness in Modern America. *Maryland Law Review* 40.

Frisch, M. H. 1986. The Memory of History. In *Presenting the Past: Essays on History and the Public,* edited by S. P. Benson et al. Philadelphia: Temple University Press.

Gabler, N. 2000. The Celebriticians. *George* (December/January):108–111, 124.

Galanter, M. 1986. The Day after the Litigation Explosion. *Maryland Law Review* 3, 46.

Galanter, M., and C. R. Epp. 1992. A Beginner's Guide to the Litigation Maze. *Business Economics* 27:33.

Gallup Organization. 1935. Do You Think Expenditures by the Government for Relief and Recovery Are Too Little, Too Great, or Just about Right? Princeton, N.J.: Gallup Organization.

———. 1999. Gallup Social and Economic Indicators: Environment. [http://www.gallup.com/poll/indicators/indenvironment.asp].

Gamson, J. 1994. *Claims to Fame: Celebrity in Contemporary America*. Berkeley: University of California Press.

Gamson, W. 1992. *Talking Politics.* Cambridge: Cambridge University Press.

Gans, H. 1979. *Deciding What's News.* New York: Vintage.

———. 1985. Are U.S. Journalists Dangerously Liberal? *Columbia Journalism Review* 24:4 (November/December).

Garfinkel, H. 1967. *Studies in Ethnomethodology.* Englewood Cliffs, N.J: Prentice-Hall.

Geertz, C. 1973. *The Interpretation of Cultures.* New York: Basic.

———. 1975. Common Sense as a Cultural System. *Antioch Review* 33 (spring):5–26.

Gilboa, E. 1990. Effects of Televised Presidential Addresses on Public Opinion: President Reagan and Terrorism in the Middle East. *Presidential Studies Quarterly* 20:43–53.

Gilens, M., and C. Hertzman. 2000. Corporate Ownership and News Bias: Newspaper Coverage of the 1996 Telecommunications Act. *Journal of Politics* 62 (2).

Gitlin, T. (1980). *The Whole World Is Watching: Mass Media in the Making and Remaking of the New Left.* Berkeley: University of California Press.

Glass, D. 1985. Evaluating Presidential Candidates: Who Focuses on Their Personal Attributes? *Public Opinion Quarterly* 49:517–534.

Glendon, M. A. 1991. *Rights Talk: The Impoverishment of Political Discourse.* New York: Free Press.

Goffman, E. 1981. *Forms of Talk.* Philadelphia: University of Pennsylvania Press.

Golding, M. P. 1963. Principled Decision Making and the Supreme Court. *Columbia Law Review* 63.

Goldman, A. I. 1986. Toward a Theory of Social Power. In *Power,* edited by Steve Lukes. New York: New York University Press.

Graber, D. 1984a. *Mass Media and American Politics.* 2nd ed. Washington, D.C.: CQ Press.

———. 1984b. *Processing the News: How People Tame the Information Tide.* New York: Longmans.

———. 1990. Seeing Is Remembering: How Visuals Contribute to Learning from Television News. *Journal of Communication* 40:134–155.

———. 1993. *Mass Media and American Politics.* 4th ed. Washington, D.C.: CQ Press.

———. 1997. *Mass Media and American Politics.* 5th ed. Washington, D.C.: CQ Press.

Graddol, D., and O. Boyd-Barrett. 1994. *Media Texts: Authors and Readers.* Clevedon, U.K.: Multilingual Matters Ltd.

Gramsci, A. 1988. *An Antonio Gramsci Reader,* edited by David Forgacs. New York: Schocken Books.

Granovetter, M. 1973. The Strength of Weak Ties. *American Journal of Sociology* 78: 1360–1380.

Greeley, L. M. 1910. The Changing Attitude of the Courts toward Social Legislation. *Illinois Law Review* 5:4.

Greenburg Research. 1994. Roper Center POLL Database.

Greenstein, F. 1982. *The Hidden-Hand Presidency: Eisenhower as Leader.* New York: Basic.

Greider, W. 1992. *Who Will Tell the People?* New York: Simon & Schuster.

Gronbeck, B. 1996. The Presidency in the Age of Secondary Orality. In *Beyond the Rhetorical Presidency,* edited by M. Medhurst. College Station: Texas A&M University Press.

Grossberg, L. 1992. *We Gotta Get out of This Place.* New York: Routledge.

Grossman, M., and M. J. Kumar. 1981. *Portraying the President: The White House and the News Media.* Baltimore: Johns Hopkins University Press.

Guensburg, C. 1998. When the Story Is about the Owner. *American Journalism Review,* 1 December.

Gunter, B. 1987. *Poor Reception: Misunderstanding and Forgetting Broadcast News.* Hillsdale, N.J.: Lawrence Erlbaum.

Gurevitch, M., and A. P. Kavoori. 1992. Television Spectacles as Politics. *Communication Monographs* 59:415–420.

Guttman, A., and D. Thompson. 1996. *Democracy and Disagreement.* Cambridge, Mass.: Belknap Press.

Habermas, J. 1989. *The Structural Transformation of the Public Sphere.* Cambridge, Mass.: MIT Press.

Hall, P., and R. Taylor. 1998. Political Science and the Three New Institutionalisms. In *Institutions and Social Order,* edited by K. Soltan, E. M. Uslaner, and V. Haufler, 15–43. Ann Arbor: The University of Michigan Press.

Hall, S. 1982. The Rediscovery of "Ideology": Return of the Repressed in Communication Studies. In *Culture, Society and the Media,* edited by M. Gurevitch, T. Bennett, J. Curran, and J. Wollacott. London: Methuen.

Hamby, A. L. 1992. *Liberalism and Its Challengers: From FDR to Bush.* 2nd ed. New York: Oxford University Press.

Handler, J. 1995. *The Poverty of Welfare Reform.* New Haven, Conn.: Yale University Press.

Hardt, H. 1993. Authenticity, Communication, and Critical Theory. *Critical Studies in Mass Communication* 10:49–69.

Hargrove, E. 1998. *The President As Leader.* Lawrence: University Press of Kansas.

Hargrove, E. C., and M. Nelson. 1984. *Presidents, Politics, and Policy.* New York: Knopf.

Harris, L. 1994. Roper Center POLL Database.

Harrison, T. Are Public Opinions Used Illegitimately? 47% Say Yes. 1995. In *Argumentation and value, Proceedings of the 9th SCA/AFA Conference on Argumentation,* edited by Sally Jackson. Annandale, Va.: SCA.

Hart, R. P. 1987. *The Sound of Leadership: Presidential Communication in a Modern Age.* Chicago: University of Chicago Press.

———. 1994. *Seducing America: How Television Charms the Modern Voter.* New York: Oxford University Press.

———. 1997. *Seducing America.* 2nd ed. New York: Oxford University Press.

———. 2000. *Campaign Talk.* Princeton, N.J.: Princeton University Press.

Hart and Teeter for NBC News and *Wall Street Journal.* 1994. Roper Center POLL Database.

Hartley, J. 1992. *The Politics of Pictures: The Creation of the Public in the Age of Popular Media.* London: Routledge.

———. 1999. *Uses of Television.* London: Routledge.

Hazlett, T. W. 1998. Assigning Property Rights to Radio Spectrum Users: Why Did FCC License Auctions Take 67 Years? *Journal of Law and Economics* 41(2):529–576.

Headliners and Legends. 1999. MSNBC: December 16.

———. 2000. MSNBC: January 27.

Heclo, H. 1996. The Sixties False Dawn: Awakenings, Movements and Post-Modern Policy Making. *The Journal of Policy History* (winter).

Henggeler, P. 1995. *The Kennedy Persuasion: The Politics of Style since JFK.* Chicago: Ivan R. Dee.

Henkin, L. 1975. DeFunis: Introduction. *Columbia Law Review* 75 (April).

Herbst, S. 1993. *Numbered Voices.* Chicago: University of Chicago Press.

———. 1995. On the Disappearance of Groups. In *Public Opinion and the Communication of Consent,* edited by T. Glasser and C. Salmon. New York: Guilford.

Herman, E. 1995. The Assault on Social Security. *Z Magazine,* 30 November.

Herman, E., and N. Chomsky. 1988. *Manufacturing Consent.* New York: Pantheon.

Hertsgaard, M. 1988. *On Bended Knee: The Press and the Reagan Presidency.* New York: Farrar, Straus, & Giroux.

Hess, S. 1986. *The Ultimate Insiders.* Washington, D.C.: Brookings.

Hikins, J. 1975. The Rhetoric of "Unconditional Surrender" and the Decision to Drop the Atomic Bomb. *Quarterly Journal of Speech* 69:250–264.

Hilgartner, S., and C. L. Bosk. 1988. The Rise and Fall of Social Problems: A Public Arenas Model. *American Journal of Sociology* 1(July):53–78.

Hill, R. A. 1994. Making Noise: Marcus Garvey *Dada* August 1922. In *Picturing Us: African American Identity in Photography,* edited by D. Willis, 181–205. New York: New Press.

Hillbruner, A. 1974. Archetype and Signature: Nixon and the 1973 Inaugural. *Central States Speech Journal* 25:169–181.

Hinckley, B. 1990. *The Symbolic Presidency: How Presidents Portray Themselves.* New York: Routledge.

Hippler, H., and N. Schwarz. 1986. Not Forbidding Isn't Allowing. *Public Opinion Quarterly* 50:87–96.

Hobsbawm, E., and T. Ranger. 1983. *The Invention of Tradition*. Cambridge: Cambridge University Press.

Hockenberry—The Bottom Line. 1999. MSNBC: 7 June.

Hofstadter, R. 1969. *The Idea of a Party System: The Rise of Legitimate Opposition in the United States, 1780–1840*. Berkeley: University of California Press.

Hogan, M. 1997. George Gallup and the Rhetoric of Scientific Democracy. *Communication Monographs* 64:161–179.

Hogan, M. J. 1996. Enola Gay Controversy: History, Memory, and the Politics of Presentation. In *Hiroshima in History and Memory*, edited by M. J. Hogan. Cambridge: Cambridge University Press.

Hotwire. 1999. MSNBC: 6 July.

Houtkoop-Steenstra, H., and C. Antaki. 1997. Creating Happy People by Asking Yes-No Questions. *Research on Language and Social Interaction* 30:285–313.

http://nationaljournal.com/members/adspotlight/2000/04/0413rgny1.htm. Accessed April 13, 2000.

Huckfeldt, R. 1999. The Social Communication of Political Expertise: Individual Judgments Regarding Political Informants. Paper presented at the Midwest Political Science Association, Chicago.

Huckfeldt, R., and J. Sprague 1995. *Citizens, Politics and Social Communication*. Cambridge: Cambridge University Press.

Huckfeldt, R., P. Beck, R. Dalton, J. Levine, and W. Morgan. 1998. Ambiguity, Distorted Messages, and Nested Environmental Effects on Political Communication. *Journal of Politics* 60(4):996–1030.

Hughes, E. J. 1962. *The Ordeal of Power: A Political Memoir of the Eisenhower Years*. New York: Atheneum.

Hunter, J. 1987. *Image and Word: The Interaction of Twentieth-Century Photographs and Texts*. Cambridge, Mass.: Harvard University Press.

Huntington, S. P. 1981. *American Politics: The Promise of Disharmony*. Cambridge, Mass.: Belknap.

Hyman, H., and P. Sheatsley. 1950. The Current Status of American Public Opinion. In *The Teaching of Contemporary Affairs*, edited by J. Payne. Washington, D.C.: Twenty-First Yearbook of the National Council of Social Studies.

Irwin-Zarecka, I. 1994. *Frames of Remembrance: The Dynamics of Collective Memory*. New Brunswick, N.J.: Transaction.

Israel, F. 1966. *State of the Union Messages of the Presidents*. Washington, D.C.: GPO.

Iyengar, S. 1991. *Is Anyone Responsible?* Chicago: University of Chicago Press.

Iyengar, S., and D. R. Kinder. 1987. *News That Matters*. Chicago: University of Chicago Press.

Jackson v. City of Joliet 715 F. 2d 1200 (7th Cir.), cert. denied, 465 U.S. 1049 (1983).

Jaffe, L. 1949. The Judicial Universe of Mr. Justice Frankfurter. *Harvard Law Review* 62.

Jamieson, K. H. 1988. *Eloquence in an Electronic Age: The Transformation of Political Speechmaking*. New York: Oxford University Press.

Jaroslovsky, R. 1994. Washington Wire. *Wall Street Journal*, 17 June.

Jensen, K. B. 1990. The Politics of Polysemy: Television News, Everyday Consciousness and Political Action. *Media, Culture and Society* 12:57–77.

Johnson, H., and D. Broder. 1996. *The System: The American Way of Politics at the Breaking Point*. Boston: Little, Brown.

Johnstone, B. 1991. Individual Style in an American Public Opinion Survey. *Language in Society* 20:557–576.

Jones, C. 1994. *The Presidency in a Separated System*. Washington, D.C.: Brookings.

Jones, S. 1993. A Sense of Space: Virtual Reality, Authenticity and the Aural. *Critical Studies in Mass Communication* 10:238–252.

Just, M., A. Crigler, and D. Alger. 1996. *Crosstalk: Citizens, Candidates, and the Media in a Presidential Campaign*. Chicago: University of Chicago Press.

Karl, T. L. 2000. Economic Inequality and Democratic Instability. *Journal of Democracy* 2(1):149–156.

Katz, E. 1996. And Deliver Us From Segmentation. *Annals of the American Academy of Political and Social Science* 546:22–33.

Keeter, S. 1987. The Illusion of Intimacy: Television and the Role of Candidate Personal Qualities in Voter Choice. *Public Opinion Quarterly* 51:344–358.

Kelly, R. 1984. Rolls Royce Chiselers. *San Diego Union-Tribune*, 22 February.

Kenworthy, T. 2000. Okla. Starts to Face up to '21 Massacre. *USA Today*, 18 February.

Kernell, S. 1997. *Going Public: New Strategies of Presidential Leadership*. 3rd ed. Washington, D.C.: CQ Press.

Key, V. O., Jr. 1955. A Theory of Critical Elections. *Journal of Politics* 17 (February):3–18.

King, B. 1986. Stardom as an Occupation. In *The Hollywood Film Industry*, edited by Paul Kerr. London: Routledge.

Kingdon, J. W. 1995. *Agendas, Alternatives, and Public Policies*. 2nd ed. New York: HarperCollins.

Kleppner, P. 1979. *The Third Electoral System, 1853–1892: Parties, Voters, and Political Cultures*. Chapel Hill: University of North Carolina Press.

Knight, J., and J. Johnson. 1994. Aggregation and Deliberation: On the Possibility of Democratic Legitimacy. *Political Theory* 22:277–296.

Koenig, L. W. 1996. *The Chief Executive*. 6th ed. Fort Worth, Tex.: Harcourt Brace College Publishers.

Kornhauser, A. 1966. The Problem of Bias in Opinion Research. In *Reader in Public Opinion and Communication*, edited by B. Berelson and M. Janowitz. New York: Free Press.

Krasnow, E. G., and L. D. Longley. 1978. *The Politics of Broadcast Regulation*. 2nd ed. New York: St. Martin's.

Krosnick, J. 1989. Question Wording and Reports of Survey Results. *Public Opinion Quarterly* 53:107–113.

Labov, W., and D. Fanshel. 1977. *Therapeutic Discourse*. New York: Academic.

Lakoff, R. 1982. Persuasive Discourse and Ordinary Conversation. In *Analyzing Discourse*, edited by D. Tannen. Washington, D.C.: Georgetown University Press.

Lammers, W. 1981. Presidential Press Conferences: Who Hides and When? *Political Science Quarterly* 96:261–278.

Lane, R. 1962. *Political Ideology*. Glencoe, Ill.: Free Press.

Larry King Live. 2000. CNN: 6 January.

Lawrence, R. G. 1996. Accidents, Icons, and Indexing: The Dynamics of News Coverage of Police Use of Force. *Political Communication* 13:437–454.

———. 2000. *The Politics of Force: Media and the Construction of Police Brutality*. Berkeley: University of California Press.

Lawrence, R. G., and T. A. Birkland. 1999. The *Exxon Valdez* and Event-Driven Policy Discourse. Paper presented at the 1999 meeting of the International Communication Association, San Francisco, Calif., May 27–31.

Lazarsfeld, P., and R. Merton. 1948. Mass Communication, Popular Taste and Organized Social Action. In *The Communication of Ideas,* edited by L. Bryson. New York: Harper.

———. 1960. Mass Communication, Popular Taste, and Organized Social Action. In *Mass Communications,* edited by W. Schramm. Urbana: University of Illinois Press.

Lazarsfeld, P., B. Berelson, and H. Gaudet. 1944. *The People's Choice.* New York: Columbia University Press.

Lee, R. 1994. Images of Civic Virtue in the New Political Rhetoric. In *Presidential Campaigns and American Self Images,* edited by A. H. Miller and B. E. Gronbeck. Boulder, Colo.: Westview Press.

Leighly, J. 1990. Social Interaction and Contextual Influences on Political Participation. *American Politics Quarterly* 18:459–475.

Leuchtenburg, W. 1983. *In the Shadow of FDR: From Harry Truman to Ronald Reagan.* Ithaca, N.Y.: Cornell University Press.

Lewis, B. 1975. *History—Remembered, Recovered, Invented.* Princeton, N.J.: Princeton University Press.

Lichter, S. R., S. Rothman, and L. S. Lichter. 1986. *The Media Elite.* Bethesda, Md.: Adler and Adler.

Lieberman, J. K. 1983. *The Litigious Society.* New York: Basic.

Lipari, L. 1999. Polling as Ritual. *Journal of Communication* 49:83–102.

———. 2000. Toward a Discourse Approach to Polling. *Discourse Studies* 2:111–139.

Lippmann, W. 1922. *Public Opinion.* New York: Macmillan.

———. 1927. *The Phantom Public.* New York: Harcourt, Brace.

Lockerbie, B., and S. Borrelli. 1990. Question Wording and Public Support for Contra Aid 1983–1986. *Public Opinion Quarterly* 54:195–208.

Los Angeles Times. 1994. Roper Center POLL Database.

Lott, D., ed. 1969. *The Presidents Speak.* New York: Holt, Rinehart, and Winston.

Lowell, L. 1950. The Nature of Public Opinion. In *Reader in Public Opinion and Communication,* edited by B. Berelson and M. Janowitz. New York: Free Press.

Lowi, T. 1985. *The Personal President: Power Invested, Promise Unfulfilled.* Ithaca, N.Y.: Cornell University Press.

Lubell, S. 1965. *The Future of American Politics.* Rev. 3rd ed. New York: Harper and Row.

Lucas, S. 1986. Genre Criticism and Historical Context: The Case of George Washington's First Inaugural Address. *Southern Speech Communication Journal* 51:354–370.

Lull, J., ed. 1988. *World Families Watch Television.* Newbury Park, Calif.: Sage.

Lupia, A., and M. D. McCubbins. 1998. *The Democratic Dilemma: Can Citizens Learn What They Need to Know?* New York: Cambridge University Press.

Machiavelli, N. 1940. *The Discourses,* trans. Christian E. Detmold. New York: Modern Library.

Maine, H. 1950. The Nature of Public Opinion. In *Reader in Public Opinion and Communication,* edited by B. Berelson and M. Janowitz. New York: Free Press.

Maltese, J. 1994. *Spin Control: The White House Office of Communications and the Management of Presidential News.* 2nd ed. Chapel Hill: University of North Carolina Press.

Mander, M. S. 1987. Narrative Dimensions of the News: Omniscience, Prophecy, and Morality. *Communication* 10:51–70.

Mannheim, J., and W. Lammers. 1981. The News Conference and Presidential Leadership of Public Opinion: Does the Tail Wag the Dog? *Presidential Studies Quarterly* 11:177–188.

Manning, B. 1977. Hyperlexis: Our National Disease. *Northwestern University Law Review* 71.

Mansbridge, J. 1980. *Beyond Adversary Democracy.* New York: Basic.

March, J. G., and J. P. Olsen. 1984. The New Institutionalism: Organizational Factors in Political Life. American Political Science Review 78:734–749.

———. 1989. *Rediscovering Institutions: The Organizational Basis of Politics.* New York: Free Press.

———. 1995. *Democratic Governance.* New York: Free Press.

Markesinis, B. S. 1990. Litigation-Mania in England, Germany and the USA: Are We So Very Different? *Cambridge Law Journal* 49:233–276.

Marsden, P. 1987. Core Discussion Networks of Americans. *American Sociological Review* 52:122–131.

Marshall, P. D. 1998. *Celebrity and Power: Fame in Contemporary Culture.* Minneapolis: University of Minnesota Press.

McCann, J. 1990. Changing Electoral Contexts and Changing Candidate Images during the 1984 Presidential Campaign. *American Politics Quarterly* 18:123–140.

McChesney, R. 1999. *Rich Media, Poor Democracy.* Urbana: University of Illinois Press.

McCombs, M., L. Danielian, and W. Wanta. 1995. Issues in the News and the Public Agenda: The Agenda-Setting Tradition. In *Public Opinion and the Communication of Consent,* edited by T. L. Glasser and C. T. Salmon, 281–300.

McCullough, D. 1992. *Truman.* New York: Simon & Schuster.

McLaughlin Group. 1999. NBC: 8 August.

Mead, G. H. 1929. The Nature of the Past. In *Essays in Honor of John Dewey, on the Occasion of His Seventieth Birthday, October 20, 1929.* New York: Henry Holt.

Medhurst, M. 1996. *Beyond the Rhetorical Presidency.* College Station: Texas A&M University Press.

Meet the Press. 1999. NBC: 3 January.

———. 1999. NBC: 21 February.

———. 1999. NBC: 4 July.

———. 1999. NBC: 8 August.

———. 1999. NBC: 5 December.

———. 2000. NBC: 6 February.

Meiklejohn, A. 1961. The First Amendment Is Absolute. *Supreme Court Review* 2.

Meilleur, M. J. 2000. The Theorist as Painkiller: Political Theory and Public Deliberation. Paper presented at the 58th annual meeting of the Midwest Political Science Association.

Melucci, A. 1989. *Nomads of the Present: Social Movements and Individual Needs in Contemporary Society.* Philadelphia: Temple University Press.

———. 1996. *Challenging Codes: Collective Action in the Information Age.* Cambridge: Cambridge University Press.

Merelman, R. 1984. *Making Something of Ourselves: On Culture and Politics in the United States.* Berkeley: University of California Press.

——. 1998. The Mundane Experience of Political Culture. *Political Communication* 15:515–535.

Messaris, P. 1994. *Visual 'Literacy': Image, Mind, and Reality.* Boulder, Colo.: Westview Press.

——. 1997. *Visual Persuasion: The Role of Images in Advertising.* Thousand Oaks, Calif.: Sage Publications.

Meyrowitz, J. 1985. *No Sense of Place: The Impact of Electronic Media on Social Behavior.* New York: Oxford University Press.

Michelman, F. 1969. On Protecting the Poor through the Fourteenth Amendment. *Harvard Law Review* 83.

Milkis, S. 1993. *The President and the Parties: The Transformation of the American Party System since the New Deal.* New York: Oxford University Press.

Miller, R. E., and A. Sarat. 1980. Grievances, Claims and Disputes: Assessing the Adversary Culture. *Law and Society Review* 15.

Miller, T. 1998. *Technologies of Truth: Cultural Citizenship and the Popular Media.* Minneapolis: University of Minnesota Press.

Miroff, B. 1998. The Presidency and the Public: Leadership as Spectacle. In *The Presidency and the Political System.* 5th ed. Washington, D.C.: CQ Press.

Mitchell, W. J. T. 1980. *The Language of Images.* Chicago: University of Chicago Press.

——. 1986. *Iconology: Image, Text, Ideology.* Chicago: University of Chicago Press.

——. 1994. *Picture Theory: Essays on Verbal and Visual Representation.* Chicago: University of Chicago Press.

Molotch, H., and M. Lester. 1974. News as Purposive Behavior: On the Strategic Use of Routine Events, Accidents, and Scandals. *American Sociological Review* 39:101–112.

Mooney, B. 1970. *The Politicians: 1945–1960.* Philadelphia: Lippincott.

Morawetz, V. 1905. The Power of Congress to Regulate Railway Rates. *Harvard Law Review* 18.

Morgan, S. E. 1988. *Inventing the People: The Rise of Popular Sovereignty in England and America.* New York: Norton.

Morris, D. 1997. *Behind the Oval Office: Winning the Presidency in the Nineties.* New York: Random House.

Morse, M. 1986. The Television News Personality and Credibility: Reflections on the News in Transition. In *Studies in Entertainment: Critical Approaches to Mass Culture,* edited by T. Modleski, 55–79. Bloomington: Indiana University Press.

Murray, A. 1997. Broadcasters Get a Pass on Campaign Reform. *Wall Street Journal,* 29 September.

Mutz, D. C. 1994. Contextualizing Personal Experience: The Role of the Mass Media. *Journal of Politics* 56:689–714.

Myrdal, G. 1944. *An American Dilemma: The Negro Problem and Modern Democracy.* New York: Harper and Brothers.

National Opinion Research Center. 1994. Roper Center POLL Database.

National School Safety Center. 1999. School Associated Violent Deaths. Westlake Village, Calif. [http://nssc1.org/savd/savd.htm].

NBC's Tartikoff; No to PAC. 1987. *Broadcasting* 33:128.

Nehamas, A. 1999. *Virtues of Authenticity.* Princeton, N.J.: Princeton University Press.

Nelson, D. N. 1998. *National Manhood: Capitalist Citizenship and the Imagined Fraternity of White Men.* Durham, N.C.: Duke University Press.

Neuman, W., M. R. Just, and A. Crigler. 1992. *Common Knowledge.* Chicago: University of Chicago Press.

Neustadt, R. E. 1980. *Presidential Power.* New York: Wiley.

———. 1990. *Presidential Power and the Modern Presidents.* New York: Free Press.

Neustadt, R. E., and E. R. May. 1986. *Thinking in Time: The Uses of History for Decision Makers.* New York: Free Press.

Newport, F. 1999. Media Portrayals of Violence Seen by Many as Causes of Real-Life Violence. Gallup News Service. [http://www.gallup.com/poll/release/pr990510.asp].

Newsstand. 1999. CNN/Time: 15 May.

Nightline. 1999. ABC: 17 February.

Noelle-Neumann, E. 1970. Wanted: Rules for Wording Structured Questionnaires. *Public Opinion Quarterly* 34:191–201.

North, D. 1981. *Structure and Change in Economic History.* New York: Norton.

Novick, P. 1999. *The Holocaust in American Life.* Boston: Houghton Mifflin.

Office of Juvenile Justice and Delinquency Prevention. 1999. OJJDP Statistical Briefing Book. [http://ojjdp.ncjrs.org/ojstatbb/qa004.html].

O'Loughlin, J., and R. Grant. 1990. The Political Geography of Presidential Speeches, 1946–1987. *Annals of the Association of American Geographers* 80:504–530.

Olson, M. 1965. *The Logic of Collective Action.* Cambridge, Mass.: Harvard University Press.

Olson, W. K. 1991. *The Litigation Explosion: What Happened When America Unleashed the Lawsuit?* New York: Truman Talley Books.

O'Muircheartaigh, C., G. Gaskell, and D. Wright. 1993. Intensifiers in Behavior Frequency Questions. *Public Opinion Quarterly* 57:552–565.

Open Secrets. 2000. Contribution List, National Association of Broadcasters, 1997–1998. [www.crp.org].

Orren, K., and S. Skowronek. 1994. Beyond the Iconography of Order: Notes for a "New Institutionalism." In *The Dynamics of American Politics: Approaches and Interpretations,* edited by L. J. Dodd and C. Jillson. Boulder, Colo.: Westview Press.

Orvell, M. 1989. *The Real Thing: Imitation and Authenticity in American Culture, 1880–1940.* Chapel Hill: University of North Carolina Press.

Pach, C., and E. Richardson. 1991. *The Presidency of Dwight D. Eisenhower.* Rev. ed. Lawrence: University Press of Kansas.

Page, B. 1994. Democratic Responsiveness? Untangling the Links Between Public Opinion and Policy. *PS: Political Science and Politics* 27:25–29.

———. 1996. *Who Deliberates?* Chicago: University of Chicago Press.

Page, B., and R. Shapiro 1992. *The Rational Public.* Chicago: University of Chicago Press.

Parenti, M. 1986. *Inventing Reality: The Politics of the Mass Media.* New York: St. Martin's Press.

Parmet, H. 1972. *Eisenhower and the American Crusades.* New York: MacMillan.

Parry-Giles, S. 2000. Mediating Hillary Rodham Clinton: Television News Practices and Image-Making in the Postmodern Age. In *Critical Studies in Mass Communication.* Washington, D.C.: National Communication Association.

Parry-Giles, S., and T. Parry-Giles. 1999. Meta-Imaging, The War Room, and the Hyperreality of U.S. Politics. *Journal of Communication* 49:28–45.

Pateman, C. 1970. *Participation and Democratic Theory*. London: Cambridge University Press.

Patterson, T. E. 1993. *Out of Order*. New York: Knopf.

———. 1998. Political Roles of the Journalist. In *The Politics of News*, edited by D. Graber, D. McQuail, and P. Norris. Washington, D.C.: CQ Press.

Pepper, R. 1995. *Letter to Senator Joseph I. Lieberman*. 5 May.

Petty, R. E., G. A. Rennier, and J. Cacioppo. 1987. Assertion versus Interrogation Format in Opinion Surveys. *Public Opinion Quarterly* 51:481–494.

Pew Research Center for the People and the Press. 1999a. Columbine Shooting Biggest Draw of 1999. [http://www.people-press.org/content.html].

Pew Research Center for the People and the Press. 1999b. Teens and Traffic Top Community Concerns. [http://www.people-press.org/content.html].

Philo, G. 1990. *Seeing and Believing: The Influence of Television*. London: Routledge.

Piven, F., and R. Cloward. 1971. *Regulating the Poor: The Functions of Public Welfare*. New York: Random House.

Pollitt, K. 1995. Subject to Debate. *The Nation,* 30 January.

Pooley, E. 1999. In a Contrary State, an Underdog Has His Day. *Time,* 26 April. [http://www.pathfinder.com/time/magazine/articles/0,3226,23285,00.html].

Popkin, S. L. 1994. *The Reasoning Voter*. Chicago: University of Chicago Press.

Popular Memory Group. 1982. Popular Memory: Theory, Politics, Method. In *Making Histories: Studies in History-Writing and Politics,* edited by R. Johnson, G. McLennan, B. Schwarz, and D. Sutton. Minneapolis: University of Minnesota Press.

Powell, W., and P. Dimaggio, eds. 1991. *The New Institutionalism in Organizational Analysis*. Chicago: University of Chicago Press.

President's Remarks on Shootings at Colorado School. 1999. *New York Times,* 21 April.

Presser, S., and M. Traugott. 1992. Little White Lies and Social Science Models. *Public Opinion Quarterly* 56:77–86.

Princeton Survey Research for Times Mirror. 1994. Roper Center POLL Database.

Radio-Television News Directors Association and Foundation. 2000. Washington, D.C. [www.rtnda.org].

Radosh, R. 1996. *Divided They Fell: The Demise of the Democratic Party, 1964–1996*. New York: Free Press.

Ragsdale, L. 1984. The Politics of Presidential Speechmaking, 1949–1980. *American Political Science Review* 78:971–984.

Ranney, A. 1962. *The Doctrine of Responsible Party Government: Its Origins and Present State*. Urbana: University of Illinois Press.

Rasinski, K. 1989. The Effect of Question Wording on Public Support for Government Spending. *Public Opinion Quarterly* 53:388–394.

Reich, R. 1997. *Locked in the Cabinet*. New York: Knopf.

Reichard, G. 1975. *The Reaffirmation of Republicanism: Eisenhower and the Eighty-Third Congress*. Knoxville: University of Tennessee Press.

———. 1982. The Presidency Triumphant. In *Reshaping America: Society and Institutions, 1945–1960,* edited by R. Bruhner and G. Reichard. Columbus: Ohio State University Press.

Robinson, J. P., and M. R. Levy. 1986. *The Main Source: Learning from Television News.* Beverly Hills, Calif.: Sage.

Roper Center for Public Opinion Research. 2000. What is POLL? Public Opinion Databank. [www.ropercenter.uconn.edu/online.html].

Rockman, B. 1984. *The Leadership Question: The Presidency and the American System.* New York: Praeger.

———. 1994. The New Institutionalism and the Old Institutions. In *Perspectives on American Politics,* edited by L. Dodd and C. Jillson. Washington, D.C.: CQ Press.

Rossinow, D. 1998. *The Politics of Authenticity. Liberalism, Christianity, and the New Left in America.* New York: Columbia University Press.

Rossiter, C. 1960. *The American Presidency.* 2nd ed. New York: Time Books.

———. 1987. *The American Presidency.* 2nd ed. Baltimore: Johns Hopkins University Press.

Rousseau, J. 1987. *Basic Political Writings,* trans. Donald Cress. Indianapolis, Ind.: Hackett.

Rudy Boards the Straight Talk Express. 2000. *National Journal Hotline.* [www.nationaljournal.com].

Ryan, H. 1988. *Franklin D. Roosevelt's Rhetorical Presidency.* Westport, Conn.: Greenwood.

Ryfe, D. 1997. *The Interactive President: Presidential Communication and Political Culture in Twentieth-Century America.* Ph.D. diss., University of California, San Diego.

———. 1999. Franklin D. Roosevelt's Fireside Chats. *Journal of Communication* 49:80–103.

Sabato, L. J. 2000. *Feeding Frenzy: Attack Journalism and American Politics.* Baltimore: Lanahan Publishers.

Safire, W. 1996. Stop the Giveaway. *New York Times,* 4 January.

Sanders, L. 1997. Against Deliberation. *Political Theory* 25:347–376.

Schaeffer, N., and D. Maynard. 1996. From Paradigm to Prototype and Back Again: Interactive Aspects of Cognitive Processing in Standardized Survey Interviews. In *Answering Questions: Methodology for Determining Cognitive and Communicative Processes in Survey Research,* edited by N. Schwarz and S. Sudman. San Francisco: Jossey-Bass.

Schattschneider, E. E. 1960/1975. *The Semisovereign People: A Realist's View of Democracy in America.* New York: Henry Holt.

Scheingold, S. 1974. *The Politics of Rights, Lawyers, Public Policy and Political Change.* New Haven, Conn.: Yale University Press.

Schiff, Frederick. 1994. Deconstructing "Attitude Structures" in Public Opinion Studies. *Critical Studies in Mass Communication* 11:287–297.

Schlesinger, A. M., Jr. 1992. *The Disuniting of America: Reflections on a Multicultural Society.* New York: Norton.

Schlesinger, P. 1978. *Putting "Reality" Together: BBC News.* London: Constable.

Schmuhl, R. 1990. *Statecraft and Stagecraft: American Political Life in the Age of Personality.* Notre Dame, Ind.: University of Notre Dame Press.

Schram, M. 1987. *The Great American Video Game: Presidential Politics in the Television.* New York: Morrow.

Schram, S. 1995. *Words of Welfare.* Minneapolis: University of Minnesota Press.

Schudson, M. 1978. *Discovering the News.* New York: Basic.

———. 1992. *Watergate in American Memory: How We Remember, Forget, and Reconstruct the Past.* New York: Basic.

———. 1997. Why Conversation Is Not the Soul of Democracy. *Critical Studies in Mass Communication* 14:297–309.

———. 1998a. *The Good Citizen: A History of American Civic Life.* New York: Free Press.

———. 1998b. In All Fairness: Definitions of Fair Journalism Have Changed over the Last Two Centuries. In *What's Fair? Media Studies Journal* (spring/summer).

Schuman, H., G. Kalton, and J. Ludwig. 1983. Context and Contiguity in Survey Questionnaires. *Public Opinion Quarterly* 47:112–115.

Schuman, H., and S. Presser. 1981. *Questions and Answers in Attitude Surveys.* New York: Academic.

Schuman, H., S. Presser, and J. Ludwig. 1981. Context Effects on Survey Responses to Questions about Abortion. *Public Opinion Quarterly* 45:216–223.

Schumpeter, J. 1950. *Capitalism, Socialism, and Democracy.* 3rd ed. New York: Harper.

Schwartz, B. 1991. Iconography and Collective Memory: Lincoln's Image in the American Mind. *The Sociological Quarterly* 32:301–319.

Schwartz, B., Y. Zerubavel, and B. M. Barnett. 1986. The Recovery of Masada: A Study in Collective Memory. *The Sociological Quarterly* 27:147–164.

Sears, D., and C. Funk. 1991. The Role of Self-Interest in Social and Political Attitudes. In *Advances in Experimental Social Psychology,* edited by Mark Zanna. San Diego: Academic.

Seelye, K. Q. 1999. Campaigns Find All Talk Turns to Littleton. *New York Times,* 20 May.

Seib, G. 1994. Washington Wire. *Wall Street Journal,* 16 December.

Senate Ethics Manual. 1996. Select Committee on Ethics, United States Senate (104th Session).

Sewell, W. 1992. A Theory of Structure: Duality, Agency and Transformation. *American Journal of Sociology* 98:1–29.

Sharp, M. P. 1933. Movement in Supreme Court Adjudication: A Study of Modified and Overruled Decisions. *Harvard Law Review* 46.

Shaw, D. L., and M. McCombs. 1977. *The Emergence of American Political Issues: The Agenda-Setting Function of the Press.* St. Paul, Minn.: West Publishing Company.

Shogan, R. 1992. *The Riddle of Power.* New York: Penguin.

Sidel, R. 1992. *Women and Children Last.* New York: Penguin.

Sigal, L. 1973. *Reporters and Officials: The Organization and Politics of Newsmaking.* Lexington, Mass.: D. C. Heath.

Sigelman, L. 1992. There You Go Again: The Media and the Debasement of American Politics. *Communication Monographs* 59:407–410.

Silverstone, R., and E. Hirsch, eds. 1992. *Consuming Technologies: Media and Information in Domestic Spaces.* New York: Routledge.

Simon, D., and C. Ostrom. 1989. The Impact of Televised Speeches and Foreign Travel on Presidential Approval. *Public Opinion Quarterly* 53:58–82.

Simon, H. A. 1957. *Models of Man: Social and Rational.* New York: Wiley.

Simonson, P. 1996. Dreams of Democratic Togetherness: Communication Hope from Cooley to Katz. *Critical Studies in Mass Communication* 13:324–342.

Skocpol, T. 1997. *Boomerang: Health Care Reform and the Turn against Government.* New York: Norton.

Skowronek, S. 1982. *Building a New American State: The Expansion of National Administrative Capacities, 1877–1920.* New York: Cambridge University Press.

———. 1993. *The Politics Presidents Make: Leadership from John Adams to George Bush.* Cambridge, Mass.: Belknap.

———. 1998. Presidential Leadership in Political Time. In *The Presidency and the Political System,* edited by M. Nelson. 5th ed. Washington, D.C.: CQ Press.

Sloan, J. W. 1991. *Eisenhower and the Management of Prosperity.* Lawrence: University Press of Kansas.

Smith, B. J. 1985. *Politics and Remembrance.* Princeton, N.J.: Princeton University Press.

Smith, E. 1993. Transmitting Race: The L.A. Riots in TV News. Paper presented at the Center for Urban Affairs and Policy Research Conference on Media, Race, and Governance. Northwestern University, Evanston, Ill., Feb. 5.

Smith, E., and P. Squire. 1990. The Effects of Prestige Names in Question Wording. *Public Opinion Quarterly* 54:97–116.

Smith, G., and C. Wales. 2000. Citizens' Juries and Deliberative Democracy. *Political Studies* 48:51–65.

Smith, H. 1988. *The Power Game: How Washington Works.* New York: Balantine.

Smith, R. M. 1997. *Civic Ideals: Conflicting Visions of Citizenship in U.S. History.* New Haven, Conn.: Yale University Press.

Smith, T. 1987a. That Which We Call Welfare by Any Other Name Would Smell Sweeter: An Analysis of the Impact of Question Wording on Response Patterns. *Opinion Quarterly* 51:75–83.

———. 1987b. The Art of Asking Questions, 1936–1985. *Public Opinion Quarterly* 51:S95–S108.

Smoller, F. 1990. *The Six O'clock Presidency: A Theory of Presidential Press Relations in the Age of Television.* New York: Praeger.

Snider, J. H. 1997. Does Media Ownership Affect Media Stands? The Case of the Telecommunications Act of 1996. Paper presented at the 25th annual Telecommunications Policy Research Conference, Washington, D.C., September 29.

———. 2000a. Local TV News Archives as a Public Good: Public Policy Implications. *The Harvard International Journal of Press/Politics* 5 (spring):2.

———. 2000b. The Cable Act of 1992: The TV Broadcasters as Political Actors. Paper to be delivered at the American Political Science annual conference, Washington, D.C., September.

Snider, J. H., and B. Page. 1997. The Political Power of TV Broadcasters: Covert Bias and Anticipated Reactions. Paper delivered at the American Political Science Association annual conference, Washington, D.C., August 29.

———. 1999a. Broadcasters and Information Policy: The Mechanisms of News Bias. Paper delivered at the Midwest Political Science Association annual conference, Chicago, Illinois, April 18.

———. 1999b. Measuring Information and Money as Interest Group Resources: The Case of the Local TV Broadcasters. Paper delivered at the Midwest Political Science Association annual conference, Chicago, Illinois, April 17.

Sniderman, P., R. Brody, and P. Tetlock. 1991. *Reasoning and Choice: Explorations in Political Psychology.* New York: Cambridge University Press.

Snyder, J. 1980. Picturing Vision. In *The Language of Images,* edited by W. J. T. Mitchell, 221–246. Chicago: University of Chicago Press.

Soltan, K., E. M. Uslaner, and V. Haufler. 1998. New Institutionalism: Institutions and Social Order. In *Institutions and Social Order,* edited by K. Soltan, E. M. Uslaner and V. Haufler. Ann Arbor: The University of Michigan Press.

Southwick, T. P. 1999. *Distant Signals: How Cable TV Changed the World of Telecommunications.* Overland Park, Kansas: Primedia.

Sparrow, B. 1999. *Uncertain Guardians: The News Media as a Political Institution.* Baltimore: Johns Hopkins University Press.

Speaker Wright, Meet Mr. Wright. 1986. *New York Times,* 10 December.

Speidel, R. E. 1958. Extraterritorial Assertion of the Direct Action Statute: Due Process, Full Faith and Credit and the Search for Governmental Interest. *Northwestern University Law Review* 52: March/April.

Stephens, M. 1998. *The Rise of the Image, the Fall of the Word.* New York: Oxford University Press.

Stoker, L. 1992. Interests and Ethics in Politics. *American Political Science Review* 86:369–380.

Strang, D., and J. W. Meyer. 1993. Institutional Conditions for Diffusion. *Theory and Society* 22:487–511.

Stuckey, M., and F. Antczak. 1998. The Rhetorical Presidency: Deepening Vision, Widening Exchange. *Communication Yearbook* 21:405–441.

Suchman, L., and B. Jordan. 1990. Interactional Troubles in Face-to-Face Survey Interviews. *Journal of the American Statistical Association* 85:232–241.

Sudman, S. 1982. The Presidents and the Polls. *Public Opinion Quarterly* 46:301–310.

Sudman, S., and N. Bradburn. 1982. *Asking Questions.* San Francisco: Jossey-Bass.

Summers, C. W. 1947. The Right to Join a Union. *Columbia Law Review* 47.

Sundquist, J. L. 1983. *Dynamics of the Party System: Alignment and Realignment of Political Parties in the United States.* Rev. ed. Washington, D.C.: Brookings.

Sunstein, C. 1987a. Constitutionalism after the New Deal. *Harvard Law Review* 101:421–510.

———. 1987b. Lochner's Legacy. *Columbia Law Review* 87:873 ff.

Swanson, D. 2000. The Homologous Evolution of Political Communication and Civic Engagement: Good News, Bad News, and No News. Paper presented at the Communicating Civic Engagement in Europe and the United States conference, Center for Communication and Civic Engagement, University of Washington, Seattle, Wash., May 19–20.

Tarde, G. 1969. *On Communication and Social Influence.* Chicago: University of Chicago Press.

Taylor, C. 1992. *The Ethics of Authenticity.* Cambridge, Mass.: Harvard University Press.

Tebbel, J., and S. M. Watts. 1985. *The Press and the Presidency: From George Washington to Ronald Reagan.* New York: Oxford University Press.

The Gallup Organization. 1999. Gallup Social and Economic Indicators: Environment. [www.gallup.com/poll/indicators/indenvironment.asp].

The News With Brian Williams. 1999. MSNBC: 8 July.

The Today Show. 1999. NBC: 17 February.

———. 1999. NBC: 19 February.

———. 1999. NBC: 4 March.

———. 1999. NBC: 4 June.

———. 1999. NBC: 10 June.

This Week. 1999. ABC: 21 February.

———. 1999. ABC: 21 November.

Thomas, D., and L. Siegelman. 1984. Presidential Identification and Policy Leadership: Experimental Evidence on the Reagan Case. *Policy Studies Journal* 12:663–675.

Thurow, G. E. 1996. Dimensions of Presidential Character. In *Beyond the Rhetorical Presidency*, edited by M. J. Medhurst, 15–29. College Station: Texas A&M University Press.

Time and Again. 1999. MSNBC: 30 January.

———. 1999. MSNBC: 27 February.

———. 1999. MSNBC: 30 May.

———. 1999. MSNBC: 6 July.

———. 1999. MSNBC: 8 July.

Tocqueville, A. 1969. *Democracy in America,* edited by J. P. Mayer, translated by George Lawrence. Garden City: Doubleday Anchor.

Today in America. 1999. MSNBC: 20 February.

Touraine, A. 1988. *The Return of the Actor: Social Theory in Postindustrial Society.* Minneapolis: University of Minnesota Press.

Tribe, L. 1973. Toward a Model of Roles in the Due Process of Life and Law. *Harvard Law Review* 83.

Tuchman, G. 1978. *Making News: A Study in the Construction of Reality.* New York: Free Press.

Tulis, J. 1987. *The Rhetorical Presidency.* Princeton, N.J.: Princeton University Press.

U.S. Congress. 1994. Welfare Reform. *Congressional Record,* 20 April.

———. 1995. Family Self-Sufficiency Act. *Congressional Record,* 19 September.

———. 1996. Republicans Have Not Run Away from the Promises Made to the American People. *Congressional Record,* 26 September.

U.S. House of Representatives Committee on Ways and Means. 1994. *Where Your Money Goes: The 1994–95 Green Book.* Washington, D.C.: Brassey's.

U.S. Senate Campaign Web. Will the Real Hillary Clinton Please Stand Up? 2000. 22 February. [http://www.rudyyes.com/contents/news/2-22-00release.html].

Vartabedian, R. 1985. Nixon's Vietnam Rhetoric: A Case Study of Apologia as Generic Paradox. *Southern States Communication Journal* 50:366–381.

Verba, S., K. Schlozman, H. Brady, and N. Nie. 1993. Citizen Activity: Who Participates? What Do They Say? *American Political Science Review* 87:303–318.

Walsh, E. 1977. The Making of a Presidential Trip. *The Washington Post,* 16 March.

Walzer, M. 1999. Deliberation—and What Else? In *Deliberative Politics: Essays on Democracy and Disagreement*, edited by S. Macedo. New York: Oxford University Press.

Warren, M. 1992. Democratic Theory and Self-Transformation. *American Political Science Review* 86:8–23.

Watson, M.A. 1990. *The Expanding Vista: American Television in the Kennedy Years.* Durham, N.C.: Duke University Press.

Weaver, D., and G. Wilhoit. 1986. *The American Journalist.* Bloomington: University of Indiana Press.

Weaver, R. K., R. Shapiro, and L. Jacobs. 1995. Trends: Welfare. *Public Opinion Quarterly* 59:606–627.

Weisbrot, R. 1990. *Freedom Bound: A History of America's Civil Rights Movement.* New York: Norton.

Weisman, S. R. 1980. "Fanatics" in Regime in Tehran Blamed by Carter for Crisis. *New York Times*, 5 July.

Weissman, A. 1974. The Discriminatory Application of Penal Laws by State Judicial and Quasi-Judicial Officers: Playing the Shell Game of Rights and Remedies. *Northwestern University Law Review* 68.

White, H. 1987. *The Content of the Form: Narrative Discourse and Historical Representation.* Baltimore: Johns Hopkins University Press.

Wicker, T. 1975. *On Press.* New York: Viking.

Wills, G. 1992. *Lincoln at Gettysburg: Words That Remade America.* New York: Simon & Schuster.

Windt, T. 1987. Presidential Rhetoric: Definition of a Discipline of Study. In *Essays in Presidential Rhetoric*, edited by T. Windt and B. Ingold. 2nd ed. Dubuque, Iowa: Kendall/Hunt Publishers.

Winfield, B. 1990. *FDR and the News Media.* Urbana: University of Illinois Press.

Wolfsfeld, G. 1997. *Media and Political Conflict: News from the Middle East.* Cambridge: Cambridge University Press.

Woodward, B. 1994. *The Agenda: Inside the Clinton White House.* New York: Simon & Schuster.

Wright Ponders PAC for NBC. 1986. *Broadcasting*, 15 December: 58.

Wyatt, R., E. Katz, and T. Liebes. 1995. The Facets of Expression Inhibition: Factors That Inhibit Talk in Public and Private Spaces in Three Cultures. Paper presented at the Annenberg Scholars Conference on Public Space, Philadelphia.

Yankelovich, D. 1991. *Coming to Public Judgment: Making Democracy Work in a Complex World.* Syracuse, N.Y.: Syracuse University Press.

Yankelovich Partners for Time, CNN. 1994. Roper Center POLL Database.

Zaller, J. 1992. *The Nature and Origins of Mass Opinion.* New York: Cambridge University Press.

———. 1994. Positive Constructs of Public Opinion. *Critical Studies in Mass Communication* 11:287–297.

———. 1998. Monica Lewinsky's Contribution to Political Science. *PS: Political Science and Politics* 31:182–189.

Zarefsky, D. 1986. *President Johnson's War on Poverty: Rhetoric and History.* Tuscaloosa: University of Alabama Press.

Zelizer, B. 1992. *Covering the Body: The Kennedy Assassination, the Media, and the Shaping of Collective Memory.* Chicago: University of Chicago Press.

———. 1998. *Remembering to Forget: Holocaust Memory through the Camera's Eye.* Chicago: University of Chicago Press.

Zerubavel, Y. 1995. *Recovered Roots: Collective Memory and the Making of Israeli National Tradition.* Chicago: University of Chicago Press.

Zetterbaum, M. 1981. Alexis de Tocqueville, 1805–1859. *History of Political Philosophy*, edited by L. Strauss and J. Cropsey. 2nd ed. Chicago: University of Chicago Press:715–736.

Zucker, L. 1977. The Role of Institutionalization in Cultural Persistence. *American Sociological Review* 42:726–743.

———. 1983. Organizations as Institutions. In *Research in the Sociology of Organizations*, edited by S. B. Bacharach. Greenwich, Conn.: JAI Press.

———. 1987. Central Concepts and Indicators of Institutionalization. *Annual Review of Sociology* 13:444–464.

———, ed. 1988. *Institutional Patterns and Organizations: Culture and Environment.* Cambridge: Ballinger.

Index

About the Contributors

Vanessa B. Beasley is an assistant professor of speech communication at Texas A & M University.

Amy Bunger is an assistant professor of criminology and criminal justice at Florida State University.

David A. Crockett is assistant professor of political science at Trinity University.

Jill A. Edy is an assistant professor of journalism at Middle Tennessee State University.

Roderick P. Hart holds the Shivers Chair in Communication & Government and is the director of the Annette Strauss Institute for Civic Participation at the University of Texas at Austin.

Jeffrey P. Jones is an assistant professor of communication and media studies at Goucher College.

Regina G. Lawrence is an assistant professor of political science at Portland State University.

Lisbeth Lipari is an assistant professor of communication at Denison University.

Shawn J. Parry-Giles is an assistant professor of communication at the University of Maryland.

David Michael Ryfe is an assistant professor of journalism at Middle Tennessee State University.

J. H. Snider has a doctorate degree from Northwestern University and is currently a Congressional Fellow.

Bartholomew H. Sparrow is an associate professor of government at the University of Texas at Austin.

Paul Waldman is a postdoctoral fellow at the University of Pennsylvania.